ETHICAL AND LEGAL ISSUES IN PROFESSIONAL PRACTICE WITH FAMILIES

WILEY SERIES IN COUPLES AND FAMILY DYNAMICS AND TREATMENT

Florence W. Kaslow, Editor

Treating the Changing Family: Handling Normative and Unusual Events
edited by Michele Harway

In-Laws: A Guide to Extended-Family Therapy
by Gloria Call Horsley

Handbook of Relational Diagnosis and Dysfunctional Family Patterns
edited by Florence W. Kaslow

Child-Centered Family Therapy
by Lucille L. Andreozzi

Strange Attractors: Chaos, Complexity, and the Art of Family Therapy
by Michael Bütz, William G. McCown, and Linda L. Chamberlain

Infertility: Psychological Issues and Counseling Strategies
by Sandra R. Leiblum

The Self in the Family: A Classification of Personality, Criminality, and Psychopathology
by Luciano L'Abate and Margaret Baggett

Painful Partings: Divorce and Its Aftermath
by Lita Linzer Schwartz and Florence W. Kaslow

Ethical and Legal Issues in Professional Practice with Families
edited by Diane T. Marsh and Richard D. Magee

Ethical and Legal Issues in Professional Practice with Families

EDITED BY

Diane T. Marsh

AND

Richard D. Magee

John Wiley & Sons, Inc.

New York • Chichester • Weinheim • Brisbane • Singapore • Toronto

Copyright © 1997 by John Wiley & Sons, Inc.

Library of Congress Cataloging-in-Publication Data:

Marsh, Diane T.
      Ethical and legal issues in professional practice with families /
by Diane T. Marsh and Richard D. Magee.
          p.   cm. — (Wiley series in couples and family dynamics and
treatment)
      Includes bibliographical references.
      ISBN 0-471-13458-9 (cloth : alk. paper)
      1. Family psychotherapy—Moral and ethical aspects.   2. Family
psychotherapy—Law and legislation—United States.   3. Family
psychotherapy—Practice.   I. Magee, Richard D., 1933–
II. Title.   III. Series.
RC488.5.M367   1997
174′.2—dc21   96-46318

Printed in the United States of America

10   9   8   7   6   5   4   3   2   1

Series Preface

Our ability to form strong interpersonal bonds with romantic partners, children, parents, siblings, and other relations is one of the key qualities that defines our humanity. These relationships shape who we are and what we become—they can be a source of great gratification, or tremendous pain. Yet, only in the mid-20th century did behavioral and social scientists really begin focusing on couples and family dynamics, and only in the past several decades have the theory and findings that emerged from those studies been used to develop effective therapeutic interventions for troubled couples and families.

We have made great progress in understanding the structure, function, and interactional patterns of couples and families—and have made tremendous strides in treatment. However, as we stand poised on the beginning of a new millennium, it seems quite clear that both intimate partnerships and family relationships are in a period of tremendous flux. Economic factors are changing work patterns, parenting responsibilities, and relational dynamics. Modern medicine has helped lengthen the life span, giving rise to the need for transgenerational caretaking. Cohabitation, divorce, and remarriage are quite commonplace, and these social changes make it necessary for us to rethink and broaden our definition of what constitutes a family.

Thus, it is no longer enough simply to embrace the concept of the family as a system. In order to understand and effectively treat the evolving family, our theoretical formulations and clinical interventions must be informed by an understanding of ethnicity, culture, religion, gender, sexual preference, family life cycle, socioeconomic status, education, physical and mental health, values, and belief systems.

The purpose of the *Wiley Series in Couples and Family Dynamics and Treatment* is to provide a forum for cutting-edge relational and family theory, practice, and research. Its scope is intended to be broad, diverse, and international, but all books published in this series share a common mission: to reflect on the past, offer state-of-the-art information on the present, and speculate on, as well as attempt to shape, the future of the field.

FLORENCE W. KASLOW
Florida Couples and Family Institute

v

About the Contributors

ANN LEE BEGLER is a partner in the Pittsburgh law firm of Begler Kowall. She received her undergraduate degree from the University of Pittsburgh in 1971 and her law degree from Duquesne University in 1975. Ms. Begler has four years of training in gestalt therapy. She has been a trained and active mediator since 1983. She has served as legal counsel, as a consultant and as a trainer in the field of legal and ethical issues related to confidentiality, expert witness testimony, dual relationships and boundary violations, and various other issues.

PEARL BERMAN, Ph.D. is a licensed psychologist who is a professor of psychology and clinic supervisor within the PsyD program at Indiana University of Pennsylvania. She received her BA in Psychology from Brandeis University in 1977 and her Ph.D. in Clinical Psychology from Bowling Green State University in 1983. Her areas of clinical and research expertise include child physical and sexual abuse, neglect, and spousal violence. She has published book chapters and presented papers in these areas.

RACHEL GOLDBERG, Ph.D. is a licensed psychologist in private practice for sixteen years specializing in children and adolescents. She was the first psychologist to be hired by Bryn Mawr College. She is a fellow of the Pennsylvania Psychological Association where she serves on the Ethics Committee and a board member of the Philadelphia Society of Clinical Psychologists and the Salvation Army. She has created groups for children who have a parent with serious mental illness. Prior to her doctoral training, Dr. Goldberg directed programs for mentally handicapped young adults. She is currently on the staff of Thomas Jefferson University.

BEVERLY J. GOODWIN, Ph.D. is an associate professor of psychology at Indiana University of Pennsylvania. She received her doctorate in psychology from the University of Pittsburgh Clinical Psychology Program. Her specialty areas are psychopathology, supervision and training, curriculum transformation, diversity issues in psychology, and relationship violence. Her current research interests are images of African Americans in the popular media and the impact of sexual victimization on women of color.

MICHAEL C. GOTTLIEB, Ph.D. practices independently in Dallas. He is a diplomate (ABPP) in Family Psychology, a fellow of the American Psychological Association (APA), and a member of the adjunct faculty at Texas Woman's University. He is a past president of the Texas Psychological Association, The American Board of Family Psychology, and The Academy of Family Psychology. Currently, he is a member of the Committee on Professional Practice and Standards of the APA. In 1996, he was selected as the Distinguished Psychologist by the Academy of Family Psychology.

BETHANY R. HAMPTON received her Ph.D. in counseling psychology at the University of Texas at Austin in 1988. Dr. Hampton is an associate professor in the Department of Psychology and Philosophy at Texas Woman's University in Denton. Her scholarship has focused on gender issues, ethics, and sexual boundary violations. As a practicing psychologist, she specializes in feminist marital and family therapy.

SAMUEL KNAPP received his Ed.D. in counseling from Lehigh University in 1982. He is currently the Professional Affairs Officer for the Pennsylvania Psychological Association.

LINDA K. KNAUSS, Ph.D. is the coordinator of clinical services at the Devereux Kanner Center in West Chester, Pennsylvania. She has also served as the director of internship training and assistant director of the Department of Psychology at Eastern State School and Hospital. In addition to a private practice in psychology, Dr. Knauss is an adjunct faculty member at Immaculata College. Dr. Knauss has held leadership positions on state and regional ethics committees. She is currently the president of The Philadelphia Society of Clinical Psychologists and will become president of the Pennsylvania Psychological Association in June 1997.

RICHARD D. MAGEE, Ph.D. is professor of psychology at Indiana University of Pennsylvania, where he directs the Center for Applied Psychology and the Family Clinic. His work involves family therapy supervision and community consultation with schools and family-based intervention programs. Dr. Magee is an approved supervisor of the American Association for Marriage and Family Therapy.

ANTHONY P. MANNARINO, Ph.D. is professor of psychiatry, MCP Hahnemann School of Medicine, Allegheny University of the Health Sciences. He is also the director of the Center for Traumatic Stress in Children and Adolescents and director of Child and Adolescent Psychiatry, Allegheny General Hospital, Pittsburgh, Pennsylvania. His clinical and research interests are the evaluation and treatment of traumatic stress in children.

DIANE T. MARSH, Ph.D. is professor of psychology at the University of Pittsburgh at Greensburg. She specializes in professional practice with people who have serious mental illness and with their families, and is a member of the American Psychological Association Task Force on Serious Mental Illness and Serious Emotional Disturbance.

JOHN P. QUIRK, Ed.D. received his doctorate from the University of Georgia in 1971. He is a professor and the doctoral coordinator in the Department of Educational and School Psychology at Indiana University of Pennsylvania. His research interests include assessment of family factors that relate to academic achievement, parent training, and family therapy for child behavior problems.

ROY SCRIVNER received his Ph.D. in counseling psychology from the University of Texas at Austin in 1974. For nine consecutive years, he served as an officer in the Texas Psychological Association, including as president in 1992. In 1977, the American Psychological Association Society for the Psychological Study of Lesbian and Gay Issues presented him with a Distinguished Professional Contributions Award for his work in lesbian, gay, and bisexual family issues. In 1987, he established the Lesbian and Gay Research Fund in the Texas Psychological Foundation. He has been employed as a full-time family therapist at the DVA Medical Center, Dallas, Texas, since 1975.

PAUL S. STRAND, Ph.D. is an assistant professor in the Department of Psychology at Indiana University of Pennsylvania. His research interests include the study of development and communication within the context of the family. Dr. Strand received his Ph.D. from the University of Tennessee and did an internship and post doctorate work at Dartmouth Medical School.

ANTHONY M. ZIPPLE, Sc.D. is a licensed psychologist and senior vice president at Vinfen Corporation in Cambridge, Massachusetts. Dr. Zipple is also an adjunct faculty member at Boston University's Department of Rehabilitation Counseling and the book review editor for the *Psychiatric Rehabilitation Journal*.

Contents

Introduction

In recent years, there have been important developments in professional ethics, family law, and practice with families. *Ethical and Legal Issues in Professional Practice with Families* explores these developments and offers practitioners new guidelines, insights, and strategies for working with families. The book has been written against a backdrop of increasing interest in family practice among both mental health and legal professionals. Within the last decade, for example, couple and family therapy has become an important focus in practice, teaching, training, research, and policy. Contributors to the book have expertise in all of these areas.

The book provides a comprehensive resource that can address the needs of the wide range of professionals who are increasingly concerned with ethical and legal issues in family practice. In fact, coverage of ethical and legal issues is sometimes mandated by professional organizations, such as the American Association for Marriage and Family Therapy, and by accrediting organizations, such as state licensing boards. Apart from these requirements, graduate students and professionals recognize the importance of competence in this area to enhance their skills as practitioners, to conform to prevailing ethical and legal standards, and to reduce professional liability.

Ethical and Legal Issues in Professional Practice with Families has a number of outstanding features. First, our contributors bring diverse backgrounds and expertise to the project. In light of the complex and changing nature of ethical, legal, and professional territories, individual practitioners cannot keep abreast of all important developments. Our book is designed to meet this need.

Second, consistent with the trend toward professional diversification in this era of managed care, we explore professional practice across various settings and discuss a variety of professional roles, including those of therapist, consultant, educator, supervisor, administrator, policy maker, researcher, and advocate. Complementing this broad perspective are chapters that cover specific topics in depth and present specialized guidelines for practitioners.

Third, several overarching themes integrate the diverse content. Throughout the book, we highlight the importance of (1) a competence paradigm for professional practice with families that emphasizes their strengths, resources, and expertise; (2) a collaborative mode of working with families; (3) the empirical foundations of professional practice; (4) a comprehensive system of mental health care; and (5) an integrated and coordinated model of service delivery.

Fourth, our contributors agree on a core set of guidelines that can foster ethical practice. Practitioners should (1) be knowledgeable about their professional code of ethics and about applicable federal and state law; (2) consult with colleagues as appropriate; (3) establish positive and collaborative relationships with clients and their families; (4) communicate effectively about ethical matters to relevant parties; (5) anticipate problems and develop strategies for their resolution; (6) document treatment carefully; and (7) remain abreast of current theory and research to ensure that their treatment is appropriate and effective.

Finally, the book offers many practical suggestions. Our readers will learn how to analyze and resolve ethical dilemmas, to enhance their practice with families, and to reduce liability and improve risk management.

Ethical and Legal Issues in Professional Practice with Families is organized into four parts. Part One focuses on general considerations that arise in professional practice with families. In "Ethical Issues in Professional Practice with Families," Diane T. Marsh examines the unique ethical issues that arise in couple and family therapy. Writing from a systemic perspective, Dr. Marsh presents a model for ethical decision making that can be used to analyze and resolve ethical dilemmas, examining the hierarchical levels of ethical rules, ethical principles, and ethical theories.

In a parallel chapter, "Legal Issues in Professional Practice with Families," attorney Ann Lee Begler begins with an overview of the legal system and notes the range of legal problems that may arise in the lives of clients. Additional topics include negligence and professional malpractice; diagnosis, competence, and referrals; confidentiality and privilege; suicide; harm to others; supervision; failure to report; and the family practice professional as court witness.

Focusing on a central concern of family practitioners in "Ethical Concerns Regarding Gender in Family Practice," Bethany R. Hampton and Michael C. Gottlieb review the literature concerned with client and family variables affected by gender and discuss the theoretical foundations of systems theory as well as their relationship to gender. Drs. Hampton and Gottlieb also describe the relationship between systems theory and gender, the influence of gender role socialization on therapists and supervisors, and the strategies that can foster a more ethical and gender-sensitive family practice.

Beverly J. Goodwin, in "Multicultural Competence in Family Practice," delineates another basic dimension of professional practice, beginning with the definition and conceptualization of multiculturalism. Dr. Goodwin then focuses on the training required for multicultural competence and the role that multicultural issues play in the delivery of services to families.

Part Two addresses professional practice with specific populations. In "Ethical Dilemmas in Working with Children and Adolescents," Rachel Goldberg specifies some ethical issues that arise in clinical work with minors, including child abuse, custody evaluation, separation and divorce, confidentiality, treatment of minors, informed consent, psychological assessment in school settings, and research with minors.

Richard D. Magee, in "Ethical Issues in Couple Therapy: Therapist Competence and Values," considers couple therapy as a significant and sought after treatment modality, noting the reasons for its elevation in professional status. He discusses ways in which the therapist's professional competence and personal value system provide a foundation for the ethical practice of couple therapy.

Addressing an important area of forensic practice, in "Working with Families with Custody and Visitation Problems," Anthony P. Mannarino examines the ethical and professional issues that clinicians encounter when working with families in which there are custody and visitation problems. Topics include definitional issues, role and professional boundaries, and practical suggestions for clinicians.

In "Ethical and Legal Issues in Lesbian, Gay, and Bisexual Family Therapy," Roy Scrivner identifies the salient ethical issues involved in providing services to these clients, with special attention to the dominant issue of clinical competence and the unique dilemmas that arise in professional practice. Dr. Scrivner uses case studies to illustrate problems commonly presented to the therapist.

John P. Quirk, in "Professional and Ethical Issues in Family-School Mental Health Interventions" addresses professional practice in school settings. He analyzes the ethical issues that may arise in connection with internal and external mental health consultation, child advocacy, systems theory, informed consent, and confidentiality.

Part Three focuses on current topics in professional practice. In "Ethical Issues in Child Maltreatment," Pearl S. Berman assists practitioners in integrating mandatory reporting of child abuse with good clinical practice. Presenting case examples, Dr. Berman illustrates the ethical issues that can arise in therapy with maltreating families and offers suggestions for their ethical and effective resolution.

In "The Recovered Memories Debate and Clinical Practice with Families," Paul S. Strand and Michael R. Nash begin with a discussion of social constructivism and the theoretical implications of false memories. Based on their review of the pertinent literature, Drs. Strand and Nash then draw several empirically validated conclusions and present some useful guidelines for dealing with the issue of repressed memories.

Diane T. Marsh, in "Serious Mental Illness: Ethical Issues in Working with Families," considers the ethical issues that arise in professional practice with families that include a member who has serious mental illness, such as schizophrenia, bipolar disorder, or major depression. Applying the model of ethical decision making delineated in Chapter 1, Dr. Marsh presents selected ethical dilemmas and assists practitioners in resolving the dilemmas in a manner that is both clinically and ethically appropriate.

In "Client Confidentiality and the Family's Need to Know: Strategies for Resolving the Conflict," Anthony M. Zipple, Susan Langle, Wayne Tyrell, LeRoy Spaniol, and Harriet Fisher provide practical suggestions for meeting the needs of families while protecting client confidentiality. Following their survey of the relevant literature, the authors offer a range of approaches for providing relevant but nonconfidential information to families and for providing confidential information in a manner that is ethically, legally, and clinically sound.

Part Four addresses some important professional issues that arise in family practice. Michael C. Gottlieb, in "An Ethics Policy for Family Practice Management," reviews the unique ethical dilemmas that arise in family practice and notes the inherent limitations to ethical rule making. Dr. Gottlieb also underscores the need for practitioner education and offers suggestions for developing a personal ethical decision-making policy.

In "Professional Liability and Risk Management in an Era of Managed Care," Samuel Knapp discusses risk management techniques for practitioners who work with families. Presenting a number of practical strategies, Dr. Knapp suggests that practitioners focus on their relationship with patients and families, anticipate problems, document carefully, and consult with knowledgeable peers.

Emphasizing the essential role of graduate programs, in "Professional Training in Ethics," Linda K. Knauss considers whether ethics should be a separate course, when in the curriculum an ethics course should be offered, and the content of and approaches to an ethics course. Dr. Knauss also examines the foundations of ethical behavior, the relationship between ethical principles and personal values, the relationships among ethical, legal, and clinical issues, and the role of continuing education.

PART ONE

General
Considerations

CHAPTER 1

Ethical Issues in Professional Practice with Families

DIANE T. MARSH

There is general agreement that the delineation and resolution of ethical issues is significantly more challenging in professional practice with families than with individuals. Indeed, the ethical complexity appears to increase geometrically in multiperson therapies, which are likely to include family members who differ in age, gender, role, needs, and desires. Moreover, when confronted with ethical dilemmas, family practitioners may find they have insufficient guidance, because ethical issues that arise in couple and family therapy are not always adequately addressed in professional ethical codes (Lakin, 1994; Patten, Barnett, & Houlihan, 1991).

From the perspective of professional practice with families, ethical codes present two general problems. First, ethical codes of the traditional mental health professions continue to reflect an individual model of practice that generalizes only partly to couple and family therapy (Margolin, 1982; Zygmond & Boorhem, 1989). In addition, unique ethical issues arise in multiperson therapies (Beamish, Navin, & Davidson, 1994; Green & Hansen, 1989). These include concerns about defining the client in couple and family therapy; obtaining informed consent from multiple family members; dealing with confidentiality; refusing to treat a family without all members present; handling values in family therapy; preserving the family; and using therapeutic strategies that involve unilateral decision making, deception, or withholding of information from families.

Especially during the past decade, practitioners have increasingly focused on ethical dilemmas that occur in professional practice with family members, including those who are not clients. A number of

3

books and chapters offer a comprehensive view of ethical issues in family therapy (Doherty & Boss, 1991; Huber, 1994; Vesper & Brock, 1991; Walrond-Skinner & Watson, 1987). The literature concerned with specific ethical concerns has also expanded. These concerns include confidentiality and privileged communications (Watkins, 1989); malpractice in family therapy (Paquin, 1988); family violence (Margolin & Burman, 1993; Tilden, Schmidt, Limandri, & Chiodo, 1994); child maltreatment (Lippitt, 1985; Sieber, 1994); family law (Zaidel, 1993); incest (Daniluk & Haverkamp, 1993); acquired immune deficiency syndrome (AIDS; Knapp & VandeCreek, 1990); duty-to-warn (Costa & Altekruse, 1994); use of conscious deception (Solovey & Duncan, 1992); diagnostic considerations (Denton, 1989); family mediation (Grebe, 1992); and managed care (Haas & Cummings, 1991).

Professional training in ethics has also received greater attention (Beamish et al., 1994; Horne, Dagley, & Webster, 1993; Smith, 1993). Practitioners are becoming more sensitive to the potential impact of clinical decisions on family members who are not clients. This issue has received substantial professional and popular attention in the area of recovered memories of sexual abuse (e.g., Kandel & Kandel, 1994). Other circumstances also mandate consideration of nonclient family members, such as parents who are serving as primary caregivers for an adult child with a developmental disability or serious mental illness (Marsh, 1992; Turnbull & Turnbull, 1990).

Family members who are not clients can be significantly affected by the decisions and behavior of clinicians. In the following vignette, a mother talks about her initial encounter with her son's therapist, who added considerably to her own anguish:

My son's therapist told me that his early relationship with me was the central problem—at the same time I was told that his prognosis was poor and he might need institutional care. At the time, I felt as if I were being told my son was dying and I was responsible for his death. It was absolutely devastating. I needed support during the most difficult period of my life. Instead, my pain was intensified by someone who passed judgment without taking the time to understand our family. (Marsh, 1994, p. 108)

A Systemic Perspective

Consistent with its roots in general systems theory, the family systems paradigm has incorporated the concept of hierarchic and integrative levels, with emphasis on the inherent interdependence among levels and on the potential impact of one level on another. Family practitioners assume that human behavior is best understood within its social context (see Imber-Black, 1991). Accordingly, their approach to services is contextually based, whether they are working with individuals, couples, families, or larger systems. This systemic perspective offers a valuable perspective for analyzing and resolving ethical dilemmas (Volker, 1994; Wendorf & Wendorf, 1985). For example, we can focus on the levels of the ecological system, the family system, family subsystems, and individual family members.

THE ECOLOGICAL SYSTEM

At the level of the ecological system, individuals and families are viewed as embedded in a larger sociocultural matrix (see Brofenbrenner, 1989). From this larger perspective, clinicians must take into account the role of social institutions, values, priorities, and policies, which can have a significant impact on family functioning. For instance, an ecological perspective is useful in conceptualizing the family experience of disability (Seligman & Darling, 1989); of chronic health problems (McDaniel, Hepworth, & Doherty, 1992); and of serious mental illness (Marsh, 1992). This broad perspective is also essential in understanding ethnic minority families (Giordano & Carini-Giordano, 1995), and gay and lesbian families (Scrivner & Eldridge, 1995).

THE FAMILY SYSTEM

Although family practitioners are sensitive to the larger context of professional practice, the family system is generally their primary unit of interest. At the level of the family system, it is important to consider family structure, functions, and characteristics. As we are regularly informed by a barrage of statistics, in recent years families have been undergoing significant change. Although the family remains the unit in which most people grow up, the traditional nuclear family—breadwinning father, homemaker mother, and children—is no longer the norm. Many other family structures have become more prevalent, including two-career, single-parent, teenage, ethnic minority, gay and lesbian, cohabiting, and blended families. Even within more traditional families, roles and relationships have been changing. Males and females are less restricted by narrow sex roles and more likely to share financial and caregiving responsibilities. Moreover, clinicians are increasingly aware of the multicultural context of the family system and its impact on professional practice.

In spite of their diversity, family systems have many generic characteristics that affect family functioning and family therapy. Steinglass (1987) has discussed these characteristics in terms of three core family systems concepts: organization, which is concerned with the consistency and patterning of family systems; morphostasis, which refers to their tendency to function as steady states over time; and morphogenesis, which pertains to the evolution of the family over time. Thus, practitioners need to be sensitive to family organization, stability, and development.

Family Subsystems

At the next level, clinicians direct their attention to family subsystems, including the parental subsystem, the marital subsystem, the sibling subsystem, and the extrafamilial subsystem. Because the impact of a family event depends partly on its timing in the lifespans of the individual and the family (Rolland, 1994), consequences are likely to differ for young and adult family members. In light of their developmental status, for example, young family members are particularly vulnerable to the adverse impact of a relative's disability, which functions as an "energy sink" that consumes energy needed for normal development (Bubolz & Whiren, 1984). Consistent with this developmental perspective, although there is strong evidence for a shared family burden, the serious mental illness of a close relative has a different impact on parents, spouses, siblings, and offspring (Marsh, 1992).

Here is the account of a woman who has a brother with schizophrenia. She talks about the impact of his mental illness on her own life:

I became the perfect child to spare my parents any more grief. I was forced to become responsible. In many ways, it forced me to accomplish things in my life I might not have otherwise done. But I have spent my life trying to run away from this problem. Feeling guilty and helpless, the unending sorrow for not being able to help. I have not felt entitled to be happy most of my adult life. (Marsh & Dickens, in press)

Individual Family Members

Finally, at the level of individual family members, clinicians are always sensitive to the unique biopsychosocial context of personal lives.

In summary, ethical practice with families must be placed in a broad context that acknowledges the ecological matrix in which the family system is embedded, the characteristics of family systems and subsystems, and the singular reality of personal lives.

A Model for Ethical Decision Making

In light of the complexity of the area, it is essential for clinicians to have a comprehensive framework for analyzing and resolving ethical conflicts. A number of models for ethical decision making are available (Steere, 1984; Volker, 1994; Woody, 1990). Kitchener (1984, 1986) has presented a model of ethical decision making that includes three hierarchically-tiered levels. The first level involves ethical rules, such as those included in professional codes of ethics and in other sets of rules or laws. The second level consists of ethical principles, which are enduring beliefs and specific modes of conduct that protect the interests and welfare of all involved. Ethical principles generally take precedence over personal and group values. Three of the most important principles in the helping professions are autonomy (freedom), beneficence (welfare of others), and nonmaleficence ("Above all do no harm").

Ethical theories comprise the third level of analysis, which can be used to resolve conflicts between ethical rules or principles. At this metalevel of analysis, the objective is to examine all possible consequences of clinical decisions. In applying the model to the resolution of ethical dilemmas, clinicians begin with the level of ethical rules. If conflicts arise among ethical rules or a particular issue is not addressed at this level, they can move to the next level of ethical principles. Similarly, if practitioners are unable to resolve the conflict at the second level, they can turn to higher level ethical theories. Thus, there is a progressive shift to an increasingly more general and abstract level until resolution of the ethical dilemma is accomplished.

Clinicians face many potential ethical conflicts in professional practice with families. For example, as Kaslow (1993) has discussed, present diagnostic systems do not include relational disorders. In the current *Diagnostic and Statistical Manual of Mental Disorders* (*DSM-IV*; American Psychiatric Association, 1994), such disorders are given V-Codes, which are generally ineligible for insurance reimbursement. As a result, couple and family therapists face the dilemma of providing a diagnosis that accurately reflects their systems approach to interpersonal problems without neglecting individual clients and without committing insurance fraud. The widespread practice of giving individual diagnoses in multiperson therapy misrepresents the focus and method of treatment and raises both ethical and legal concerns (Kaslow, 1996).

In addition, practitioners may need to address conflicts between ethical rules or principles, since, for instance, we are not free to harm others; conflicts among various members of the family, who may differ regarding a given course of action, such as a divorce; and conflicts between the clinician and the family, who may disagree about the advisability of family therapy. I will explore each level of analysis, beginning with the ethical rules contained in the codes of mental health professions, including the American Psychological Association (APA), the American Psychiatric Association, the National Association of Social Workers, the American Association for Marriage and Family Therapy, and the American Counseling Association.

For purposes of illustration, my discussion will be based on the APA Ethics Code (American Psychological Association, 1992). In addition to six general principles, which establish aspirational goals for psychologists, the APA Ethics Code includes specific ethical standards, which set forth enforceable rules. Following a consideration of the general principles, I will briefly discuss selected ethical standards that have particular relevance to professional practice with families.

The Level of Ethical Rules: APA General Principles

The following general principles will be considered: competence, integrity, professional and scientific responsibility, respect for people's rights and dignity, concern for others' welfare, and social responsibility. Some essential elements of each principle are presented, noting certain issues that are likely to arise in professional practice with families.

COMPETENCE

With respect to the principle of competence, the APA Ethics Code mandates that psychologists maintain high standards of competence, recognize the boundaries of their competence, and provide only services for which they are qualified. When providing services in new areas or involving new techniques, they develop the necessary competencies for effective practice through appropriate study, training, supervision, and consultation.

Several general competencies are needed for effective family practice, including familiarity with family psychology, family therapy,
psychopathology, individual and family assessment, cultural diversity,
gender concerns, and developmental and individual differences. Most
practitioners have some familiarity with each of these areas. In addition, certain competencies are important in specific cases, including
those that involve child maltreatment, domestic violence, gay and lesbian relationships, substance abuse, divorce mediation, child custody,
sex therapy, serious mental illness, chronic health problems, disability,
school psychology, and forensic practice. Each of these specialized areas
may be essential for effective professional practice with some clients.
Clinicians may choose to develop the requisite competencies or refer to
a colleague with expertise in a given area.

INTEGRITY

Psychologists are required to promote integrity in the science, teaching, and practice of psychology; to be honest, fair, and respectful of
others; to be aware of personal beliefs, values, needs, and limitations;
to clarify professional roles; and to avoid potentially harmful multiple
relationships. Each of these mandates poses potential problems with
families. For example, the use of strategic or paradoxical approaches
raises ethical questions in light of their potential for manipulation and
deception (Betts & Remer, 1993). Problems with these interventions include possible conflicts with informed consent, integrity, and contract
law (Henderson, 1987); an adverse impact on the therapeutic alliance,
which is strengthened by therapist empathy, respect, genuineness, and
honesty (Solovey & Duncan, 1992); and the modeling of a deceptive
therapeutic relationship.

The values of practitioners inevitably influence couple and family
therapy, which may involve divorce, sex roles, extramarital affairs, and
other issues likely to elicit a personal response (e.g., Margolin, 1982).
Although value-free therapy is not possible, clinicians who are aware
of their personal values can avoid or minimize problems by discussing
potential problems with clients, consulting with colleagues, or making
a referral to another practitioner. It is also important for clinicians to
remain sensitive to issues concerning professional roles and multiple
relationships in light of the potential for changing circumstances and
relationships in family therapy, as in the case of unsuccessful marital
therapy that is followed by an acrimonious divorce involving a custody
dispute. More generally, they must avoid improper and potentially

harmful multiple relationships, including personal, scientific, professional, and financial relationships that may undermine therapy.

PROFESSIONAL AND SCIENTIFIC RESPONSIBILITY

This principle requires psychologists to uphold professional standards
of conduct, to clarify professional roles and obligations, to accept appropriate responsibility for their behavior, to adapt methods for differing
clients, to consult with professionals and institutions as appropriate,
and to make appropriate referrals to prevent or avoid unethical conduct.
Consistent with the systemic perspective discussed earlier, family practitioners regularly consult with, refer to, and cooperate with other professionals and institutions to serve the best interests of their clients.

Consultation is an essential element of effective professional practice with families. In a given case, practitioners may need to consult
with the health care system, the mental health system, the educational
system, the child welfare system, or the juvenile justice system. For instance, the concept of wraparound services for children and adolescents with serious emotional disturbance implies that appropriate
services will be coordinated to meet all of their diverse needs in the
community. Similarly, the national initiatives of the Community Support Program (CSP) and the Child and Adolescent Service System Program (CASSP) are predicated on the concept of a comprehensive
system of care that includes a range of services, as well as provisions
for effective service delivery (see Marsh, 1992).

Consistent with this conception of a comprehensive system of care,
family practitioners may serve on formal or informal teams designed
to offer clients a range of services that are delivered in an individualized, coordinated, integrated, and continuous manner. Consultation
with colleagues may offer assistance in developing a system of care for
particular clients, in addressing problems or impasses in therapy, and
in resolving ethical concerns. Clinicians also have a responsibility to
make appropriate referrals. Referrals should be made when personal
competence is insufficient, when personal values interfere with professional practice, or when the welfare of the client is better served.

RESPECT FOR PEOPLE'S RIGHTS AND DIGNITY

This principle requires psychologists to respect the fundamental
rights, dignity, and worth of all people; and to be sensitive to cultural,
individual, and role differences. With respect to families, it is important for clinicians to apply this principle to the family system, family

subsystems, and individual family members, including minor children. Clinicians also need to be sensitive to the dimensions of difference that characterize particular families and family members, including age, gender, race, ethnicity, national origin, religion, sexual orientation, disability, language, and socioeconomic status.

Although these considerations apply to all clients, they assume greater importance for practitioners who work with ethnic minority families (Task Force, 1991). Unfortunately, relatively few graduate programs in the mental health professions offer satisfactory training in multicultural competence. Gender also merits special consideration in family practice, which takes place against a backdrop etched by a history of discrimination and unequal power, as well as by the prevalence of sex role stereotypes, of sexual harassment, and of rape, sexual abuse, and domestic violence. Although family practitioners initially focused on the issues of women in therapy (e.g., Weiner & Boss, 1985), there has been increasing attention to the issues of men (e.g., Meth & Pasick, 1990).

CONCERN FOR OTHER'S WELFARE

Psychologists are mandated to contribute actively to the welfare of others, to resolve conflicts so as to avoid or minimize harm, and to be sensitive to issues of power and authority. This principle poses inherent problems for family practitioners, who must strive to balance the needs of the family system with those of individual family members. There are circumstances when the best interests of family members are incompatible or when a given course of action, such as a divorce, may have a different impact on the welfare of particular family members. Although family practitioners generally consider the client to be the family as a whole, the needs of individuals sometimes take precedence over the needs of the family unit, as in the case of child maltreatment or domestic violence. Under these circumstances, clinicians face the challenge of choosing the course of action that results in the least amount of avoidable harm to all relevant parties (as required by the ethical theory of utilitarianism; see subsequent discussion of ethical theories).

SOCIAL RESPONSIBILITY

This principle requires psychologists to be aware of responsibilities to community and society, to strive to advance human welfare and the science of psychology, and to contribute a portion of professional time. These requirements have implications for family practitioners, who are encouraged to play a constructive role in their communities and the larger society, to promote research with families, and to undertake pro bono work with families. This principle is also consistent with an advocacy role for professionals, who may choose to advocate for individual clients, for changes in the service delivery system, for professional objectives, for laws and social policies that advance human welfare, or for social and political causes.

The Level of Ethical Rules: Selected APA Ethical Standards

In addition to the aspirational goals specified in the general principles, the APA Ethics Code includes specific ethical standards, which cite enforceable rules. I will explore some important elements of two ethical standards of particular relevance to families: Therapy (Standard 4) and Privacy and Confidentiality (Standard 5).

THERAPY

As early as feasible, psychologists are required to discuss appropriate issues with clients (see the following discussion of informed consent), to provide information about supervision, and to make reasonable efforts to answer questions and avoid misunderstanding. When working with multiple family members, practitioners should strive to communicate effectively with all members of the family. Clinicians are also mandated to clarify lines of responsibility, especially when there are multiple therapists, consultants, or live supervisors or teams.

Practitioners are required to obtain appropriate informed consent to therapy or related procedures, using language that is reasonably understandable to participants. Informed consent generally implies that the person has the capacity to consent, has been informed of significant information concerning the procedure, and has freely and without undue influence expressed consent. It is usually prudent to document consent.

From a legal perspective, Bray, Shepherd, and Hayes (1985) have specified the three elements of informed consent: (a) legal capacity, which requires that the client be competent and of minimum legal age; (b) comprehension of information, which requires that the client receive information about potential benefits and risks of the procedure, risks of forgoing the procedure, and available alternatives; and (c) voluntary agreement, which requires that the client be permitted to act freely in giving consent and to withdraw from participation without penalty. These elements also apply to family participation in research (Heatherington, Friedlander, & Johnson, 1989), and to the use of electronic recording or observers, a mandate that is not always honored in professional practice (e.g., Brock & Coufal, 1989).

Information that can be conveyed to families is inherently limited because of uncertainty regarding the behavior of individual family members and the consequences of specific interventions (Heatherington et al., 1989). Nevertheless, general agreement exists about the information that should be provided to potential clients (see Corey, Corey, & Callanan, 1993). In addition to information about potential risks and benefits, clinicians should discuss the nature and anticipated length of therapy, their professional background, fees, confidentiality, supervision, diagnostic labeling, audio- or videotaping of sessions, record keeping and access to files, and potential multiple relationships. Therapists should take care to ensure that children, adults, and elderly family members are able to understand information that is provided.

Family members should also be informed that therapy can result in increased family stress and disruption and in unintended (and perhaps undesirable) consequences (see Huber, 1994). For example, therapy-induced change in one family member can have an adverse impact on family relationships, and confrontation with long-denied problems, such as substance abuse, can provoke anger and conflict. Although a temporary increase in distress may be necessary for constructive long-term change, families should be aware of the potential for unexpected developments in family therapy.

Practitioners are required to establish which individuals are clients; to clarify the relationship with each person; and to clarify and adjust, or withdraw from, potentially conflicting roles. With multiple clients, roles can be renegotiated at any time, but must be clear at all times, as when there is a shift from marital therapy to a divorce proceeding. Similarly, policies need to be clarified regarding matters such as the handling of "family secrets" involving confidences shared by one family member, such as an extramarital affair (e.g., Margolin, 1982). As long as policies are discussed at the outset of therapy, clinicians may elect to refuse to keep secrets, to reserve the right to decide how to use information, or to establish multiple confidential relationships.

Communication with nonclients should also be clarified, especially in cases where other family members may be significantly affected by decisions made in therapy. For instance, when the client is an adult child with a chronic medical or mental illness whose parents are serving as primary caregivers, a collaborative relationship with families offers substantial benefits for all parties (e.g., Petrila & Sadoff, 1992). Under these circumstances, parents are not clients themselves, although they may have occasional contact with the therapist, who can assist them in understanding and coping with the illness, in providing a supportive environment at home, and in enhancing their relative's treatment and rehabilitation. At the same time, the boundaries of confidentiality need to be negotiated to reflect the right of clients to a confidential therapeutic relationship, as well as the rights of their family caregivers.

As specified in the section covering forensic activities, clinicians avoid performing multiple and potentially conflicting roles in their forensic work. For example, a court-ordered custody evaluation is not protected by confidentiality and requires an objective evaluation of the family. In contrast, therapy with the child involved in the custody dispute is protected by confidentiality and necessitates a subjective relationship with the child. Thus, to avoid potential conflict, practitioners should generally restrict their involvement to one of these roles. When it appears that they may be called on to perform potentially conflicting roles, practitioners need to clarify role expectations and the extent of confidentiality in advance to the extent feasible, and thereafter as changes occur. This policy will assist practitioners to avoid compromising professional judgment and objectivity and to avoid misleading others regarding their role.

PRIVACY AND CONFIDENTIALITY

Initially, it is important to distinguish among confidentiality, which is a professional ethical standard that offers protection against unauthorized disclosures; privileged communication, which is a legal right that offers protection under certain circumstances from having confidences revealed during legal proceedings without permission; and privacy, which is a constitutional right to protection against invasion of privacy. In the course of clinical practice, professionals may find themselves dealing with all of these concerns. Given the focus of this chapter, however, I will address only the ethical standard of confidentiality.

This standard requires psychologists to discuss relevant limitations on confidentiality at the beginning of therapy, and thereafter as new circumstances warrant. Limitations may result from the presence of other people in group, couple, and family therapy; or from applicable laws, institutional rules, or professional or scientific relationships. They also need to discuss any foreseeable uses of information generated through their services.

Practitioners are required to take reasonable precautions to maintain confidentiality and to minimize intrusions on privacy. For example, written and oral reports should include only germane information, and information should be shared only for appropriate purposes and with relevant individuals. In addition, clinicians should maintain appropriate confidentiality in record keeping. In the case of multiple clients, such as family members, records may be kept individually or comingled. In either case, family members need to be informed at the outset about record-keeping practices, as well as procedures necessary to release records and to disclose confidential information.

Confidential information should be disclosed without the consent of the individual only as mandated by law, or where permitted by law for a valid purpose, such as to provide needed professional services, to obtain appropriate professional consultations, to protect the client or others from harm, or to obtain payment for services. Clinicians may also disclose confidential information with the appropriate consent of the client, unless prohibited by law. When consulting with colleagues, practitioners should protect the confidentiality of the relationship unless they have obtained the prior consent of the client or the disclosure cannot be avoided, and they should share information only to the extent necessary to achieve the purposes of the consultation. In the case of multiple clients, each legally competent party needs to provide consent for disclosure of confidential information, as in the case of participants in marital therapy who decide to divorce.

The Level of Ethical Principles

Family practitioners who turn to professional codes for resolution of their ethical dilemmas sometimes find these guidelines to be contradictory and ambiguous. Under these circumstances, they can shift to the second level of ethical principles for assistance. Three ethical principles will be considered: autonomy, beneficence, and nonmaleficence (see Steere, 1984).

AUTONOMY

Autonomy is concerned with the freedom of individuals to act in accordance with their beliefs as long as they do not impede the freedom of others. When making decisions about participation in treatment or research, clients must be allowed to make autonomous decisions and to be in possession of all relevant information. Thus, they are free to choose their degree of participation, to decline to participate at all, to set or alter goals, and to withdraw without undue pressure (see Lakin, 1988). Although this principle would appear to insure the right of families to make an informed choice about their participation in therapy, ethical conflicts may arise between autonomy (informed consent) and beneficence (welfare of the client).

Based on the assumption that family involvement is essential for effective treatment of children and adolescents, for example, an agency or individual practitioner may require families to participate in family therapy as a condition for obtaining treatment for their child. In my research, 50% of parents of children with serious emotional disturbance reported receiving mandatory family therapy (Marsh, Koeske, & Schultz, 1993). Such an institutional policy may increase the potential for negative treatment effects when the needs and desires of family members are ignored. Here is the description of one mother who was subject to a requirement of family therapy:

When I put her into the hospital, the doctor told me that we had to come to mandatory family therapy twice a week. We had to go to these sessions in order to be able to visit our daughter. It was an extreme waste of my time. . . . It was not helping me out at all. . . . What I needed was information about my daughter and what to do about her. (Marsh, 1992, pp. 57–58)

As this mother suggests, a more flexible approach to working with families may be best. Certainly, family involvement in a child's treatment is likely to promote the welfare of the child and the family. But family therapy is not the only means of involving families, who may benefit from educational programs and support groups for themselves or from sessions designed to address their needs, increase their understanding of their child, improve their coping skills, and enlist their assistance with the treatment plan. This flexible and collaborative approach is consistent with the principles of autonomy, because families are permitted to determine the nature of their involvement, and of beneficence, because their involvement is likely to enhance their child's treatment and strengthen their family.

Conflicts may also arise when a family requests individual therapy for a member and the clinician believes it is in the best interest of the family to participate in marital or family therapy. In fact, there is empirical support for the general effectiveness of family therapy (Markus, Lange, & Pettigrew, 1990), and for the superiority of marital therapy or family therapy in certain cases (Gurman & Kniskern, 1991). When a clinician considers family therapy to be the most suitable course of action for a particular family, he or she can explain the rationale for family therapy and encourage their participation. If disagreement persists regarding the appropriate course or some family members decline to participate, the clinician may choose to honor the client's preference or to make a referral to another practitioner or agency, so that willing family members are not denied treatment. At the same time, clinicians are not obliged to provide treatment if they believe it would be ineffective or counterproductive.

BENEFICENCE

Elements of beneficence include the duty to contribute actively to the good of others and to offer the intervention that provides the most benefits for the lowest cost. Thus, clinicians should conduct a cost-benefit analysis of various alternatives and discuss this analysis with potential clients. In some cases, consistent with the principle of least intervention (Thompson, 1990), clinicians may recommend against psychotherapy, perhaps referring the client to nonclinical services, such as an educational program or support group. As Lewis (1989) has discussed, it is important not to overprescribe therapy for problems that a family may be capable of resolving without professional assistance or that may be transitional in nature.

The objective is to recommend the optimal match between the needs, desires, and resources of particular clients and the available services. For example, families who have a member with serious mental illness consistently rate educational and supportive resources as more helpful than psychotherapy, including family therapy (Marsh, 1995). Thus, a referral for nonclinical services would appear to be the initial intervention of choice for most of these families. More intensive forms of intervention, including family therapy, can be recommended for families whose needs are not met through nonclinical intervention.

The importance of an optimal match is illustrated by the following vignettes. Both of these mothers received psychotherapy themselves during the course of their child's treatment. The first mother found therapy a good match for the needs of her family members, who were facing problems in many areas of their lives:

I was in mental health [treatment] myself for attempting suicide after my husband left me and a combination of a lot of things. I have had a great deal of counseling, which has helped me very much. I have been mentally abused by my husband and so have my children. Counseling has made us all stronger. (Marsh, 1992, p. 197)

The second mother does not appear to be an appropriate candidate for psychotherapy. She needed the knowledge, skills, and support to cope more effectively with her son's schizophrenia and found therapy a poor match for her needs:

I went to see the therapist specifically to see how I was going to live through my pain and how to deal with my son's mental illness. He wanted me to deal with my childhood, something I had already dealt with. My son's illness wasn't caused by my childhood. I didn't feel he was willing to help me with my goals, so I quit after three sessions. (Marsh, 1992, p. 207)

NONMALEFICENCE

Nonmaleficence is the directive to do no harm, which is defined broadly to include a range of negative consequences. Intentional harm is prohibited, and exposure to risk of harm is permissible only when a risk-benefit analysis indicates that the likelihood of positive consequences outweighs the potential for harm. Thus, clinicians should conduct a risk-benefit analysis to ensure that the chosen course offers the maximum benefits at lowest risk. Nonmaleficence generally takes precedence over other ethical rules and principles, including autonomy (since we are not free to harm others), privacy and confidentiality (since we may forfeit our rights to privacy and confidentiality if there is risk of harm), and beneficence (if there is a greater likelihood of harm than of benefit in therapy).

Researchers who investigate therapeutic outcome often define risk in terms of negative treatment effects, which are adverse consequences that result from the therapy. As Strupp and Hadley (1985) have discussed, negative treatment effects can result from inappropriate use of therapy, undertaking of unrealistic tasks or goals, loss of trust in therapy and the therapist, deficiencies in assessment or technique, presence of certain therapist or client qualities, problems in the client-therapist relationship, and breaches in confidentiality.

In the following vignette, a mother describes a number of negative effects that resulted from her contacts with professionals:

I felt so battered after my experiences with professionals. When my daughter was hospitalized, we were placed in family therapy without even being consulted, something we neither needed nor wanted. And the comments of various professionals suggested that they held us responsible for our daughter's problems, adding to our feelings of guilt and responsibility. . . . [M]y husband and I both felt drained and violated by our experiences. We needed understanding and support during that period. Instead, our experiences with professionals added to our problems. (Marsh, 1992, p. 212)

In addition, some special risks are associated with family therapy (e.g., Anderson, 1986; Hare-Mustin, 1980). For example, problems can arise from the application of conceptual models that ignore the expressed needs of families, that foster learned helplessness, or that incorporate pejorative assumptions about families. Lakin (1988) has described conceptual models as "maps of the soul" that guide clinical intervention (p. 34). As he points out, ethical problems arise when these models obscure or override the needs and desires of clients. Here is one mother's description of her encounters with professionals:

One of the most difficult things to deal with during my daughter's hospitalization was the distortion of our family experience. . . . [I]t was as if we were cardboard figures thrust into clichés about families that had little to do with us as a real family. All of this distortion added to our confusion and vulnerability. And when I tried to discuss our family or to correct their distortions, their theoretical assumptions seemed to take precedence over our reality. We would have been better off if we had been left alone to regroup and heal by ourselves. (Marsh, 1992, p. 24)

Problems can also arise from use of authoritarian help-giving models that promote paternalism and encourage dependency, passivity, and low self-esteem (e.g., Miller, Scott, & Searight, 1990). Indeed, in contrast with the generally accepted goal of client empowerment, such models are often disempowering for clients. The following mother recounts her experiences in therapy:

I feel now that it was a mistake to get into therapy. . . . I was not mentally ill and did not need treatment or analysis. . . . Nor was it constructive for me to become a patient or to become involved in a process that seemed to emphasize my vulnerability and to drain my energy. I needed to feel healthy and strong and intact, the very things that were undermined by what happened in therapy. (Marsh, 1992, p. 204)

Further risks are associated with the application of conceptual models that incorporate unsupported assumptions of family dysfunction or pathogenesis (e.g., Carr, 1990). Such models can add significantly to the problems of families already experiencing considerable distress (e.g., Marsh, 1992). Here are the words of two siblings who found themselves in family therapy simply because they happened to have a brother or sister with a serious mental illness. They also shared the experience of having their own anguish intensified by professionals who held their families accountable for the illness:

I was 16 when my 14-year-old brother had his first psychotic episode. He was hospitalized for most of my adolescence. His illness was the most devastating episode of my entire life. I was ashamed, I was afraid, I was confused. I was involved in family therapy sessions that put the blame on the family. It was awful.

I was part of a twins and siblings study. I recall no help for my pain. The viewpoint at that time was that the illness was caused by faulty parenting. I am angry at the doctors for blaming my parents, which hurt them as much as the tragedy of losing a daughter to mental illness. God knows, it pretty much destroyed my parents. (Marsh & Dickens, in press)

Other sources of negative treatment effects in family therapy include premature confrontation with "loaded" issues, unnecessary escalation of family distress, changes in one family member that unbalance the family system, untimely challenges to the family's predominant mode of interaction, pressure to make disclosures, and failure to resolve conflicts provoked in sessions (Huber, 1994). The risk of these negative effects can be reduced by a skillful therapist. Other risks can be minimized by assisting families to make an informed choice about their participation in therapy and by collaborating with them to develop a mutually acceptable treatment plan that addresses their expressed needs. Such an approach is likely to maximize the likelihood of a positive response to therapy, such as the following:

Family therapy occurred in a hospital setting during the initial hospitalization. It seemed mostly an opportunity for the psychiatrist, social worker, and psychiatric nurse to observe family interactions and may have been helpful in our son's treatment. Individual and marital therapy [were] helpful in resolving problems which were exacerbated by the serious mental illness of my son. Trying to change is never easy, but overall it was helpful. (Marsh, 1992, p. 199)

The Level of Ethical Theories

If practitioners find they cannot resolve an ethical conflict at the level of ethical rules or principles, they can shift to the third level of ethical theories. This metalevel of analysis facilitates resolution of ethical conflicts through an examination of all possible consequences of decisions. Many ethical theories have been proposed, including the Golden Mean, Judeo-Christian doctrine, empathetic reciprocity, Kant's Categorical Imperative, utilitarianism, and causalism (Turnbull & Turnbull, 1990). As Kitchener (1986) has discussed, many twentieth-century ethicists have defined ethical decisions in terms of the theories of universalizability and utilitarianism. Namely, ethical decisions are those (a) that are consistent with those that individuals would make under the same circumstances for themselves or others whom they love (universalizability), or (b) that produce the least amount of avoidable harm to all pertinent individuals (utilitarianism).

The theory of universalizability asserts that a decision is ethical if it can be unambiguously generalized to all similar cases and if it is consistent with decisions individuals would make personally. One problem with this theory is the difficulty of finding "similar" cases when, from a clinical perspective, each family is necessarily understood in terms of its uniqueness. Moreover, this theory offers little specific assistance in resolving conflicts between ethical rules or principles.

Utilitarian theory requires that all possible benefits be weighed against all possible costs for all affected individuals. Thus, the scope of ethical practice is all family members, including those who are not clients. Following an assessment of the potential impact of a decision on the family system and all individual members, the ethical course of action is that which results in the least amount of avoidable harm. Such a family-systems orientation is compatible with current standards of practice in the area of developmental disabilities (e.g., Turnbull & Turnbull, 1990). It is also consistent with emerging case law, including a recent case in which substantial damages were awarded to a father who claimed that his daughter's therapist had implanted false memories of childhood sexual abuse.

Conclusion

There are a number of ethical guidelines for professional practice with families. First, practitioners should be knowledgeable about their professional code of ethics, as well as applicable federal and state law. They should ensure that their own behavior is consistent with these ethical and legal standards, keep abreast of new ethical and legal developments, maintain a high level of professional competence, and consult with colleagues as appropriate.

Second, family practitioners should communicate effectively with families. Relevant topics include information required for informed consent, as well as office policies and procedures, fees, record keeping, confidentiality, professional roles and obligations, and relationships with family members.

Third, current scientific and professional information provides an essential foundation for effective practice with families. For example, clinicians should be familiar with empirical support for specific interventions, with the individual and family variables that can affect treatment outcome, and with professional guidelines on specific topics, such as custody evaluation and recovered memories.

Fourth, an initial role as a family consultant offers practitioners an opportunity to assist families in making an informed choice about their use of services. The objective is to achieve an optimal match between the needs, desires, and resources of particular families and the available services. Thus, good clinical practice requires a careful process of systematic treatment selection for particular clients.

Fifth, consistent with the ethical principles of beneficence and nonmaleficence, clinicians should undertake cost-benefit and risk-benefit analyses to ensure that the chosen course of action provides the most benefits for the lowest cost and with the fewest risks.

Sixth, the risk of negative treatment effects should be minimized, including those associated with the absence of informed consent, the application of conceptual models that incorporate unsupported assumptions of family pathogenesis or dysfunction, coercive methods for gaining family treatment compliance, and deceptive and manipulative interventions.

Finally, the overarching consideration in professional practice is the relationship between the clinician and the family. Indeed, it is this interpersonal context that appears to be most closely related to therapeutic outcome. A constructive alliance is likely to be promoted by a respectful and empathic attitude toward families, an emphasis on their strengths and expertise, an understanding of their phenomenological reality, and an effort to meet their expressed needs.

References

American Psychiatric Association. (1994). *Diagnostic and statistical manual of mental disorders* (4th ed.). Washington, DC: Author.

American Psychological Association. (1992). Ethical principles of psychologists and code of conduct. *American Psychologist, 47,* 1597–1611.

Anderson, C. M. (1986). The all-too-short trip from positive to negative connotation. *Journal of Marital and Family Therapy, 12,* 351–354.

Beamish, P. M., Navin, S. L., & Davidson, P. (1994). Ethical dilemmas in marriage and family therapy: Implications for training. *Journal of Mental Health Counseling, 16,* 129–142.

Betts, G. R., & Remer, R. (1993). The impact of paradoxical interventions on perceptions of the therapist and ratings of treatment acceptability. *Professional Psychology: Research and Practice, 24,* 164–170.

Bray, J. H., Shepherd, J. N., & Hays, J. R. (1985). Legal and ethical issues in informed consent to psychotherapy. *American Journal of Family Therapy, 13,* 50–60.

Brock, G. W., & Coufal, J. D. (1989, March/April). Ethics in practice. *Family Therapy Networker,* p. 27.

Brofenbrenner, U. (1989). Ecological systems theory. *Annals of Child Development, 6,* 187–249.

Bubolz, M. M., & Whiren, A. P. (1984). The family of the handicapped: An ecological model for policy and practice. *Family Relations, 33,* 5–12.

Carr, A. (1990). Failure in family therapy: A catalogue of engagement mistakes. *Journal of Family Therapy, 12,* 371–386.

Corey, G., Corey, M. S., & Callanan, P. (1993). *Issues and ethics in the helping professions* (4th ed.). Pacific Grove, CA: Brooks/Cole.

Costa, L., & Altekruse, M. (1994). Duty-to-warn guidelines for mental health counselors. *Journal of Counseling and Development, 72,* 346–350.

Daniluk, J. C., & Haverkamp, B. E. (1993). Ethical issues in counseling adult survivors of incest. *Journal of Counseling and Development, 72,* 16–22.

Denton, W. H. (1989). DSM-III-R and the family therapist: Ethical considerations. *Journal of Marital and Family Therapy, 15,* 367–377.

Doherty, W. J., & Boss, P. G. (1991). Values and ethics in family therapy. In A. S. Gurman & D. P. Kniskern (Eds.), *Handbook of family therapy* (Vol. 2, pp. 606–637). New York: Brunner/Mazel.

Giordano, J., & Carini-Giordano, M. A. (1995). Ethnic dimensions in family treatment. In R. H. Mikesell, D. D. Lusterman, & S. H. McDaniel (Eds.), *Integrating family therapy: Handbook of family psychology and systems theory* (pp. 347–356). Washington, DC: American Psychological Association.

Grebe, S. C. (1992). Ethics and the professional family mediator. *Mediation Quarterly, 10,* 155–165.

Green, S. L., & Hansen, J. C. (1989). Ethical dilemmas faced by family therapists. *Journal of Marital and Family Therapy, 15,* 149–158.

Gurman, A. S., & Kniskern, D. P. (1991). Family therapy outcome research: Knowns and unknowns. In A. S. Gurman & D. P. Kniskern (Eds.), *Handbook of family therapy* (Vol. 1, pp. 742–775). New York: Brunner/Mazel.

Haas, L. J., & Cummings, N. A. (1991). Managed outpatient mental health plans: Clinical, ethical, and practical guidelines for participation. *Professional Psychology: Research and Practice, 22,* 45–51.

Hare-Mustin, R. T. (1980). Family therapy may be dangerous for your health. *Professional Psychology, 11,* 935–938.

Heatherington, L., Friedlander, M. L., & Johnson, W. F. (1989). Informed consent in family therapy research: Ethical dilemmas and practical problems. *Journal of Family Psychology, 2,* 373–385.

Henderson, M. C. (1987). Paradoxical process and ethical consciousness. *Family Therapy, 14,* 187–193.

Horne, A. M., Dagley, J. C., & Webster, C. B. (1993). Strategies for implementing marriage and family counselor training in counselor education programs. *Counselor Education and Supervision, 33,* 102–115.

Huber, C. H. (1994). *Ethical, legal, and professional issues in the practice of marriage and family therapy* (2nd ed.). New York: Merrill.

Imber-Black, E. (1991). A family—larger-system perspective. In A. S. Gurman & D. P. Kniskern (Eds.), *Handbook of family therapy* (Vol. 2, pp. 583–605). New York: Brunner/Mazel.

Kandel, M., & Kandel, E. (1994, May). Flights of memory. *Discover,* pp. 32–38.

Kaslow, F. (1993). Relational diagnosis: Past, present and future. *American Journal of Family Therapy, 21,* 195–204.

Kaslow, F. (1996). *Handbook of relational diagnosis and dysfunctional family patterns.* New York: Wiley.

Kitchener, K. S. (1984). Intuition, critical evaluation and ethical principles: The foundation for ethical decisions in counseling psychology. *Counseling Psychologist, 12,* 43–55.

Kitchener, K. S. (1986). Teaching applied ethics in counselor education: An integration of psychological processes and philosophical analysis. *Journal of Counseling and Development, 64,* 306–310.

Knapp, S., & VandeCreek, L. (1990). Application of the duty to protect HIV-positive patients. *Professional Psychology: Research and Practice, 21,* 161–166.

Lakin, M. (1988). *Ethical issues in the psychotherapies.* New York: Oxford University Press.

Lakin, M. (1994). Morality in group and family therapies: Multiperson therapies and the 1992 ethics code. *Professional Psychology: Research and Practice, 25,* 344–348.

Lewis, W. (1989). How not to engage a family in family therapy. *Journal of Strategic and Systemic Therapies, 8,* 50–53.

Lippitt, D. N. (1985). The ethical task in family therapy. *Family Therapy, 12,* 297–301.

Margolin, G. (1982). Ethical and legal considerations in marital and family therapy. *American Psychologist, 37,* 788–801.

Margolin, G., & Burman, B. (1993). Wife abuse versus marital violence: Different terminologies, explanations, and solutions. *Clinical Psychology Review, 13,* 59–73.

Markus, E., Lange, A., & Pettigrew, T. F. (1990). Effectiveness of family therapy: A meta-analysis. *Journal of Family Therapy, 12,* 205–221.

Marsh, D. T. (1992). *Families and mental illness: New directions in professional practice.* New York: Praeger.

Marsh, D. T. (1994). The psychodynamic model and services for families: Issues and strategies. In H. P. Lefley & M. Wasow (Eds.), *Helping families cope with mental illness* (pp. 105–128). Newark, NJ: Harwood Academic.

Marsh, D. T. (1995). Families and serious mental illness: Ethical issues in professional practice. *Family Psychologist, 11*(1), 17–19.

Marsh, D. T., & Dickens, R. M. (in press). *Troubled journey: Coming to terms with the mental illness of a sibling or parent.* New York: Tarcher/Putnam.

Marsh, D. T., Koeske, R. D., & Schultz, K. (1993). Services for families: A NAMI CAN Survey. *Innovations and Research, 2*(4), 53–54.

McDaniel, S. H., Hepworth, J., & Doherty, W. J. (1992). *Medical family therapy: A biopsychosocial approach to families with health problems.* New York: Basic Books.

Meth, R. L., & Pasick, R. S. (1990). *Men in therapy: The challenge of change.* New York: Guilford.

Miller, T. R., Scott, R., & Searight, H. R. (1990). Ethics for marital and family therapy and subsequent training issues. *Family Therapy, 17,* 163–171.

Paquin, G. W. (1988). The malpractice of family therapy: An analysis of two "schools." *Law and Psychology Review, 12,* 21–59.

Patten, C., Barnett, T., & Houlihan, D. (1991). Ethics in marital and family therapy: A review of the literature. *Professional Psychology: Research and Practice, 22,* 171–175.

Petrila, J. P., & Sadoff, R. L. (1992). Confidentiality and the family as caregiver. *Hospital and Community Psychiatry, 43,* 136–139.

Rolland, J. S. (1994). *Families, illness, and disability: An integrative treatment model.* New York: Basic Books.

Scrivner, R., & Eldridge, N. S. (1995). Lesbian and gay family psychology. In R. H. Mikesell, D. D. Lusterman, & S. H. McDaniel (Eds.), *Integrating family therapy: Handbook of family psychology and systems theory* (pp. 327–345). Washington, DC: American Psychological Association.

Seligman, M., & Darling, R. B. (1989). *Ordinary families, special children: A systems approach to childhood disability.* New York: Guilford.

Sieber, J. E. (1994). Issues presented by mandatory reporting requirements to researchers of child abuse and neglect. *Ethics and Behavior, 4,* 1–22.

Smith, R. L. (1993). Training in marriage and family counseling and therapy: Current status and challenges. *Counselor Education and Supervision, 33,* 89–101.

Solovey, A. D., & Duncan, B. L. (1992). Ethics and strategic therapy: A proposed ethical direction. *Journal of Marital and Family Therapy, 18,* 53–61.

Steere, J. (1984). *Ethics in clinical psychology.* New York: Oxford University Press.

Steinglass, P. (1987). A system view of family interaction and psychopathology. In T. Jacobs (Ed.), *Family interaction and psychopathology* (pp. 25–65). New York: Plenum.

Strupp, H. H., & Hadley, S. W. (1985). Negative effects and their determinants. In D. T. Mays & C. M. Franks (Eds.), *Negative outcome in psychotherapy and what to do about it* (pp. 20–55). New York: Springer.

Task Force on the Delivery of Services to Ethnic Minority Populations. (1991). *Guidelines for providers of psychological services to ethnic, linguistic, and culturally diverse population.* Washington, DC: American Psychological Association.

Thompson, A. (1990). *Guide to ethical practice in psychotherapy.* New York: Wiley.

Tilden, V. P., Schmidt, T. A., Limandri, B. J., & Chiodo, G. T. (1994). Factors that influence clinicians' assessment and management of family violence. *American Journal of Public Health, 84,* 628–633.

Turnbull, A. P., & Turnbull, H. R. (1990). *Families, professionals, and exceptionality: A special partnership* (2nd ed.). Columbus, OH: Merrill.

Vesper, J. H., & Brock, G. W. (1991). *Ethics, legalities, and professional practice issues in marriage and family therapy.* Boston: Allyn & Bacon.

Volker, T. (1994). Value analysis: A model of personal and professional ethics in marriage and family counseling. *Counseling and Values, 38,* 193–204.

Walrond-Skinner, S., & Watson, D. (Eds.) (1987). *Ethical issues in family therapy.* New York: Routledge & Kegan Paul.

Watkins, S. A. (1989). Confidentiality and privileged communications: Legal dilemma for family therapists. *Social Work, 34,* 133–136.

Weiner, J. P., & Boss, P. G. (1985). Exploring gender bias against women: Ethics for marriage and family therapy. *Counseling and Values, 30,* 9–23.

Wendorf, D. J., & Wendorf, R. J. (1985). A systemic view of family therapy ethics. *Family Process, 24,* 443–453.

Woody, J. D. (1990). Resolving ethical concerns in clinical practice: Toward a pragmatic model. *Journal of Marital and Family Therapy, 16,* 133–150.

Zaidel, S. (1993). Ethical issues in family law. *Medicine and Law, 12,* 263–270.

Zygmond, M. J., & Boorhem, H. (1989). Ethical decision making in family therapy. *Family Process, 28,* 269–280.

CHAPTER 2

Legal Issues in Professional Practice with Families

ANN LEE BEGLER

Our cultural fascination with the legal system has heightened the interplay between law and mental health. All of the reasons the law appears to have a growing presence in our lives may never be apparent. Yet, given that presence, to maintain an effective practice, it is essential for mental health professionals who work with families to have a sound base of knowledge about the ways in which the law and their work intersect. Families who are in treatment are often dealing with many legal issues. The practitioner is continually impacted by potential areas of malpractice. Mental health practitioners are potential court witnesses. This chapter highlights the importance of the concentric circles that bring law and family practice together.

Overview of the Legal System

Before addressing specific legal issues that emerge in the context of a professional practice with families, it is helpful to first understand the framework within which conflict is handled within the traditional legal system.

The American legal system is a system of rules designed to regulate behavior in society. In theory, it has been designed *to insure the determination of truth.* Inherent in the system is the belief that if truth can be found, justice will result. The court system is divided between actions related to criminal conduct and civil actions for damages. In criminal cases, the parties to the action are the accused and the state. The criminal system addresses alleged violations of criminal laws—crimes against the state. The potential outcome of a criminal case is conviction and punishment.

Cases that come before the civil court system do not involve crimes against the state. In civil cases, parties to a lawsuit can be individuals or private or public entities. The primary goal of a civil action is to determine if one has been injured and, if so, to award monetary compensation for that injury. Civil courts also address family law issues, such as divorce and custody. Sometimes these issues are related to the purported establishment of economic justice within the family structure; other proceedings focus on the needs, welfare, and custody of children. This chapter focuses on civil court issues and the interplay between that system and mental health practitioners.

Within the structure of the system, it is assumed that one person involved in a legal conflict is right and the other wrong or, said differently, that one person has been harmed and the other caused that harm. Thus, participants in the legal system are defined as adversaries, each oppositional to the other, and each attempting to achieve a result that is favorable to that person.

The legal system is designed to be objective. A trial is the ultimate forum where decisions are made, but several steps take place before a case reaches a trial. Often, an attorney will first informally investigate the facts that underlie a possible lawsuit. If the attorney believes a suit is justified and that it has a reasonable likelihood of success, a formal document called a *complaint* is filed on behalf of the person bringing the lawsuit (the *plaintiff*). This document sets forth the facts that are alleged and the harm that has been done. The person who has been sued (a *defendant*) files a formal written response (an *answer*). Those steps may be followed by several preliminary determinations a court may be asked to make on various legal issues. The parties, through their respective attorneys, then gather information under a set of guidelines and rules called *discovery*. This information can be sought by asking that certain questions be answered in writing—these are called *interrogatories*. Discovery can include a process where oral testimony is taken before a court reporter (who types and transcribes the testimony) from witnesses before a trial. This is called a *deposition*. There can also be requests to inspect documents and places. There can be requests for formal examinations and evaluations as well.

Ultimately each side presents its information *(evidence)* to a third party through the introduction of testimony and documents. That third party, which can be a judge or a jury, has the job of listening to the evidence, assessing the credibility of people who testify, determining the facts, and then applying certain legal rules and theories to those facts to reach a just conclusion. Again, by design, the participants do not make decisions; instead, by being in the adversarial system, participants give that power to the judge or the jury.

Following the determination made at trial, either side may find reasons to have the initial decision reviewed by higher courts. These reviews are based on an examination of the transcribed testimony from the trial. The higher courts do not hear witnesses, nor do the judges on those courts gather new evidence. The higher courts can affirm the initial decision, reverse the initial decision, or send a case back to the trial court for an additional review and a new proceeding. When this occurs, the process begins again and the new decision can also be reviewed through appeals within the structure of the court system. The process of litigation, from the time an attorney and client decide to bring a lawsuit until final completion, may take only a few months, but most often a final determination is not reached until several years have passed.

These are important considerations for the mental health professional to understand, as the design and theory that underlie the legal system are inherently different from the design and theory underlying most mental health disciplines. For most mental health practitioners working with families, whether as counselors, social workers, psychologists, or psychiatrists, the primary goal is to support the client in learning how to make decisions and choices that are self-directed and that lead the client to a healthier and more satisfying life. Often the process itself is designed to be self-empowering to the client. An effective mental health practitioner knows that there is rarely *one* truth and that the truth for each person is different. Most practitioners know that today's truth can be tomorrow's question. Finding *the* truth and *reaching justice* are not typical ends that are sought in the delivery of mental health services. Although objective feedback may sometimes be useful to the client, the process itself is not objective in nature. In fact, the therapeutic process is, by necessity, subjective and focuses on the personal experience of each individual client.

Therefore, when the mental health professional has reason to interface with the legal system, it is useful to remember that, traditionally, the interests, goals, and processes are quite different from those to which the practitioner may be accustomed. Although in recent years there has been some movement toward a more evolved legal system that incorporates concepts of therapeutic jurisprudence (legal outcomes that have a therapeutic impact), until that evolution takes place in some fundamental way, the conflicts between the mental health and legal systems will, by necessity, remain. However, if the mental health professional develops an understanding of the values and processes inherent in the legal system, the mental health professional will better be able to address legal issues as they emerge and demand attention. Many mental health professionals falter at the first step as they are shaken to find the legal system cannot come close to offering what the mental health practitioner expects. The opportunity to adjust expectations, however, can allow the practitioner the insight necessary to maneuver through the legal system in a manner less fraught with turmoil and risk.

Legal Problems in the Lives of Clients

A mental health professional who has some understanding about these types of legal issues and the legal processes families can face can work more effectively with the families. Additionally, without at least some working knowledge of legal issues, the family therapist is susceptible to making recommendations as part of treatment that, although therapeutically sound, may have potential negative legal consequences for the client. When this occurs, not only may the therapeutic relationship suffer, but the professional is vulnerable to later complaints of malpractice.

What kinds of legal issues do families face? Perhaps the most common issue is divorce. Many couples seek marriage and family counseling before they actually separate. Couples frequently discuss how the separation will occur. Issues related to custody of the children also arise in the context of therapy. Some therapists have been known to work with couples on interim arrangements for financial support. Yet practical, everyday decisions people make about these matters can have serious legal consequences.

In many states, the actual date on which a couple physically separates has certain consequences. In Pennsylvania, for example, the date of separation is the date that is the dividing line between marital and nonmarital assets. The family therapist, with the best of therapeutic intentions, can advise a couple that it would be helpful to create a physical separation so the couple can more clearly see and understand their relationship. However, if the therapist is unfamiliar with the law, and if the clients have not first sought legal advice, the separation can be problematic. Assume the couple separates, and a month after separation, one spouse is granted certain stock options where that spouse works. Had the couple remained living together, those assets would have been subjected to a division between the spouses. Separation may have changed the character of the property. Suppose the family therapist supports an arrangement of shared custody during the separation. Legally, the creation of such an arrangement can have a long-term legal impact. Although the family practitioner had only the mutual interest of the parents in mind, and the interests of the children, this type of therapeutic guidance can have legal consequences. If one of the parties later feels harmed by actions taken at the suggestion of the therapist or is in fact harmed, the relationship has been jeopardized, and litigation against the practitioner could result.

Divorce is not the only issue that arises in the context of family therapy. Some families are struggling with legal issues related to the care of elderly family members. These issues might involve the development of an estate plan or decisions related to extreme medical interventions. These legal issues can generate intense anxiety and family members may turn to the family practitioner for help. Or the elderly family member may be questioning whether to treat children differently as part of an estate plan. Again, in trying to help the family member, the practitioner is faced with counseling issues that have legal implications.

Many couples are dealing with issues of infertility and adoption. Other families are working on issues related to the inability to acquire appropriate education for children with disabilities. Parents may have to make decisions about hospitalizing children with difficult mental disorders. Older clients may have issues related to social security. Some family members may be working on issues related to discrimination on the job, or work-related injuries that are compensable through worker's compensation. These are just a few examples of the types of legal concerns families face. Often, decisions are related to other life transitions for family members. The support and assistance of a family practitioner can play a critical part in the family's ability to maneuver through these difficult legal decisions.

To be effective in working with families, the practitioner needs to feel comfortable with the legal aspects and should be moderately adept at helping to discern legal issues, making timely and appropriate referrals. The professional working with families plays a significant role in helping family members frame expectations and understand limitations. It is important to know what can reasonably be expected within the legal system. Making the mistake of believing a client's path in the legal system will be congruent with the therapeutic path will only result in misinformation and unhelpful guidance.

Negligence and Professional Malpractice

Mental health practitioners complain that the therapeutic interventions they choose to use with clients are increasingly determined by their perception of how a judge or jury might some day view their conduct. Many mental health practitioners feel caught in the legal fray. Lawsuits are filed by clients who are unhappy with their treatment. Lawsuits, encouraged by certain advocacy groups, are being brought against therapists by family members even when clients remain satisfied. Mental health professionals are beginning to consider their own lawsuits against health care providers for impinging on their ability to provide mental health care, and against others for slander and defamation as a result of suits that have been filed against them. Our society has become more litigious; mental health professionals are not immune from this movement toward the courts.

Although in reality claims of malpractice against mental health practitioners generally are far fewer than malpractice claims against other types of health care providers (Carson, Karns, Taragin, Trout, & Wilcsek, 1992), the rate of claims against psychiatrists doubled between 1970 and 1980 (Perr, 1985). This trend is also affecting nonpsychiatric mental health disciplines (Smith, 1994; Watkins & Watkins, 1989). Not only are claims increasing in frequency, but also notable are increases in the size of monetary awards granted (Robertson, 1988). Lawsuits against mental health practitioners, including those working with families, can be based on conduct that is allegedly negligent, as well as misconduct that is intentional, such as assault and battery, and purposely directed toward the client.

Malpractice lawsuits against mental health professionals are generally grounded on legal principles of negligence (Simon & Sadoff, 1992). The person who brings such a lawsuit (the plaintiff) has the burden of proving four fundamental elements: (1) that there was a duty owed by the professional to the plaintiff; (2) that there was a breach of that duty by the professional; (3) that the plaintiff suffered a legally recognizable injury; and (4) that the injury was a direct result of the breach of the professional's duty, or, said differently, the breach was the proximate cause of the injury. As with any negligence case, the ultimate issue will be whether the professional acted reasonably—whether the professional violated a standard of care.

Several potential areas of negligence and possible malpractice emerge for professionals who work specifically with families. Although they do not differ from those areas of vulnerability for all mental health practitioners, they need to be viewed and understood within the context of a family-oriented practice. Problems may arise in the following major areas: diagnosis, competence, and referrals; confidentiality and privilege; assessment of the risk of suicide or self-harm; assessment of the risk of harm to others; sexual contact and other boundary violations; use of alternative therapies; supervision; and failure to make statutory reports.

DIAGNOSIS, COMPETENCE, AND REFERRALS

When a client first comes to see a practitioner, the mental health professional must diagnose what is wrong and make some assessment as to whether he or she has the requisite skills to act as a therapist for this person, couple, or family. The diagnosis will be influenced by the professional's training and the "school" the professional follows. However, a family therapist must be careful that a commitment to a particular mode of practice does not screen out other possibilities. Even if the issues presented by the client seem to be appropriate for the therapist's approach, there may be other issues that emerge that require recognition and referral.

For instance, assume the family therapist has adopted a family-systems approach for the practice of family therapy. The family therapist is quite adept at helping clients (1) understand their role within the system and (2) focus on the impact of their behavior within the construct of the system. However, what if one of the clients in the family has a recognizable addiction to alcohol? If this particular treating professional has no expertise in the field of addiction, the professional may have to refer the client to another professional for an evaluation and follow-up treatment. Additionally, the professional may need to evaluate his or her own abilities to sufficiently treat this person and this family.

A similar situation could arise where the mental health professional makes a determination that one client's sluggishness, lack of energy, and tendency to become isolated is no more that a slight situational depression related to a recently identified problem in the family. What happens if the family practitioner fails to consider the possibility of a long-standing, biologically-based depression, and fails to even suggest a referral for possible consideration of medication? There are many examples that raise the issue of diagnosis, competency, and referrals. This is an area where ongoing self-assessment is critical.

A professional can be found liable for malpractice based on a failure to adequately diagnose a client if that failure leads to injury of the client (Slawson & Guggenheim, 1984). Also, if a referral is made, the family practitioner must make the referral to a competent person and must handle the referral and transfer of the client in a competent manner. If the person to whom the client is referred acts incompetently and injures the client, the family practitioner who made the referral can be held liable. Likewise, once therapy has begun, if the therapist neglects to see the client, fails to make a reasonable referral (as necessary), or fails to act appropriately in effectuating the actual transfer of the client, the family practice professional may be deemed to have abandoned the client and is vulnerable to claims of malpractice.

CONFIDENTIALITY AND PRIVILEGE

Most professional organizations have professional codes of ethics that mandate the mental health professional maintain the confidences of a client. The American Psychological Association, the American Psychiatric Association, the Association of Marriage and Family Therapists, the National Association of Social Workers, and the American Counseling Association all have such a requirement. For professionals working with families, the issue of confidentiality is an area that requires particular sensitivity and clarity.

This ethical duty to maintain confidentiality has also been found to be a legal duty. If it is breached, and if, as a result, the client is injured, the professional may be liable for malpractice. These types of lawsuits can be brought under a general theory of negligence; for breach of contract, assuming confidentiality was explicitly expressed or implicit in the relationship; or for an intentional invasion of privacy. When a legal action is filed, the client does not have to choose among these possibilities. All of them can be alleged and pursued.

At the outset of a relationship with a client, the family therapist should explain the nature of confidentiality and clearly define the commitment to confidentiality for the client. The information provided should also contain any limitations on confidentiality. This can be a particularly confusing area for those who work with couples or multiple family members, as there are various forms of family therapy and each approach treats privacy and secrets differently (Watkins, 1989). Some family therapists will not act as a therapist for the family if they see a particular individual family member; other therapists will see the individuals in the family, and the family as a unit. What happens when the therapy changes from individual therapy to family therapy? What are the rules regarding confidentiality under these circumstances? If the therapist's view is that all can be shared, and the client is in disagreement, the therapist must make a careful assessment as to whether he or she has the capacity to provide ongoing therapy within this limitation.

Unfortunately, one of the most egregious breaches of client confidentiality in therapy with families occurs when the professional discusses cases with other people, including members of the therapist's family. This so-called *pillow talk* is one of the most common areas of complaints submitted to the Association of Marriage and Family Therapists (AMFT) ethics committee (Baker & Patterson, 1990). In a study done by Pope (Pope, Tobachnick, & Keith-Spiegel, 1987) almost two-thirds of therapists surveyed self-reported engaging in behaviors that jeopardized their clients' privacy.

It is dangerous to permit clients to make assumptions about the treatment of confidentiality in family therapy. Clients are entitled to know if the therapist will share information with clients' other family members. Breaches of confidentiality are a high-risk area for any therapist working with more than one family member. The family therapist should define the parameters of confidentiality within the family structure, and also, for the family, within the context of the larger world.

Many clients may assume that the therapist's duty to maintain confidentiality is absolute. That is not the case. In many states, therapists are mandated to report certain events such as the abuse and neglect of children who come before them. In certain circumstances, a therapist is relieved of the duty to maintain a confidence if the therapist believes, in the exercise of reasonable judgment, that the client is about to physically harm himself or herself, or another person.

The mental health professional should always make sure clients know about any exceptions to confidentiality. Although it may be sufficient to transmit this information orally, the safest way for the therapist to define this issue is to do it in writing. It can be incorporated into a specific written contract for services or contained in a brochure. Discussions with the client regarding confidentiality and exceptions to confidentiality should always be noted in the client file.

Confidentiality and privilege are not the same. Privilege is a status that is conferred by law. It is a protected status that a client can assert to prevent his or her therapist from testifying in a legal proceeding. Not all therapeutic relationships are covered by the concept of privilege. Most states recognize a privilege in a client's relationship with a psychiatrist or a licensed psychologist. Some states have also passed privilege statutes applicable to licensed social workers. Other states have passed general psychotherapeutic privilege statutes. Privilege only protects information from being shared in a legal proceeding. The right to raise the issue of privilege always belongs to the client.

The duty of a therapist to maintain client confidentiality is much broader. Unless a therapist has the consent of a client, the duty to protect confidentiality applies when a letter is received requesting records. It applies if an attorney or any other person calls to talk. The duty to protect confidentiality even applies if a mental health professional receives a subpoena seeking records or testimony in court. Therefore, if a family practitioner receives a subpoena, records cannot merely be turned over, nor can testimony be freely given. Unless the professional has a release from a client, the duty to maintain the client confidence is ongoing. If a release is given, it must be given freely and voluntarily. To be effective, consent must be fully informed. Consent should always be in writing, and the professional should discuss all possible ramifications of the release with the client. Those discussions should be well documented in the client file.

If the therapist does not have a release, then the therapist may have an obligation to independently challenge the subpoena that has been issued for records and testimony. The professional should immediately notify the client about the subpoena. If for some reason the client cannot be located, and if the professional does appear in court, the professional must assert the duty of confidentiality, and to the extent privilege is applicable, raise it on behalf of the client. Generally, if a subpoena is received, the practitioner should consult legal counsel.

When a client learns that confidentiality has been breached, trauma to the client can be significant. Many clients in family therapy are already having difficulty managing current relationships in their lives. It is not uncommon for family therapy processes to foster an examination of the client's family of origin, and through that process the client learns where the ability and inability to trust were first formulated. In some families, early childhood traumas have broken the bonds of trust early in life. For some clients, learning to restore the ability to form trusting relationships is the crux of therapeutic work. When the bond of trust is broken through the failure to maintain client privacy, the resulting harm can be severe, and the legal liability falling on the mental health practitioner can be extensive.

Suicide or Self-Harm

A therapist must act reasonably in assessing the risk of suicide and self-harm. The therapist can be liable if a client harms himself or herself. Although a mental health professional is not required to prevent all suicide, reasonable steps must be taken to do so (Berman & Cohen-Sandler, 1983; Smith, 1994). The risk of suicide and the risk of a client's harming another are perhaps two of the most difficult assessments the family practitioner will have to make. This difficulty is compounded as the duty to assess and act, within reason, is juxtaposed with the professional's duty to maintain confidences and respect the client's right to privacy. The client also has certain rights to be free from restraint and to be free from the risks associated with certain treatments, such as medication and electroconvulsive therapies.

To reach a determination that a practitioner was derelict in his or her duty toward a client, a court must determine that the practitioner failed to possess the degree of skill possessed by others similarly qualified, to exercise reasonable care, and to use his or her best judgment. Fortunately, courts do recognize that custodial care decisions are complex; they do not demand protection at any cost (Gutheil, Bursztajn, & Brodsky, 1984).

The problem of assessment in these cases is heightened by the need for the practitioner to differentiate between acute and chronic suicidal states. Deciding where a patient stands on this continuum and determining the level of intervention that is appropriate is difficult terrain. Litman (1989) suggests that the practitioner approach decisions in this area against the framework of being able to posture a legally viable defense. He suggests doing and documenting the following:

1. Discussing the chronic risk with the client and possibilities for management of that risk;
2. Discussing certain approaches that might be warranted;
3. Informing and involving the family; and
4. Considering a second opinion.

Litman acknowledges that consideration of all of these options may lessen the practitioner's anxiety, and notes such a reduction as an important part of the treatment of the chronically suicidal client, as anxiety on the part of the therapist can heighten the anxiety of the client (Cantor & McDermott, 1994; Litman, 1989). If, during this process, the practitioner decides that he or she cannot continue, then a termination of treatment or transfer of treatment must be conscientiously and carefully adopted. Again, the treating professional's breach of duty in managing termination is always a potentially viable lawsuit waiting to happen.

Harm to Others

Mental health professionals have a duty to take reasonable steps to protect others from harm that can be perpetrated by dangerous clients. This duty to warn first emerged in the now landmark case of *Tarasoff v. Regents of the University of California* (1976). Although the parameters of the duty to warn differ from state to state, most jurisdictions do have some law, whether by statute or decisional case law, that imposes some aspect of this duty on mental health professionals.

The early cases in this area focused on protection of an identifiable victim from acts of physical violence by a client. In the context of work with families, it is easy to see how frequently this risk must be assessed by the practicing professional. In recent years, the prevalence of violence within the family has become more widely known and recognized. Most homicide victims are killed by someone they know. The high incidence of violence within the family has caused most states to enact laws designed to provide the victim with restraining orders and household evictions.

When the professional working with families is confronted with threatened acts of violence toward another by a client, the therapist must exercise professional judgment in determining to what degree the targeted victim is at risk. Even if the client is advised in advance that such threats may require the breach of the therapist's commitment to maintain confidentiality, such a breach may ultimately mark the end of the therapist-client relationship. The client may not be receptive to other therapeutic treatment, and thus the possibility of longer term change may diminish. This makes the judgment of the therapist a difficult one to balance. As with many others that can lead to potential malpractice, the duty to warn requires careful risk assessment.

Many mental health professionals are familiar with the duty to warn in the context of potential physical violence and have openly discussed that issue with clients. An emerging area in the field of mental health, related to one's duty to warn, is to question whether the mental health professional has a duty to warn when he or she becomes aware of life-threatening transmittable illnesses, such as the HIV virus. Again, the duty to warn in such circumstances is typically regulated by individual states. For example, California has enacted a law that protects a physician from liability for disclosing HIV test results to a spouse, or sexual or needle-sharing partner of an HIV-positive patient (Knapp & VandeCreek, 1990).

The impact of this issue will be most greatly felt by those family practitioners who work with traditional and nontraditional families in high-risk populations. It is not uncommon for persons infected with the HIV virus to seek the services of a mental health professional. Infected persons are at greater risk for neuropsychiatric disorders, and there is evidence of increased depression and suicide risk (Clark, 1990; Marsak, Tierney, & Hardiff, 1988; Searight & Pound, 1994).

Assessing dangerousness has always been a difficult task (Melton, 1987; Melton, Petrila, Poythress, & Slobogin, 1987). Yet, even before the Tarasoff decision, cases that held physicians liable for failure to warn family members and close associates of a patient's communicable disease existed (Falk, 1988). The mental health professional must make an assessment when working with clients who engage in high-risk behaviors; that assessment, however, must consider whether the client is able to work cooperatively with the therapist over time and move in a direction, with support, where the client will be self-revealing to others. Some clients may never be able to follow that path, including clients who suffer from dementia or who are unable to manage impulse control, as is correlative with addiction, severe depression, or other symptoms or illnesses. In such instances, the therapist may be obligated to warn those who are within a foreseeable zone of harm or to take some action that will prevent the client from having access to those people.

Sexual Contact with Clients and Boundary Violations

A mental health professional who becomes sexually involved with a client is subject to civil liability (*Doe v. Samaritan Counseling Center,* 1990; Epstein, 1989). In recent years, this has become one of the most common types of lawsuits filed against mental health professionals. Some states have passed laws that make this behavior criminal and create criminal penalties for it. Although it is possible for a lawsuit to be brought on the basis of an intentional tort such as assault and battery, many insurance policies refuse to cover acts that are intentional or criminal. Most cases filed against mental health professionals for sexual misconduct are formulated on theories of negligence that allege the therapist breached a duty to the client by failing to properly manage transference (Cummings & Sobel, 1985; Jorgenson, Bisbing, & Southerland, 1992; Morin, 1989; Smith, 1994). Given the nature of the therapeutic relationship, consent is not a defense to these actions.

For professionals working with families, sexual involvement with a client may result in a lawsuit not just by the client, but also by the client's spouse to whom the practitioner may also owe a duty of care. In the past, the mental health professional's duty to third parties has been limited to Tarasoff situations because the law generally disfavored most kinds of litigation by third parties who were held to be outside the zone of foreseeable risk. Over the years, however, courts have begun to expand the tort of infliction of emotional distress to protect third parties who were in a particular relationship with the primary person who was harmed by another's conduct. As litigation related to negligence in mental health treatment has expanded, the duty to third parties has become increasingly recognized. In 1988, the California Supreme Court allowed damages for emotional distress to the patient of a psychiatrist after the psychiatrist had a sexual relationship with the patient's spouse (*Richard H. v. Larry D.*, 1988). And in *Marlene F. v. Affiliated Psychiatric Medical Clinic, Inc.* (1989), the California Supreme Court held the clinic and the therapist liable to a mother for the injury of emotional distress experienced by the mother after her son was sexually molested by the therapist.

Mental health professionals, including those who work with families, are also vulnerable to other lawsuits based on the alleged violations of boundaries other than those related to sexual contact. In many instances, these suits are also premised on mismanagement and negligence in managing the transference phenomenon. Lawsuits for boundary violations may also be premised on the lack of informed consent.

Peterson (1994) identifies several common types of boundary violations. These include incidences where the therapist asks the client to act in a professional capacity for the therapist (such as an accountant), to clean the therapist's house, to give the therapist some advice about the therapist's life, or to engage in other behaviors that create a role reversal between therapist and client. In essence, the therapist structures the relationship according to the needs of the therapist and the therapist looks to the client for gratification (Peterson, 1994). It can be more difficult to base a lawsuit on these more general boundary violations because it is harder for a plaintiff to define the accepted standard of care (Simon, 1992). However, as professional organizations alter their own internal ethical codes to account for dual relationships and other boundary violations, a more clearly articulated standard of care is likely to develop. Further, in situations involving such boundary violations, other clearly defined duties are often breached as well. Therefore, although it may be difficult to sustain a legal action resulting from nonsexual boundary violations, it may be that boundary violations inherently lead to failure to refer, abandonment of the client, and failure to properly terminate the relationship. All of those acts do fall well within breaches of certain standards of care that must be maintained by practitioners.

Alternative Therapies

Simon (1992) notes there are more than 450 different schools of psychotherapy, and the number is constantly increasing. Radical departures from customary practice may be considered a lack of due care as a matter of law (Simon, 1992).

Even therapy modalities that may not be seen as extremely radical, present delicate legal issues. For instance, in working with families, some professionals may determine that forms of behavior therapy are appropriate for certain clients and family members. These therapies include practices such as reinforcement, token economy, directed behavior out of sessions, and a range of other specific behaviors directed by the therapist and performed, at that direction, by the client. Some form of behavioral therapy is commonly used by those professionals who adopt a family-systems approach. In helping the client understand the impact of the client's behavior on the family system, the therapist may direct the client to experiment with alternative behaviors. Because alternative behavior is so specifically directed by the mental health professional, if litigation does occur, the plaintiff has an increased ability to show the therapist's directive as being a direct cause of the harm (Goisman & Gutheil, 1992).

Some family therapists adopt a behavioral therapy plan that includes incorporating a family member as an auxiliary therapist. This serves as a tacit endorsement of that family member's capability. If, as a result of the therapeutic bond between the primary therapist and auxiliary therapist, a disruption occurs in the original family relationship, there may be a resulting action against the primary therapist. Behavioral therapies may also result in flooding sessions that are not properly handled. Moreover, in situations involving directed sexual techniques for sexual dysfunction, behavioral directives may be misperceived as sexual misconduct (Goisman & Gutheil, 1992).

In addition to innovative therapies, more mental health practitioners are becoming familiar with a range of holistic health practices. In some instances, these practices are being used to augment counseling a client receives. These techniques raise many potential malpractice issues. Many holistic approaches combine mind-body processes. A client must be well informed and understand possible outcomes of these approaches. Informed consent is critical. Proper monitoring and assessment must occur or the professional may be held liable for failure to make a proper referral if a particular holistic approach is not yielding results.

An issue that arises in the context of holistic practices is, again, determination as to the applicable standard of care. Although litigation against holistic practitioners has not been dramatic in terms of numbers, there have been cases against naturopaths, acupuncturists, and others, such as chiropractors and podiatrists, who are neither physicians nor surgeons, yet a standard of care comparable to physicians and surgeons has been determined to be appropriate by the courts (Rian, 1983). Although in time the law may recognize the consensual nature of the relationship between a holistic practitioner and client, the law has not advanced to the degree where differentiated standards of care have been articulated.

For family practice professionals who incorporate processes such as hypnotherapy, guided imagery, body movement therapies, and other innovative approaches, it is important to provide clients with sufficient information to enable them to give well-informed consent to these processes. In terms of risk management, use of innovative approaches should be fully discussed with the client, and these discussions should be well documented. The practitioner must be skilled at managing whatever occurs during the use of these processes and cannot rely on an assertion that it was the responsibility of the client to control the outcome.

Supervision

Professionals who work with families often find themselves in the role of supervising other practitioners. Although cases alleging negligence in supervision are not many, this is a growing area of potential liability. When an attorney contemplates the filing of a malpractice action, part of the attorney's job is to investigate and consider all possible occurrences of malpractice. Because part of the attorney's job in representing the allegedly injured person is to maximize that person's opportunity to collect compensation for that injury, it makes sense that the attorney will file suit against all possible persons.

For consent to treatment to be informed, a client must be educated concerning the supervision used by the therapist. The practitioner should ensure a client knows the practitioner is in supervision, something about how the supervision process works, the identity of the supervisor, and any other information necessary for giving an informed consent.

It is not sufficient for one who is identified and defined as a supervisor to merely sign off on claim forms. Not only is such an action the possible equivalent of insurance fraud, but it violates the duty the supervisor owes to the client to truly supervise the service that is being provided. Some mental health professionals who work as supervisors have the mistaken belief that their duty extends only to actual cases brought to supervision by the treating professional. That is not the case. If the practitioner always knew which cases to take to supervision, then supervision itself might not be necessary. The purpose of supervision is to guide the practitioner. The job of the supervisor is to oversee all of the practitioner's cases. The job of the supervisor is to create sufficient opportunity so that problem areas can become apparent (Smith, 1994).

Just as the failure to properly supervise can be actionable in the courts, so too can the failure to seek proper supervision when the practitioner knows or should know he or she is in trouble. Even if the duty to seek supervision is not clearly part of an existing standard of care, the use of regular supervision is one of the best risk management and prevention tools that can be used. It is important to select a supervisor who is qualified and competent. Practitioners in private practice do not generally have access to regularly mandated supervision; however, it is possible to work out a contractual consultation or supervision contract with another professional. When difficult issues arise in treatment with a client, a couple, or members of the family, these issues should be noted in the file. The practitioner should also note contacts with the supervisor, the issues discussed in supervision, suggestions of the supervisor, and comments regarding related follow-up by the practitioner. The supervisor should make comparable documentation.

Failure to Report

Most states have laws that require mental health professionals to report incidences related to the abuse and neglect of children. There are penalties for the failure to report. If a child is harmed, or if the injury to a child is exacerbated by the professional's failure to report, civil liability will probably result. Not only are there reporting requirements for the abuse of children, some states are requiring the reporting of abuse of elderly family members and others.

In setting forth limitations on the duty of confidentiality, the legal obligation to report is one of the primary exceptions that should be noted by the mental health professional. Some have argued that mental health professionals should not be mandated reporters under these laws. The theory is that revealing the obligation to report to a client will, by necessity, stop clients from self-revealing, and thus make effective therapy or protection impossible. If the real goal is to stop acts of abuse and violence, then treatment is necessary, and if reporting lessens one's willingness to be in treatment, then the entire system is self-defeating. Despite the sense this argument makes, the legal system as we know it has generally been unwilling to adopt this approach, and the failure to report generally results in clear liability.

Additional Considerations

The prior sections provide an overview of several areas of potential malpractice that can impact professionals working with families. These areas are not exhaustive. Although I have referenced issues of informed consent, I've done so only as consent relates to releases regarding confidentiality and to the use of more innovative kinds of treatment. The issue of informed consent is always a focal point in any therapeutic relationship and there are obviously many other instances where the issue of consent can arise for the family practitioner. Likewise, in this overview I did not focus on possible negligence in prescribing drugs or in the use of electroconvulsive therapies. These areas commonly involve psychiatrists or other physicians, and do not normally impact the family therapist.

Developing sound practice habits and practicing good risk management are essential tools for any mental health practitioner. It is important to be familiar with applicable ethical codes and licensing requirements. It is also important to take advantage of literature and continuing education, and to arrange for competent supervision. Working with families can be energizing and exciting; it can also be overwhelming. Self-care is a critical component in effectively managing a practice. Key factors in averting malpractice claims include taking time to be self-reflective, taking time to properly keep records, taking time to find the right consultants, and making time to continually work with the client to explore how the relationship is working for the client.

Empirical experience teaches that actual litigation is a product of the malignant synergy of a bad outcome coupled with bad feelings; that is, only when elements of hostility, antagonism, frustration, anger, dissatisfaction, and feelings of betrayal and abandonment are present does the bad outcome actually provoke litigation (Goisman & Gutheil, 1992). Although a claim of malpractice does not always result in a lawsuit, and although the professional may have many good and adequate legal defenses to any action that is brought, litigation is generally costly, both financially and emotionally. It takes considerable time, focus, and attention.

The Family Practice Professional as Court Witness

A practitioner is always in the position of being a potential court witness. A client, through legal counsel, may request supporting testimony. A party opposing a client's legal position may attempt to compel a professional's testimony. An attorney may approach a professional to testify as an expert witness in a matter unrelated to any client of the practitioner.

Any time a treating professional appears at a deposition or in court, the therapeutic relationship with a client is at risk. Attorneys often fail to understand this risk. Clients often underestimate this risk.

Any professional who is asked to testify or produce records should fully discuss these issues with the client and the client's counsel. There may be times that the records contain information that can be injurious to the client. The practitioner may ultimately provide testimony that contains perceptions the client is surprised to hear. An attorney's job is to attain a legal victory. This is done, in part, by attempting to raise questions about the credibility of opposing witnesses, including the mental health practitioner. Observing even the appearance of a therapist's loss of power on a witness stand can be traumatic for the client.

If a professional has never been in court, and does not understand the adversarial nature of the legal process, there may be a real temptation to testify. This is particularly true if the professional has information that truly could assist the client's legal effort. However, given the risks involved, a careful assessment must be made. If testimony is given, it should never be done without thorough advance preparation. The professional should meet with the client and client's counsel and review records and testimony. At times, the family practitioner will have to educate the client's attorney. Most attorneys know little about mental health issues. A thorough collaboration is essential to effective court testimony.

If someone in legal opposition to a client attempts to compel the professional to produce records or testimony, the professional must adhere to processes and procedures that protect the confidences of the client. This issue has been discussed to some extent as part of the discussion on malpractice issues. The professional must not be swayed by argumentative and persuasive legal counsel. Again, the professional should always be prepared and meet with the client's attorney before testimony is given.

If a family practitioner is approached to testify as an expert, the professional must first determine whether he or she has the requisite expertise in a given area. The qualifications to be an expert will vary among jurisdictions. Regardless of what the legal requirements might be, a mental heath professional should never agree to provide expert testimony unless the professional is an expert. The professional should have sufficient background as a clinician or researcher. An expert must be familiar with current literature and research in the field. If actual evaluations are involved, the professional must know and understand all ethical guidelines applicable to evaluation processes.

Many legal actions can become *battles of experts*. When that occurs each side attempts to bolster the credibility of its own expert and to raise questions about the credibility of the other's expert. There are organizations that offer special education and training in the field of forensics. Any mental health professional who intends to make expert court testimony a regular part of practice should certainly form some affiliation with such an organization and be prepared to practice under ethical guidelines applicable to a forensic practice.

It would be worthwhile for a family practitioner to consider the prospect of testifying in court before the opportunity arises. It is harder to make determinations about testifying at the last minute, or during a client's legal crisis. Each professional might consider spending some time of self-reflection about this prospect. Decide in advance how to work with a client, how to talk to an attorney about a meeting, how records should be kept in case this occurs, and how comfortable you will be as a witness. This is one more time when prevention and risk management are extremely worthwhile.

Conclusion

The law impacts professionals who work with families. There are many legal issues that need to be addressed. Managed care brings its own set of legal problems and risks. Institutions, whether hospitals, clinics, or mental health agencies, must contend with a range of legal issues related to treatment and service. Special problems exist for private practice partners and professionals sharing space.

Our society has become litigious. A movement away from the adversarial process and toward alternatives such as mediation has begun, yet each year more court cases are filed in all areas of the law. Courtrooms are in the movies, on television, and in best sellers. Until we develop a culture that says cooperation has a greater value than winning, the law and mental health systems and professionals will continue to intersect. This chapter endeavors to make that intersection a little more understandable.

References

Baker, L. C., & Patterson, J. E. (1990). The first to know: A systemic analysis of confidentiality and the therapist's family. *American Journal of Family Therapy, 18,* 295–300.

Berman, A. L., & Cohen-Sandler, R. (1983). Suicide and malpractice: Expert testimony and the standard of care. *Professional Psychology: Research and Practice, 14,* 6–19.

Cantor, C. H., & McDermott, P. M. (1994). Suicide litigation: From legal to clinical wisdom. *Australian and New Zealand Journal of Psychiatry, 28,* 431–437.

Clark, M. E. (1990). AIDS prevention: Legislative options. *American Journal of Law and Medicine, 16,* 107–153.

Cummings, N. A., & Sobel, S. B. (1985). Malpractice insurance: Update on sex claims. *Psychotherapy, 22,* 186–188.

Doe v. Samaritan Counseling Center, 791 P.2d 344 (Alaska, 1990).

Falk, T. C. (1988). AIDS public health law. *Journal of Legal Medicine, 9,* 529–546.

Goisman, R. M., & Gutheil, T. G. (1992). Risk management in the practice of behavior therapy: Boundaries and behavior. *American Journal of Psychotherapy, 46,* 533–541.

Gutheil T. G., Bursztajn, H., & Brodsky, A. (1984). Malpractice prevention through the sharing of uncertainty: Informed consent in the therapeutic alliance. *New England Journal of Medicine, 311,* 49–51.

Jorgenson, L., Bisbing, S. B., & Southerland, P. K. (1992). Therapist and patient sexual exploitation and insurance liability. *Tort and Insurance Law Journal, 27,* 595–614.

Knapp, S., & VandeCreek, L. (1990). Application of the duty to protect H.I.V. positive patients. *Professional Psychology: Research and Practice, 21,* 161–166.

Krowther, C., Dare, C., & Wilson, J. (1990). Why should we talk to you? You'll only tell the court! On being an informer and a family therapist. *Journal of Family Therapy, 12,* 105–122.

Litman, R. E. (1982). Hospital suicides: Lawsuits and standards. *Suicide and Life Threatening Behaviors, 12,* 212–220.

Litman, R. E. (1989). Long-term treatment of chronically suicidal patients. *Bulletin of the Menninger Clinic, 53,* 215–228.

Marlene F. v. Affiliated Psychiatric Medical Clinic, Inc., 770 P.2d 278 (California, 1989).

Marsak, R. M., Tierney, H., & Hardiff, K. (1988). Increased risk of suicide in persons with AIDS. *Journal of the American Medical Association, 259,* 1333–1337.

Melton, G. B., Petrila, J. D., Poythress, N. G., & Slobogin, C. (1987). *Psychological evaluations for the courts* (pp. 197–204). New York: Guilford.

Morin, L. A. (1989). Civil remedies for therapist/patient sexual exploitation. *Goldgate University Law Review, 19,* 401–434.

Perr, I. N. (1985). Psychiatric malpractice issue. In S. Rachlin (Ed.), *Legal encroachment on psychiatric practice* (pp. 47–59). San Francisco, CA: Jossey-Bass.

Peterson, M. R. (1994). Client harm and professional accountability: A feminist model. *Journal of Feminist Family Therapy, 6,* 49–67.

Pope, K., Tobachnick, B., & Keith-Spiegel, P. (1987). The beliefs and behaviors of psychologists as therapists. *American Psychologists, 42,* 993–1006.

Rian, H. M. (1983). An alternative contractual approach to holistic health care. *Ohio State Law Journal, 44,* 185–217.

Richard H. v. Larry D., 243 Cal. Rptr. 807 (California, 1988).

Searight, H. R., & Pound, P. (1994). The HIV-positive psychiatric patient and the duty to protect: Ethical and legal issues. *International Journal of Psychiatry and Medicine, 24,* 259–270.

Simon, R. I. (1992). Negligent treatment. In *Clinical psychiatry and the law* (2nd ed., pp. 385–487). Washington, DC: American Psychiatric Press.

Simon, R. I., & Sadoff, R. L. (1992). *Psychiatric malpractice: Cases and comments for clinicians* (2nd ed.). Washington, DC: American Psychiatric Press.

Smith, S. R. (1994a). The legal liabilities of mental health institutions. *Administration and Policy and Mental Health, 21,* 379–394.

Smith, S. R. (1994b). Liability and mental health services. *American Journal of Orthopsychiatry, 64,* 235–251.

Taragin, M. I., Wilczek, A. P., Karns, M. E., Trout, R., & Carson, J. L. (1992). Physician demographics and the risk of medical malpractice. *American Journal of Medicine, 93,* 537–542.

Tarasoff v. Regents of the University of California, et al., 551 P.2d 334 (1976).

Watkins, S. A. (1989). Confidentiality: An ethical and legal conundrum for family therapists. *American Journal of Family Therapy, 17,* 291–302.

Watkins, S. A., & Watkins, J. C. (1989). Negligent endangerment: Malpractice in the clinical context. *Journal of Independent Social Work, 3,* 35–50.

CHAPTER 3

Ethical Concerns Regarding Gender in Family Practice

BETHANY R. HAMPTON and MICHAEL C. GOTTLIEB

The family serves as the primary institution for the socialization of children. Gendered behavior is learned within the context of family interaction through clear role expectations and proscriptions that may encourage or inhibit individual growth and development. People acquire these culturally based gendered experiences as children and act them out in their personal and family relationships as adults. In some cases, these inculcated expectations can result in various types of dysfunction for persons of either gender both intrapersonally and interpersonally.

Family practitioners bring the sum of their gendered experience and history as individuals to the therapy session. This learning may include sexist bias transmitted through their family of origin as well as training experiences in systems theory that has been criticized for promoting sexism in some of its treatment approaches.

Systems theory has become increasingly popular as a theoretical basis for family therapy and has spawned numerous specific treatment approaches. One fundamental assumption of systems theory is that individuals can affect larger systems. This notion implies that a family's well-being may be affected by the dysfunctional behavior of one of its members. Constricted gender-role socialization may be one such cause. For example, stereotyped attitudes and expectations may limit individual growth and promote personal dysfunction. A family's healthy response to stress may be obstructed by confining gender-role expectations.

The confluence of these issues raises serious ethical questions for family practitioners. After stating our assumptions, we shall review the literature on these subjects and examine their implications for ethical practice. We will discuss the relevant data regarding client and family variables affected by gender, the theoretical foundations of systems theory and their relations to gender, and the influence of gender-role socialization on therapists and supervisors. We conclude with recommendations for a more ethical and gender-sensitive family practice.

Assumptions

Our work is grounded in feminist theory. This perspective produces specific assumptions that underlie our work.

1. Both women and men suffer, albeit in different ways, in family life as a result of constricting gender-role socialization.
2. Although some changes have occurred in recent years, the contemporary American family largely retains a patriarchal structure.
3. We recognize that the definition of "family" is changing rapidly to include many differing types of family structures. For the purpose of this chapter, we will confine ourselves to addressing ethical and gender issues in monogamous heterosexual relationships.
4. Gottlieb (this volume) notes that certain ethical decisions may produce different treatment outcomes and that various clinical judgments may generate differing ethical dilemmas. Similarly in feminist analysis, ethics are considered inseparable from clinical issues (Brown, 1991) because both evolved from the understanding that intrapsychic and interpersonal dynamics operate within a political context. As a result, ethical and clinical issues often blur into one another such that clear distinctions between them become difficult. We present these issues in a manner that is meaningful to us, but such distinctions are arbitrary.

Client Variables

West and Zimmerman (1991) noted that "a person's gender is not simply an aspect of what one is, but more fundamentally, it is something that one does, and does recurrently, in interaction with others" (p. 27). Thus, the "doing" of gender is infused into the fabric of daily life. Here we discuss the general notion of gender-role socialization, the specific gender roles of women and men, and how these roles affect our interaction with one another.

Gender-Role Socialization

We understand gender roles as social constructions that carry expectations for gender-typed behavior. Weiner and Boss (1985) suggested that gender constructions are a cultural control mechanism that influence power relationships. If that is so, gender roles may be a vehicle for the maintenance of gender inequities, a phenomena that is deeply ingrained in our culture and pervades all social and familial relationships.

A systemic perspective of gender argues that gender-role socialization may be both beneficial and harmful. For example, prescribed gender roles may help individuals tolerate the anxiety of novel and ambiguous social situations. In this sense, gender-role socialization provides guidelines for appropriate social behavior. On the other hand, Lazerson (1992) reported that men and women show different patterns of illness and rates of mortality that reflect the influence of gender socialization, such as higher rates of depression in women and alcoholism in men.

There is a plethora of research that documents the deleterious effects of adherence to rigid gender norms for both men and women. To highlight a few examples, O'Neil (1981) noted that the male socialization process can contribute to interpersonal problems, work-related conflicts, and impaired health. More specifically, Harrison, Chin, and Ficarrotto (1992) argued that a strident male sex role is inherently stressful and may be lethal for men as evidenced by shorter life expectancy, higher rates of heart disease and cancer, and death from suicide and accidents. Finally, Pleck, Sonenstein, and Ku (1993) reported that a traditional masculine ideology is associated with a host of problem behaviors in adolescent males, such as delinquency, substance use, school problems, and sexual activity.

With regard to women, Walrond-Skinner (1987) found that the overuse of prescription drugs by women may be a result of the distress and abuse they suffer related to the female gender role. Similarly, Amaro (1995) suggested that the subservience of women placed them at greater risk for HIV infection.

Additional support for these conclusions comes from androgyny research, which has shown that higher levels of functioning are associated with greater gender-role flexibility (Cook, 1987). Scher, Stevens,

Good, and Eichenfield (1987) concluded that having a nontraditional role, in the sense of an enlarged family role, is good for men's mental health. Similarly, Bernard (1972) found that women who work outside the home fare better than those who do not. Finally, greater self-esteem and other indices of mental health have been associated with a more nontraditional gender role orientation (Cook, 1987).

Taken together, these findings suggest that traditional gender-role stereotyping may have pervasive and adverse consequences for men, women, and their interrelationships. As an ethical matter, it behooves family practitioners to be familiar with this body of knowledge and to address its inhibiting and dysfunctional aspects when it arises.

FEMALE GENDER ROLE

Conventional images of femininity include passivity as a socially reinforced ideal (Nadelson & Notman, 1992). "For women, many psychological problems are generated by a social definition of gender that promotes passivity and dependency on a narrow personal set of reinforcers" (Walrond-Skinner, 1987, p. 78). As a result, it is not surprising that women present themselves more frequently for counseling, suffer from higher rates of depression and other forms of mental illness, and have hospitalization rates far in excess of those for men (Braverman, 1988b).

Amaro (1995) argued that women's disempowered status as a group facilitated their vulnerability to violence in relationships with men. Violence and its threat are tools used by dominant groups to control subservient groups. Sheffield (1995) coined the term *sexual terrorism* to describe the control that fear of rape has on women's behavior even among women without histories of sexual assault.

These compelling data have led some to suggest that it is the female gender role itself that fosters the helplessness and dependency found in many psychiatric conditions (Walrond-Skinner, 1987). Braverman (1988b) concluded that the very material conditions of women's lives place them at risk for psychological difficulties, and Hare-Mustin (1978) cautioned that the widespread unhappiness and depression of women may reflect a cultural problem rather than an individual one.

More recent theories of women's psychological development have emphasized the importance of relationships for women's well-being (Gilligan, Ward, & Taylor, 1988). Although marital and family commitments may represent the ultimate fulfillment of a woman's need for connection, numerous studies have demonstrated the liabilities of marriage for women (Luepnitz, 1988). Luepnitz further reports that such interdisciplinary scholars as Durkheim from sociology and Degler from history have concluded that the traditional family as an institution may survive at the expense of mothers.

The notion of the family as harmful to women is supported by the finding that women who work outside the home seem to fare better than those who do not (Bernard, 1972). However, when women engage in paid employment outside the home while raising children, they frequently suffer from role conflict and role overload. In part, these difficulties may be due to the continuing inequity in the division of labor between husbands and wives in dual-career homes (Crosby & Jaskar, 1993). These authors concluded that women have expanded their roles to include paid employment, but have not been released from the expectations and responsibilities of being full-time wives and mothers. Such data lead Hochschild (1992) to describe women as the primary victims in dual-career families and Scanzoni and Fox (1980) to conclude that marriage functions as a more effective support system for men than for women. Taken together, these findings question the conventional wisdom that families are systems that promote the good of all its members.

MALE GENDER ROLE

The burgeoning interest in men's roles reflects a reaction to the lack of attention given the male experience in family life, family systems theory, and family therapy. Traditionally, men were socialized to dominate, control, and subordinate women in order to maintain their power and masculine role in relationships (O'Neil, 1981). Boys were socialized in ways that promoted a sense of masculine entitlement and abuse of power (Avis, 1990). Pleck (1980) provided several explanations for why men oppress women. Not only does power over women provide men with benefits and privileges, but oppression also may be due to their intrapsychic needs. He contends that men want power over women as adults because as boys they experienced the oppressive effects of female power. Pleck also provided a third explanation, which is that men perceive women as holding two kinds of power over them, expressive and masculinity-validating power. The actual or threatened loss of these two resources leads men to frantic attempts to reassert their power over women. In contrast to how such feelings lead men to treat women, such circumstances also lead men to feel dependent upon women. This feeling is in sharp contrast to the male gender role prescription of being both dominant and independent and requires that male dependence remain hidden beneath a superficial masculine overlay (Gilbert, 1987).

Pittman (1991b) observed that many men struggle with the legacies of the models of masculinity with which they were raised. For example, masculinity is frequently defined in terms of career success, which places undue pressure on men in the occupational world and has adverse effects on health and relationships. Masculinity is at other times defined as freedom from female control; this absence of control in turn impairs cooperative styles of relating. Pittman called for a new definition of masculinity built on connection with others.

Accomplishing this goal will be difficult because men must learn about masculinity from their fathers who frequently are physically or psychologically unavailable. Hence the masculine ideal in our culture has become one of emotional distance leading to the phenomenon described by many as "father hunger." At the same time, many men are struggling to become the fathers they never had (Pittman, 1991a) by participating more actively in the details of housework and child care, and liberating themselves from traditional and rigid adherence to the provider role (Brooks, 1992).

Attention to the gender socialization of men has mushroomed in the last decade as indicated by a number of new publications, men's studies programs in universities, and gender-issues symposia at professional conferences. This heterogeneous men's movement has had developmental stages similar to those of the women's movement, such as consciousness-raising activities and public educational forums.

Recently, some groups have developed sophisticated organizational structures with missions of expanding gender role options for men and providing a forum for addressing gender-based personal experiences. For example, in 1995 the American Psychological Association (APA) added a division devoted to studying men's issues. Some groups try to address these issues themselves rather than relying on women to facilitate communication and affectively validate them. Men must learn to expand their functioning themselves.

If men can learn to express emotion and better understand their masculinity, then the pressures they feel to control women may diminish. Unfortunately, behavior patterns have not yet changed. Even when men's attitudes do change, there may be no greater involvement in family life. Family therapists can be instrumental in addressing these issues when they arise in relationships.

GENDER ROLE SOCIALIZATION AND RELATIONAL FUNCTIONING

Many feminists have argued that the family is the central arena for the exploitation of women (Goldner, 1988). In part, this is because women seek greater intimacy in their relationships, whereas men tend to avoid it. Furthermore, traditional norms and stereotypes also foster the underinvolvement of men in the family and the overresponsibility of women for the well-being of both marriage and family. Finally, men have been socialized to use power and control directly, whereas women have been socialized to use indirect and passive means to control interpersonal relationships (O'Neil, 1981). Weiner and Boss (1985) have gone so far as to conclude that gender roles are the cultural control mechanisms that inform all power relationships.

Philpot (1990) noted that with greater awareness of feminist issues, tension surrounding gender issues is frequently pronounced in couples seeking therapy. Couples often present with "communications problems." Women complain that men do not take enough responsibility for household tasks and are not expressive or emotionally available to them. Men complain that their wives lack understanding of the financial burdens they feel and are unresponsive to their sexual needs. When women feel that their husbands are not listening to them, they may repeat themselves, leading to accusations of nagging to which men often respond with greater distance. In a prospectively designed study of couples, Gottman (1991) associated *stonewalling*, which he characterizes as the masculine defense of withdrawing from an interaction, with the dissolution of the marriage. This study provides poignant support for the potentially destructive effects of stereotyped, gendered interactional patterns in couple functioning.

To complicate matters further, Scher (1989) has noted that the male gender role creates numerous barriers to successful treatment. First, men need to be both in control and unlike women. Therefore, in therapy, men may feel disadvantaged and vulnerable and may struggle to maintain power and control over the therapeutic situation. Second, men may compete with the therapist for power as a result of their struggle with the intimacy inherent in the therapeutic encounter. Third, men bring their sense of instrumentality to therapy and often place excessive demands on therapists for measurable progress, a notion that has received some empirical support from the work of Allgood, Bischoff, Smith, and Salts (1992). Finally, Scher believed that most men are *father-wounded*, a condition that surfaces in feeling unloved and inadequately nurtured. Men may try to use the nurturance provided by the therapist to satisfy this need. A therapist, unaware of this iatrogenic risk, may find his or her neutrality compromised if he or she aligns with the man at the expense of the woman. All of these interpersonal dynamics may work against success in the psychotherapy where trust, self-disclosure, and self-exploration are required.

These data argue that prescribed social and cultural norms, gender roles, and interpersonal processes can contribute to dysfunctional relationships. If so, the issue of gendered behavior has basic and vital implications for family practitioners who wish to treat relational disorders.

Theoretical Models

Family systems therapy has been severely criticized from a feminist perspective. Many of the problems that have been raised can be understood as a result of "beta bias" (Hare-Mustin, 1978), in which gender and its implications have been overlooked in the formulation of basic theory and subsequent data interpretation. In this section, we discuss these matters beginning with Bateson's original thinking, problems with basic concepts such as circularity and complementarity, therapeutic neutrality, and use of the therapist's power. Finally, we will review the work of both classical theorists and postmodern thinkers in this context.

ORIGINS

Bateson (1980) dismissed the existence of power, suggesting that it was the myth of power that led to destruction and other social ills. Many who followed Bateson were also resistant to thinking of marital and family problems as imbalances of power, assuming that the family member who expressed the pain had been arbitrarily chosen by the family to represent the distress of the entire system.

The notion of an "identified patient" was based on the assumption that all family members were equal players with equal opportunities for action. Therefore, it is internally inconsistent to imbue one family member with greater power than another because systems cannot be controlled unilaterally by one component. The assumption of an equal playing field also led to concepts such as circularity and complementarity, which present serious problems for feminist thinkers.

CIRCULARITY AND COMPLEMENTARITY

Circularity is a term used to describe a system's recursive behavioral patterns. Systems theory assumed that all members are equally responsible for the maintenance of these patterns. The concept of complementarity arose to resolve the inconsistency in the assumption that all system members are equally responsible despite an observed inequality between partners in some interactions. The notion of complementarity assumes that there is some hidden strength in weakness. If a therapist makes such an assumption, he or she may ascribe a positive connotation to inequality, thereby permitting it to continue, and use the notion of circularity as a justification.

Is it ethically appropriate to hold women equally responsible when they have fewer options and resources? The concepts of circularity and complementarity ignore realistic differences in power among system members. For example, could the cycle of battering be repunctuated so that the battered woman is now held accountable for provoking her husband's aggression because the therapist assumes that they are equally responsible? On this point, Luepnitz (1988) sardonically wrote that "women do participate in their own abuse, but not as equals" (p. 163).

NEUTRALITY

Therapeutic neutrality refers to a clinical decision by the therapist not to take one family member's side against another so that each one may experience the therapist's allegiance equally. In some cases, this approach can be quite beneficial, but in others it may be unethical, illegal, and even dangerous (Braverman, 1988a).

By maintaining neutrality, the therapist may tacitly support traditional oppressive relationships that silence and devalue women. Feminist critics (e.g., Bograd, 1992) have also argued against the assumption that it is countertherapeutic to impose one's values and politics on clients. They contend that just as it is impossible not to communicate, so it is impossible not to take a stand; a "neutral" position is inevitably a political one. When an authority remains silent, it is tantamount to consent (Goodrich, Rampage, Ellman, & Halstead, 1988; Walters, Carter, Papp, & Silverstein, 1988). Doherty and Boss (1993) went so far as to claim that "the myth of value neutrality in therapy is dead" (p. 611).

Bograd (1992) questioned the naiveté of some family psychologists who choose a neutral stance in working with abusive men, whose motive may be to gain control of the therapy rather than to achieve a nonviolent, egalitarian relationship. Bograd resolved the dilemma by recognizing that part of the therapist's role is one of social control. She suggests that family therapists openly acknowledge they are conducting therapy and exerting social control by challenging social values and behaviors that are external to the therapist's belief systems.

POWER OF THE THERAPIST

Despite Bateson's initial denial of the existence of power, structural and strategic theorists went on to develop models of family therapy based on power. Structural family therapy is founded on the concept of hierarchy and power; it is the imbalance, misuse, or inappropriate application of power that is central to family dysfunction (Madanes, 1986). Haley (1976) also recognized the role that power played in interpersonal relationships, suggesting that symptoms were communications that controlled the behavior of others. He conceptualized symptoms as "power tactics" that could control the therapeutic relationship and recommended the use of strategic techniques to defuse the symptom's instrumentality.

In a political analysis of family therapy, Carpenter (1992) argued that the professional has the power to define the problem. Therefore, naming gender issues as a problem and targeting certain individuals or groups to receive services is within the therapist's authority.

Family therapists have paid little attention to how therapists make both sound clinical judgments and thoughtful ethical decisions regarding the use of their power. This is unfortunate because the results of such decisions determine who is served, what is to be accomplished, and which risks will be incurred in order to gain desired benefits.

For example, a woman presents for treatment reporting that she is being physically abused by her husband. She wants help in extracting herself from the relationship. She has no money and asks the therapist to bill her husband. What is the therapist to do? If the therapist agrees, does he or she not risk losing power and control over the treatment process?

Selected Theoretical Issues

Feminist writers have been critical of family systems theorists, and few have been spared. Here we review criticism of Bowen, Minuchin,

strategic approaches, and postmodern thinkers, and conclude with recommendations some scholars have offered.

MURRAY BOWEN

Bowen's concept of differentiation, as the hallmark of adulthood, maturity, and mental health, is founded on the male value of separation
and autonomy (Hare-Mustin, 1978). As a result, he has been indicted
for patriarchally promoting values that do not apply to women (Luepnitz, 1988). Furthermore, he has been criticized for pathologizing maternal connections (Goodrich et al., 1988; Luepnitz, 1988), and for
diagnosing mothers as overinvolved and "fused" without consideration of individual family structure or sociohistorical context.

Systems theory is based on a fundamental appreciation of context.
At its inception, family therapists roundly criticized other psychotherapists for their lack of attention to such obvious issues. It is ironic that
Bowen errs in the same direction by decontextualizing maternal behavior and describing family systems as closed, thereby failing to
grasp the larger context.

SALVADOR MINUCHIN

Minuchin's Structural Family Therapy has been charged with overre-
liance on expecting mothers to change (Luepnitz, 1988). According to
Luepnitz, although Minuchin does confront fathers at times, his tendency to unbalance systems through the mother is more pervasive.
Goldner (1988) noted that although it is the mother who was supposed
to change, restoration of parental authority often became an effort to
restore authority to fathers. By expecting only women to change, family therapists risk placing the responsibility for family well-being on
women, allowing men to continue to abdicate.

Criticism also has been leveled at Minuchin's construct of enmeshment (Goodrich et al., 1988). Although ostensibly gender-neutral in its
characterization of systems lacking optimal boundaries, enmeshment
has been overused to describe mother-child relationships, thereby de-
valuing women's skills at intimate relating.

STRATEGIC APPROACHES

Luepnitz (1988) noted that the literature of strategic therapy committed beta error (Hare-Mustin, 1978) by ignoring gender as a category.

Even the language of strategic therapy emphasizes warfare, tactics, and doing battle with family symptoms, all of which reflect a masculine cultural bias. Similarly, "strategic therapists think of their work not as healing but as fixing or even selling" (Luepnitz, 1988, p. 83).

At a practical level, paradoxical strategies and "one-upsmanship" may be useful with male clients who are accustomed to taking charge. Allgood and colleagues (1992) provided empirical support for a gender difference in the use of "resistance-using" techniques, with male clients responding with greater resistance. However, such approaches may have little utility for women, who tend to maintain more subordinate positions in the outside world (Doherty & Boss, 1993). For example, would a strategic purist so value problem resolution that he or she would resolve symptoms at the expense of endorsing submissiveness in a wife?

POSTMODERN PERSPECTIVES

More recent theoretical developments in family therapy (e.g., Michael White's narrative therapy) have been categorized as postmodern approaches (Mills & Sprenkle, 1995). These second-order cybernetics or social constructionist approaches are primarily language-focused and challenge the idea of an objective family system to be observed by an independent observer. The role of the therapist has shifted from that of an expert to one of a collaborator whose impressions are incorporated into the meaning system of the family. Although feminists have warmed to the theme of conversation over intervention (Mills & Sprenkle, 1995), the notion that even the most painful realities are open to cognitive reconstruction is troublesome to feminist sensibilities. Social injustice is not to be reframed away. As discussed previously, the narrative therapist's "neutral" stance can implicitly endorse sexist bias and therapeutic responsibility can be abdicated.

In response to the problems raised in this section, some recommendations have been offered. Bograd (1988) points to the need for a positive language of connection and intimacy to transcend the pathologizing of women's preferred interactional styles. More specifically, Goldner (1988) believes that family therapy theory has denied the issue of gender. She recommends that concepts of gender and gender inequality be integrated into the formal infrastructure of our family therapy theories. As a starting point, she suggests that we understand gender as hierarchically organized with men typically dominant over women; recognize how gender and its power actively constructs family life; and examine how gender contributes to the structure of intimate relationships.

Therapist and Supervisor Variables

In a postmodern analysis, Hare-Mustin (1994) suggests that through "dominant discourse" our gender schemas become activated, influence our perceptions of clients and their interactions, and affect our functioning as gendered individuals. This issue was investigated by The American Psychological Association Task Force on Sex Bias and Sex Role Stereotyping in Psychotherapeutic Practice (1975). The following biases were found to be prevalent among therapists:

1. The assumption that remaining in a marriage results in better adjustment for women;
2 The belief that a child's problems and child-rearing are primarily women's responsibility;
3. The demonstration of less interest and sensitivity in a woman's career than a man's;
4. The display of a double standard in regard to the sexual activities of husbands and wives; and
5. The fostering of wives' needs being deferred to their husbands'.

In this section, we review issues regarding the gender-role socialization of family therapists and their supervisors.

GENDER-ROLE SOCIALIZATION OF FAMILY THERAPISTS

Shay (1993) discussed the problems inherent in couples therapy that require that two of the three parties share the same gender. This "unstable triad" produces an inherent imbalance, which results in important transference and countertransference dilemmas. Shay details the therapeutic dynamics involving male therapists that may advantage and disadvantage both husbands and wives.

Okun (1989) suggests that therapist blind spots are created by gendered cognitive schemas. Because men are socialized into positions of privilege and dominance and women into subordinance, a therapist's gender affects his or her capacity to engage in intimate relationships and to assume power with clients.

Okun (1989) believes that power is the underlying force in gender differences. She believes that female therapists experience relational power in their ability to form and sustain nurturing relationships. On the other hand, female therapists often must struggle to exercise their authority with families and may fear punishment if they do so. At the same time, they must take care to avoid deferring to their male clients (Carlson, 1987). For example, female therapists often experience lack of respect and questioning of their credentials and competence simply by virtue of their being female. It is not surprising that in a survey of marital and family therapists, female therapists were found to be more "gender sensitive" than were male therapists (Meth, 1990).

Because male power comes as a birthright, men are typically more comfortable in positions of power. The challenge for many male therapists has been to gain comfort with the expression of affect and experience of intimacy required by the therapeutic encounter.

Doherty and Boss (1993) identified the issues of therapist emotional reactivity and projection regarding gender as directly relevant to ethical practice. "The gender debate in family therapy has provoked so much emotional reactivity precisely because of its potential for projection and distortion" (p. 631). The source of these countertransferential reactions seems rooted in the gender role socialization of therapists through their family-of-origin as well as general cultural influences. As a result, feelings, beliefs, and behaviors regarding gender are continually aroused in family therapists on both conscious and unconscious levels (Okun, 1989).

Nutt and Gottlieb (1993) suggest that the gender role socialization of male and female therapists can predict bias in their treatment applications. For example, male therapists may be more directive as a function of their socialization to be instrumental, whereas females may be more oriented toward connection and the expression of feelings based on their value of being relational.

The research findings on this issue are mixed. Shields and McDaniel (1992) found that male therapists were more verbally active, directive, and instrumental in their verbal interactions with families than were female therapists, and Hyde (1991) found that men exhibited higher activity levels. However, Newberry, Alexander, and Turner (1991) found no gender differences in structuring behavior in their sample of male and female family therapy trainees. Additionally, both groups of researchers reported no significant differences in joining skills (Shields & McDaniel, 1992) or use of support (Newberry et al., 1991) between male and female therapists as gender socialization patterns might predict.

In a sequential analysis, Newberry et al. (1991) demonstrated some gender-linked patterns in the interaction between therapists and families. They found that fathers responded more positively than mothers when therapists used structuring behavior, suggesting that male clients were more comfortable with therapies demanding less affective expression. They also found that female therapists received a more supportive response from clients following supportive behaviors than did male therapists, although it was apparent that male therapists received no pressure from families to avoid relationship behaviors. These researchers concluded that female therapists are reinforced by families for their use of gender stereotypic behavior, more so than are their male counterparts.

Nutt and Gottlieb (1993) also suggested that the treatment effectiveness of same-gender clients might be limited by shared gender "blind spots." For example, female therapists may engage female clients with closeness and focus on feelings when recommendations for instrumental behavior might be more helpful. Similarly, male therapists may focus on activity with male clients when cultivation of emotional expressivity might be better.

Hare-Mustin (1978) noted that gender role stereotypes require that men always appear competent. This rigid role prescription may make it more difficult for male therapists to recognize and acknowledge gender biases or other failings in themselves in the presence of a male client. Furthermore, social norms that emphasize men's need for control could foster power struggles between client and therapist that might interfere with the therapeutic process. Finally, since closeness and sexuality are so closely linked for men, homophobic feelings may arise in one or both as the dyad begins to feel attached. Such feelings could easily interfere with the treatment process, especially if they were denied.

Further research is required to tease apart the complex interaction of client/therapist gender in the family therapy process. For example, research has documented that behavior that violates gender prescriptions is generally negatively evaluated by others (Fiske & Stevens, 1993). This finding may indicate that clients will resist when their therapists behave in nonstereotypic fashion, particularly their female therapists.

Therapists are trained to meet the needs of their clients and must overcome some personal limitations in order to do so. But therapists are also products of a gendered culture. In this respect, they share the challenge of fulfilling their responsibilities despite their gender role socialization.

GENDER-ROLE SOCIALIZATION OF SUPERVISORS AND TRAINERS

Very little work has been published regarding gender issues in family therapy supervision. Here we review the work to date.

Kaiser (1992) identified the double bind that female family therapy supervisors may experience. "Women in authority who present themselves as primarily nurturing are often seen as being unclear thinkers, whereas those who present themselves as in charge are seen as dangerous" (p. 287). On the other hand, male supervisors enjoy a double source of power. They have the formal power of being an authority and the informal power of being male. Kaiser expressed concern for the intimidation female supervisees may feel with male supervisors. Also, caution is required in the classical cotherapy model. A female trainee and a male supervisor may model the unequal distribution of power found in many marital relationships.

Although the gender of the therapist has been empirically examined in studies of individual and family therapy outcome (Gurman & Kniskern, 1993), gender as a process variable in family therapy supervision has received little investigative attention. Philpot (1990) recommended that gender sensitivity be modeled in supervisory relationships. For example, a female student can be drawn out who might be reluctant to express her opinion in deference to a male supervisor. Doing so may help to minimize the hierarchical nature of both therapy and supervisory relationships.

Ethical Concerns

All mental health professionals are primarily obliged to their clients. They are to do what is best and avoid harm in the process (Beauchamp & Childress, 1983). Unfortunately, most ethics codes are designed for working with individuals (Woody, 1988). The recent revision of the APA *Ethical Principles and Code of Conduct* (APA, 1992) offers a first step in addressing these issues but many remain unresolved. Similarly, ethics codes have been slow to incorporate recent gender research. In this respect, the APA code is a notable exception.

Gender-sensitive family practice represents a unique confluence of complex and vexing ethical dilemmas. Family practitioners accept this obligation as a part of their daily work despite a paucity of ethical guidelines to assist them. The literature we reviewed focused on theory and practice. Except for the feminist critique of systems theory, it has devoted little attention to the myriad of ethical implications the interaction of theory and practice generates. We cannot review all of those issues here, but we will highlight some of the more salient dilemmas.

Gender

From what set of ethical assumptions do we conduct gender-sensitive family practice? Do we assume that spouses have equal power in their relationship? Although this makes ethical sense, it may be empirically incorrect. On the other hand, do we assume that a wife has relatively less power by the very fact that she is female? Although this assumption is more likely to be correct, is it ethically permissible to make an a priori assumption that a client's autonomy is compromised by virtue of her gender alone?

For example, what are we to do when presented with a couple in which a woman is being abused? We are enjoined to foster our client's autonomy (APA, 1992; Beauchamp & Childress, 1983), but what if she is not able to act in her own behalf, fearing further abuse? Could doing the ethically correct thing by encouraging her autonomy result in harm to her?

To make matters worse, this decision must be made within a larger context. The therapist is equally obligated to the abusive husband who is also his or her client. He may consider therapist support of his wife's autonomy harmful to him. Furthermore, how can a gender-sensitive therapist maintain her or his obligation and loyalty to someone who abuses and objectifies women? In short, how are we to know when gender becomes a relevant clinical matter and when it must be considered in our ethical decision making?

Systems Theory

Serious questions have been raised regarding the role of gender in systems-oriented therapy. Strategic and structural approaches have been soundly criticized for making paternalistic assumptions about how families ought to function within preconceived norms and for directly influencing them in that direction. The autonomy of clients was often violated when a therapist took control and did what he or she thought was best without consulting the family. These practices continued for many years independent of the growing work on gender issues. Only in recent years have modifications been suggested.

Some theorists may be forgiven for not taking account of gender because their theories were developed before the women's movement began. This cannot be said for more recent postmodern approaches that present numerous ethical issues regarding gender. For example, these theories view problems as "simply the result of each member of a problem system holding too tightly to one troublesome way of seeing a situation" (Mills & Sprenkle, 1995, p. 370). They view the therapist as a "co-creator of reality" who should take a "not knowing position" (Anderson & Goolishian, 1992), and leave preconceived notions about clients and an ultimate standard of their health out of the therapy room (Atkinson & Heath, 1990).

Such notions raise serious questions regarding how a therapist is to meet his or her ethical obligations to utilize current scientific knowledge to assist one's clients. Consider the following:

A couple presents complaining that the woman is depressed. The husband is a very traditional male who wants prompt answers and recommendations for his wife's condition. She speaks little, even in response to direct questioning, and repeatedly defers to her husband.

A postmodern approach may create various iatrogenic risks in such a situation. A therapist's "know nothing" role may frustrate a well-intentioned husband who is genuinely interested in helping his wife and result in postponing needed pharmacotherapy. In addition, the therapist may inadvertently perpetuate abuse if she or he fails to inquire about the possibility.

Must therapists think through every implication of each new theory that arises before using it? Do therapists risk immobilizing their decision making because of all the information they must first consider? If a therapist zealously holds to a particular theoretical position, how does he or she avoid the risk of abdicating his or her ethical responsibility to do what is best for the client?

THERAPISTS

In the process of producing a theoretical orientation toward practice, feminism has also critically evaluated the very society in which therapists try to help their clients adjust (Sprenkle & Bischof, 1994). While we support this criticism, it creates an ethical dilemma for conscientious professionals. Specifically, how can we ensure that we understand the influence of gender? How can we evaluate such matters for ourselves when we are part of the problem? In other words, how do we transcend our own culture in order to understand the limitations it places upon us? Must we change who we are? And even if we agree that such changes are necessary, how are we to go about accomplishing them? Consider the following:

A male psychologist with 30-years' experience treating families wishes to expand his knowledge regarding gender issues. He has never thought much about the question but likes to keep up with current developments so he can offer the highest quality service to his clients. What is this man to do? Will going to a weekend workshop suffice? How will he know when he has acquired sufficient knowledge? Who will help him decide what, if any, changes he must make in his practice and personal life?

On the other hand, what about a female family psychologist who works in a pediatric oncology department of a children's hospital? What difference do gender issues make in her professional life? Although awareness of gender issues may be important for her personally, is such information relevant to the ethical practice of helping gravely ill children?

Supervision

Supervisors should address gender-related issues with supervisees when the issues arise. Unfortunately, there are no studies or ethical guidelines regarding how one should conduct this process. Consider the following examples:

A male supervisor meets with his female first-semester practicum student. She plays an audiotape of an initial interview with a family. As he listens, the supervisor becomes concerned that the student has not been direct enough in her questioning of the family and even avoided obvious issues with the father. He courteously but directly confronts her with his observations. She immediately dissolves into tears and leaves the room.

A male, advanced graduate student is being supervised by a new female faculty member. In reviewing his cases, she begins to suspect that he is too hasty in his judgments and may be overconfident of his abilities. She waits a number of weeks to confirm her impression before bringing it to his attention. To her surprise, the student becomes indignant and attacks her competence.

We have noted only a sample of the ethical dilemmas created by the interaction of family practice and gender issues. There are numerous others. We are mindful that raising these issues does not resolve them. Our hope is that bringing them to light will help practitioners to be more effective, avoid harm, and adhere to higher ethical standards. In support of those goals, we offer the following recommendations.

Recommendations for Ethical Practice

The ethical issues raised in conducting gender-sensitive family practice are complex and may seem daunting. It is not our intention to discourage this type of practice. Rather, we hope to encourage others to join us in practicing from this orientation. Our goal is to inform the reader in the hope that quality of practice and ethical decision making will be enhanced. Some general principles that individual practitioners may use to assist them toward that end include:

1. To practice in family therapy requires advanced knowledge, training, and skill. It also entails a greater degree of professional responsibility and more complex, ethical decision making. Those who choose to practice in this area should be aware of these additional requirements in order to fulfill their clinical and ethical responsibilities to their clients.

2. The *Ethical Principles and Code of Conduct* of the American Psychological Association (APA, 1992) provides guidelines for ethical conduct. Although the latest revision addresses some issues related to having multiple clients, the code remains primarily focused on working with individuals. Psychologists must take additional steps to supplement their knowledge if they choose to work with couples and families.

3. Family practitioners must recognize that gender is a fundamental dynamic in all relationships. They should be able to evaluate presenting problems within that larger interactional context and understand individuals within the context of their gender-based roles.

4. Mental health professionals have an obligation to refrain from practice if they are psychologically impaired. Similarly, we contend that they also have an obligation to examine their own gendered experience when there is reason to believe that it will interfere with their ability to function effectively as professionals.

   Furthermore, self-examination will enhance professional functioning. For example, a practitioner who can flexibly alter treatment approaches to suit client needs through the application of both instrumental and affective means is in a better position to effect change than one who cannot. Similarly, by having sympathy and respect for gendered learning, therapists can empower both men and women to make new choices that can transcend the limitations of their gendered experiences.

5. Family practitioners are obliged to offer the best and most appropriate treatment available to their clients. Accordingly, practitioners are consumers of both empirical and theoretical developments. They have an affirmative obligation to evaluate both scientific research and emerging theory from a gender-sensitive perspective and to identify those issues that confer benefit as well as create risk for their clients.

   All theories of therapy have limitations. No one approach can apply in all situations. It is never appropriate to practice from a particular theoretical perspective when it is clinically contraindicated for the client. In such cases, one must use the approach that is most likely to benefit the client or make a referral to another practitioner.

6. As part of their training, students are expected to sample and eventually adopt a theoretical perspective from which to do their clinical work. These choices are often made based on personal appeal and the influence of mentors. Trainers are obliged to teach their students how to critically evaluate a given theory just as they do empirical research. This evaluation should include a critical evaluation of its empirical basis, its risks and benefits, and the particular ethical dilemmas it may raise.

7. The ethical issues surrounding family practice supervision have been sorely neglected. We have not examined the impact of our supervisory practices on supervisees or their clients in any systematic fashion. Until this knowledge becomes available, supervisors must carry on with their work and still try to avoid harm. The little data available argues that supervisors assume the existence of gender bias in themselves, their supervisees, and the families being treated and take active steps to address it.

8. No clear boundary exists between good ethical decision making and sound clinical judgment. A decision based on sound ethical principles may compromise treatment, and good clinical judgment can create serious ethical dilemmas (Gottlieb & Handlesman, 1996). To minimize such problems, the family practitioner is urged to anticipate the types of dilemmas frequently encountered in his or her particular practice situation and develop a policy to deal with them. Developing such a policy will lead to greater treatment effectiveness and fewer ethical dilemmas (Gottlieb, this volume).

Conclusion

Engaging in gender-sensitive family practice requires expertise in two independent lines of scholarly thought and practice. Practicing in this way is both rewarding and effective despite the unique ethical dilemmas created by their interaction. We have tried to explain some of these dilemmas and offer initial guidelines for those interested in this exciting practice area.

References

Allgood, S. M., Bischoff, R. J., Smith, T. A., & Salts, C. J. (1992). Therapist interventions: Do they really influence client resistance? *American Journal of Family Therapy, 20,* 333–340.

Amaro, H. (1995). Love, sex, and power. *American Psychologist, 50,* 437–447.

American Psychological Association. (1992). Ethical principles and code of conduct. *American Psychologist, 47,* 1597–1611.

American Psychological Association Task Force. (1975). Report of the task force on sex bias and sex-role stereotyping on psychotherapeutic practice. *American Psychologist, 30,* 1169–1175.

Anderson, H., & Goolishian, H. (1992). The client is the expert: A not-knowing approach to therapy. In S. McNamee & K. J. Gergen (Eds.), *Therapy as social construction: Inquiries in social construction* (pp. 25–39). London: Sage.

Atkinson, B. J., & Heath, A. W. (1990). Further thoughts on second-order family therapy—This time it's personal. *Family Process, 29,* 145–155.

Avis, J. M. (1990, November/December). Gender consciousness must transform theory, practice, training, research. *Family Therapy News,* p. 3.

Bateson, G. (1980). *Mind and nature.* New York: Bantam Books.

Beauchamp, T. L., & Childress, J. F. (1983). *Principles of biomedical ethics.* New York: Oxford University Press.

Bernard, J. (1972). *The future of marriage.* New York: Bantam Books.

Bograd, M. (1988). Enmeshment, fusion or relatedness? A conceptual analysis. In L. Braverman (Ed.), *Women, feminism and family therapy* (pp. 65–80). New York: Haworth.

Bograd, M. (1992). Values in conflict: Challenges to family therapists' thinking. *Journal of Marital and Family Therapy, 18,* 245–256.

Braverman, L. (Ed.). (1988a). *A guide to feminist family therapy.* New York: Harrington Park Press.

Braverman, L. (Ed.). (1988b). *Women, feminism, and family therapy.* New York: Haworth.

Brooks, G. R. (1992, July). Men's studies: The next decade. *Society for the Psychological Study of Men and Masculinity Newsletter, 1,* 1–2.

Brown, L. S. (1991). Ethical issues in feminist therapy. *Psychology of Women Quarterly, 15*, 323–336.

Carlson, N. L. (1987). Woman therapist: Male client. In M. Scher, M. Stevens, G. Good, & G. A. Eichenfield (Eds.), *Handbook of counseling and psychotherapy with men* (pp. 39–50). Newbury Park, CA: Sage.

Carpenter, J. (1992). What's the use of family therapy? *Australian/New Zealand Journal of Family Therapy, 13*, 26–32.

Cook, E. P. (1987). Psychological androgyny: A review of the research. *The Counseling Psychologist, 15*, 471–513.

Crosby, F. J., & Jaskar, K. L. (1993). Women and men at home and at work: Realities and illusions. In S. Oskamp & M. Costanzo (Eds.), *Gender issues in contemporary society* (pp. 143–273). Newbury Park, CA: Sage.

Doherty, W. J., & Boss, P. G. (1993). Values and ethics in family therapy. In A. S. Gurman & D. P. Kniskern (Eds.), *Handbook of family therapy* (Vol. 2, pp. 606–637). New York: Brunner/Mazel.

Fiske, S. U., & Stevens, L. E. (1993). What's so special about sex? Gender stereotyping and discrimination. In S. Oskamp & M. Costanzo (Eds.), *Gender issues in contemporary society* (pp. 173–196). Newbury Park, CA: Sage.

Gilbert, L. A. (1987). Female and male emotional dependency and its implications for the therapist client relationship. *Professional Psychology: Research and Practice, 18*, 555–561.

Gilligan, C., Ward, J. V., & Taylor, J. M. (1988). *Mapping the moral domain.* Cambridge, MA: Harvard University Press.

Goldner, V. (1988). Generation and gender: Normative and covert hierarchies. *Family Process, 27*, 17–31.

Goodrich, T. J., Rampage, C., Ellman, B., & Halstead, K. (1988). *Feminist family therapy.* New York: Norton.

Gottlieb, M. (1997, this volume).

Gottlieb, M., & Handlesman, M. (in press). *Ethical decision making and clinical judgment: At the crossroad.* Manuscript in preparation.

Gottman, J. M. (1991). Predicting the longitudinal course of marriages. *Journal of Marital and Family Therapy, 17*, 3–7.

Gurman, A. S., & Kniskern, D. P. (Eds.). (1993). *Handbook of marital and family therapy* (Vol. 2). New York: Brunner/Mazel.

Haley, J. (1976). *Problem-solving therapy.* San Francisco: Jossey-Bass.

Hare-Mustin, R. (1978). A feminist approach to family therapy. *Family Process, 17*, 181–194.

Hare-Mustin, R. (1994). Discourse in the mirrored room: A postmodern analysis of therapy. *Family Process, 33*, 19–35.

Harrison, J., Chin, J., & Ficarrotto, T. (1992). Warning: Masculinity may be dangerous to your health. In M. S. Kimmel & M. A. Messner (Eds.), *Men's lives* (pp. 271–285). New York: Macmillan.

Hochschild, A. (1992). The second shift. In M. S. Kimmel and M. A. Messner (Eds.), *Men's lives* (pp. 511–515). New York: Macmillan.

Hyde, J. S. (1991). *Half the human experience.* Lexington, MA: Heath.

Kaiser, T. L. (1992). The supervisory relationship: An identification of the primary elements in the relationship and an application of two theories of ethical relationships. *Journal of Marital and Family Therapy, 18,* 283–296.

Lazerson, J. (1992). Feminism and group psychotherapy: An ethical responsibility. *International Journal of Group Psychotherapy, 42,* 523–546.

Luepnitz, D. A. (1988). *The family interpreted.* New York: Basic Books.

Madanes, C. (1986). *Behind the one-way mirror.* San Francisco: Jossey-Bass.

Meth, R. L. (1990, November/December). Therapists asked to challenge self, clients. *Family Therapy News, 1,* p. 7.

Mills, S. D., & Sprenkle, D. H. (1995). Family therapy in the postmodern era. *Family Relations, 44,* 368–376.

Nadelson, C. C., & Notman, M. T. (1992). The impact of the new psychology of men and women on psychotherapy. *Review of Psychiatry, 10,* 608–625.

Newberry, A. M., Alexander, J. F., & Turner, C. W. (1991). Gender as a process variable in family therapy. *Journal of Family Psychology, 5,* 158–175.

Nutt, R. L., & Gottlieb, M. C. (1993). Gender diversity in clinical psychology: Research, practice, and training. *The Clinical Psychologist, 46,* 64–73.

Okun, B. (1989). Therapists' blind spots related to gender socialization. In D. Kantor & B. F. Okun (Eds.), *Intimate environments: Sex, intimacy, and gender in families* (pp. 129–162). New York: Guilford.

O'Neil, J. M. (1981). Male sex role conflicts, sexism, and masculinity: Psychological implications for men, women, and the counseling psychologist. *The Counseling Psychologist, 20,* 61–80.

Philpot, C. (1990, Summer). Gender-sensitivity in clinical psychology programs. *The Family Psychologist, 6*(3), 39.

Pittman, F. (1991a, February). Man enough. *New Woman, 1,* 40.

Pittman, F. (1991b). The secret passions of men. *Journal of Marital and Family Therapy, 17,* 11–23.

Pleck, J. H. (1980). Men's power with women, other men and society: A men's movement analysis. In E. H. Pleck & J. H. Pleck (Eds.), *The American man* (pp. 417–433). Englewood Cliffs, NJ: Prentice-Hall.

Pleck, J. H., Sonenstein, F. J., & Ku, L. C. (1993). Masculinity ideology and its correlates. In S. Oskamp & M. Costanzo (Eds.), *Gender issues in contemporary society* (pp. 85–112). Newbury Park, CA: Sage.

Scanzoni, J., & Fox, G. L. (1980). Sex roles, family and society: The seventies and beyond. *Journal of Marriage and the Family, 43,* 20–33.

Scher, M. (1989, August). *Effect of gender role incongruities on men's experience as clients in psychotherapy.* Paper presented at the annual meeting of the American Psychological Association, New Orleans, LA.

Scher, M., Stevens, M., Good, G., & Eichenfield, G. A. (Eds.). (1987). *Handbook of counseling and psychotherapy with men.* Newbury Park, CA: Sage.

Shay, J. J. (1993). Should men treat couples? Transference, countertransference, and sociopolitical considerations. *Psychotherapy, 30,* 93–102.

Sheffield, C. J. (1995). Sexual terrorism. In J. Freeman (Ed.), *Women: A feminist perspective* (pp. 1–21). Mountain View, CA: Mayfield.

Shields, G. C., & McDaniel, S. H. (1992). Process differences between male and female therapists in a first family interview. *Journal of Marital and Family Therapy, 18,* 143–151.

Sprenkle, D. H., & Bischof, G. P. (1994). Contemporary family therapy in the United States. *Journal of Family Therapy, 16,* 5–23.

Walrond-Skinner, S. (1987). Feminist therapy and family therapy. In S. Walrond-Skinner & D. Watson (Eds.), *Ethical issues in family therapy* (pp. 71–86). London: Routledge & Kegan Paul.

Walters, M., Carter, B., Papp, P., & Silverstein, O. (1988). *The invisible web.* New York: Guilford.

Weiner, J. P., & Boss, P. (1985). Exploring gender bias against women: Ethics for marriage and family therapy. *Counseling and Values, 30,* 9–23.

West, C., & Zimmerman, D. H. (1991). Doing gender. In J. Lober & S. A. Farrell (Eds.), *The social construction of gender* (pp. 13–37). Newbury Park, CA: Sage.

Woody, R. H. (1988). *Fifty ways to avoid malpractice.* Sarasota, FL: Professional Resource Exchange.

CHAPTER 4

Multicultural Competence in Family Practice

BEVERLY J. GOODWIN

M ary Rogers (1996), in her anthology *Multicultural Experiences, Multicultural Theories*, traces the beginnings of the multiculturalism philosophy to "the second wave of the civil rights movement that shaped American society during the 1950s and 1960s" (p. 1). At that time, attention became focused on racial inequalities within many segments of society, including the field of counseling and psychotherapy. One societal response was the passage of Title VII of the Civil Rights Act of 1964. Employment discrimination based on race, color, sex, or national origin was banned, and the Equal Employment Opportunity Commission was created. When the U.S. Commission on Mental Health identified racism as the number one mental health problem in the United States in 1965, some in the counseling and psychotherapy field responded with a call for increased multicultural sensitivity and competence.

Even though multiculturalism has been a buzzword in the mental health field for almost half a century (Ivey, Ivey, & Simek-Morgan, 1993; Okun, 1992; Sue & Sue, 1990), several decades passed before its importance was recognized in the field of family practice (Hardy & Laszloffy, 1992; Ho, 1987; Ivey et al., 1993; *Manual on Accreditation*, 1988; McGoldrick, Pearce, & Giordano, 1982; Preli & Bernard, 1993; Saba, Karrar, & Hardy, 1990; Sue & Sue, 1990). Therefore, it is safe to say that:

Historically, the field of family therapy has paid little attention to issues of ethnic, cultural, and, especially, racial differences. . . . Therapists' training will need to be broadened to include greater racial sensitivity. (Hardy & Las-zloffy, 1992, p. 364)

Although family practice was slow to acknowledge the importance of multicultural competence (e.g., Boyd-Franklin, 1989; Hardy & Las-zloffy, 1992; McGoldrick et al., 1982; Preli & Bernard, 1993), hundreds of publications have been published on the subject. Authors frequently offered recommendations on how best to train multiculturally competent practitioners.

This chapter reviews a portion of the literature on multicultural competence in family practice, with a focus on (a) how multiculturalism is defined; (b) how multicultural competence is conceptualized; and (c) how multiculturalism has transformed the curriculum in training programs. Recommendations for future efforts in the area of family practice training are offered.

How Multiculturalism Is Defined

Within the mental health field, the multiculturalism movement is a product of the belief that traditional counseling and psychotherapy have limitations when the client is culturally different. Donald Cheek (1976), one of the first advocates for culturally appropriate therapeutic techniques, referred to some traditional techniques as being "White techniques" because they are not effective when working with African-Americans. Katz and Ivey (1977) asserted that "racism undermines the goals of the helping field to the detriment of White and Third World helpees" (p. 485). They reviewed programs and techniques that were designed to deal with racism in individuals and groups. They also provided a description of their own program, which "combines the concept of white-on-white training with a systematic step-by-step curricular-affective program of racism awareness training" (p. 487).

Within the field of family practice, multiculturalism has been viewed primarily through the contextual lens of ethnicity (Giordano & Carini-Giordano, 1995; McGoldrick et al., 1982; McGoldrick, Preto, Hines, & Lee, 1991). An important tenet espoused by those embracing this position is that "ethnicity and family life are so intertwined that one cannot reflect on one without considering the other" (Giordano & Carini-Giordano, 1995, p. 355). The same could be said regarding the role that race and social class play in our understanding of family life

(Boyd-Franklin, 1989, 1995; Hines, 1988). Boyd-Franklin (1993) identified "race and class as two of the most complex and emotionally loaded issues in this country" (p. 361).

The work of these authors is representative of activities that set the stage for multicultural training and therapy. Each one of them addresses the topic of multiculturalism, but how exactly is it defined?

Virginia Cyrus (1993) provides one definition of multiculturalism:

The multiculturalism theory views American culture as a combination of many subsocieties. Multiculturalism claims that each group retains some of its customs and traditions, that these are accepted as valid and valuable, and that all groups coexist. (p. 4)

A more political conceptualization comes from Mary Rogers (1996), who describes multiculturalism as growing:

out of the realization that the "price of admission" to the bourgeois civil societies of the West remains indefensibly high for many groups of people and out of reach for other groups. Full admission entails assimilation. It requires "different" people to compromise or even abandon their distinctiveness by conforming their public behavior to bourgeois tastes and to act as if they fully shared the culture of straight men in the white Protestant middle classes. Unwilling or unable to pay such prices, members of many groups get cast as our society's "Others." (p. 1)

This point of view stresses that cultural differences do exist and that they will continue to exist. Multiculturalism rejects suggestions that the assimilation and melting pot theories characterize life in the United States (Cyrus, 1993; Rogers, 1996). Instead of downplaying cultural differences, the multicultural perspective encourages us to learn to live with them and points out the sociopolitical implications of particular differences (Katz, 1985; McGoldrick, 1993; Rowe & Grills, 1996).

Beginning in the 1980s, demographers began to announce the "darkening" of America by predicting that the majority would become the minority early in the next century. Cultural sensitivity was no longer a luxury but a necessity. Professional organizations began to pass propositions and resolutions on creating a climate within the profession and within training institutions to address the issue of multiculturalism (e.g., American Association for Marriage and Family Therapy, 1991; American Psychological Association, 1986a, 1986b, 1987).

How Multicultural Competence Is Conceptualized

Derald Wing Sue (1978) used the phrase *culturally effective counselor* to describe those who were sensitive to cultural differences in the therapist-client relationship. He proposed a set of characteristics to distinguish those who are culturally effective counselors from those who are not, challenging others to add to the list. Patricia Arredondo-Dowd and John Gonsalves (1980) specify five characteristics of culturally effective counselors:

1. Culturally effective counselors understand their own values and assumptions of human behavior and recognize that those helped by others may differ.
2. Culturally effective counselors realize that no theory of counseling is politically or morally neutral.
3. Culturally effective counselors understand that external sociopolitical forces may have influenced and shaped culturally different groups.
4. Culturally effective counselors are able to share the world view of their clients rather than being culturally encapsulated.
5. Culturally effective counselors are truly eclectic in their counseling, using counseling skills because of their appropriateness to the experiences and lifestyles of the culturally different. (p. 657)

These authors envision the culturally effective counselor as having counseling, cultural, linguistic, and pedagogical competencies and possessing teaching, bilingual, and life skills.

By 1982, the list of characteristics was expanded from 5 to 11 (D. Sue et al., 1982) by the Division of Counseling Psychology of the American Psychological Association (APA), which has an interest in not only producing culturally sensitive counselors but also in providing guidelines for their professional development.

In 1990, Derald Sue and David Sue refined the list by specifying competencies in three domains. They also listed the characteristics appropriate for each of the three areas, cautioning that the list is tentative and probably will be increased over time. Thus, their works have been aimed at eliminating barriers to effective therapy with culturally different clients and producing culturally skilled providers.

Paul Pedersen (1987) considered the issue of multicultural competence. Writing on cultural biases in both facilitators and students, he had a tremendous impact on training and development efforts. He listed what he considers to be the 10 most frequent examples of cultural bias seen in the literature that interfere with the development of culturally skilled practitioners. His list includes the following: (a) assumptions regarding normal behavior, (b) emphasis on individualism, (c) fragmentation by academic disciplines, (d) dependence on abstract thinking, (e) overemphasis on independence, (f) neglect of client's support systems, (g) dependence on linear thinking, (h) focus on changing individual, not system, (i) neglect of history, and (j) dangers of cultural encapsulation. Pedersen believes all of these assumptions must be challenged before therapists can be effective in providing services to a culturally diverse clientele.

There are many reviews available, offering multicultural training models (Corvin & Wiggins, 1989; Pope-Davis, Reynolds, Dings, & Ottavi, 1994; Preli & Bernard, 1993).

Corvin and Wiggins (1989) identify three general characteristics of training models:

1. A basic assumption that an individual's ethnic or cultural background significantly influences his or her worldview and the way in which he or she experiences and understands life and its problems.
2. An emphasis on learning about various cultural groups (i.e., cultural worldviews) so that there is some understanding of how an individual from a particular group may experience life and its problems.
3. A focus on teaching counseling skills and interventions appropriate for use with members of various ethnic groups. (p. 105)

Pope-Davis and colleagues (1994) propose a model of multicultural competency involving:

an awareness of one's own biases and cultural assumptions, content knowledge about cultures different from one's own, an accurate self-assessment of one's multicultural skills and comfort level, an appropriate application of cultural knowledge to the counseling process, and an awareness of the cultural assumptions underlying the counseling process. (p. 466)

Preli and Bernard (1993), borrowing from Bernard and Goodyear (1992), proposed a similar model, but with more specificity. Taking an interdisciplinary approach, they have identified six training philosophies for family therapy training programs:

1. A *pluralistic philosophy* with an open-mindedness to all cultural perspectives;

2. An emphasis on acquiring *cultural knowledge* of multicultural, as well as intragroup, differences;

3. A focus on *consciousness raising* to sensitize trainees to biases and racism;

4. An acquisition of *multicultural skill training* in a laboratory setting to facilitate success in working with a multicultural clientele;

5. An expectation that trainees have some close *contact with minorities* in some life experience; and

6. An opportunity to participate in a supervised *practicum or internship with minorities.* (pp. 7–8)

Although these models view multicultural competence as important, much of the attention in the literature does not consider the institutional changes necessary to complete the task at hand. With time, a change occurred in the literature, which shifted from the identification of individual competencies to institutional or systemic concerns. The ethical ramifications of ignoring multicultural competence became an increasing focus of discussion in the literature. This interest is seen in the *Code of Ethics* of the American Association for Marriage and Family Therapy (1991) and the *Ethical Principles of Psychologists and Code of Conduct* of the APA (1992).

There have been other institutional responses as well, for example, in 1986, the APA Council of Representatives adopted language for the revised standards for the accreditation of graduate programs. The *Criteria for Accreditation Handbook* (APA, 1986a) stipulates minimum requirements that psychology departments must meet in preparing students to function in a multicultural society. In particular, programs must foster an appreciation for and knowledge of cultural and individual differences.

Programs must develop knowledge and skills in their students relevant to human diversity such as people with handicapping conditions, of differing ages, genders, ethnic and racial backgrounds, religions, and life-styles, and from differing social and individual backgrounds. (p. 4)

The revised accreditation standards for marriage and family therapy programs (*Manual on Accreditation,* 1988) address the issue of multiculturalism. Training programs are expected to emphasize "issues of gender and ethnicity as they relate to marital and family therapy" (p. 13). Both manuals provide general requirements in relation to multiculturalism and the core curriculum. The logistics, however, are omitted; each training program must decide how to implement the requirements.

Again, the institutional response avoids an exploration of the affective component. Yet this is the truly hard work, requiring substantial effort and innovation. Instead, much of the attention has been focused on students acquiring a cultural knowledge of a racial/ethnic group—a cognitive task—which is no easy feat either. Below some issues in developing a quality core curriculum on multiculturalism are explored.

How Multiculturalism
Has Transformed Training Programs

One way to evaluate a curriculum on cultural diversity is to assess the extent to which appropriate material is included in a given publication. For example, Brown, Goodwin, Hall, and Jackson-Lowman (1985) developed a categorization system for college textbooks. They classified readings on the continuum of inclusion-exclusion, describing the extent and the manner in which issues regarding diversity are addressed.

Subclassifications include Integration, Tokenism, Segregation, and Exclusion. The category of Integration is utilized when information on diversity is presented throughout the book. Tokenism refers to a textbook that includes information on diversity only in a few places and that provides few references. Segregation applies when information on diversity is presented in chapter(s) devoted exclusively to multiculturalism. Exclusion is used to indicate that there is no material on the topic of diversity. According to Brown et al., few textbooks are truly inclusive in their orientation.

The curriculum was also transformed through implementation of systemic changes within the core curriculum. Elaine Copeland (1982) and Peggy McIntosh (1983, 1990) explored different ways the curriculum can be transformed to incorporate a multicultural perspective. Copeland's review of the literature on counseling psychology identified four basic models for providing multicultural information to students: (a) the separate course model; (b) the area of concentration model; (c) the integration model; and (d) the interdisciplinary model.

Two of the models, the separate course and integration models, deserve further attention because the former is probably the most popular and the latter is probably the most comprehensive and consummate model available to us.

The *separate course model* is probably the easiest to design. It involves adding one course on diversity to an existing training program. Depending on the mission of a training program, the contents, design, goals, and objectives of the course might vary. Elizabeth Davis-Russell (1990) sees some variability within this model.

In some places, the course's focus has been on a single, ethnic minority population, . . . because that population represents the largest minority group in the area. In other areas, . . . where the representation of four ethnic minority groups . . . is large, some institutions, using the separate-course model, have developed a course inclusive of the four ethnic minority groups. (p. 175)

This model does not lend itself to an intensive study of an ethnic minority group. Copeland believes that if only one course is offered it must include a historical overview of minorities and a theoretical perspective, so that students are able to develop both cognitive and affective skills simultaneously. It would be optimal if students could also have an opportunity to gain experiences in cross-cultural and interracial settings.

The *integration model* is implemented by adding a cultural knowledge component to all courses in the core curriculum; it involves a thorough overhaul of all courses and field experiences (Davis-Russell, 1990). In this model, multicultural training is no longer an elective but a program mission, requiring the involvement of all participants in the program, including students, faculty, clinical supervisors, and administrators. In order for this model to be successful, considerable motivation, time, and resources are necessary. Adopting this model shows a serious commitment to developing multicultural competencies in all students who matriculate through a program. For example, Troy (1990) provides an outline of the curriculum of a Psy.D. program that incorporates such a model.

McIntosh takes another direction in her curricular transformation efforts, focusing on the philosophy of the curriculum. She proposes an Interactive Phase Theory containing five interactive phases. In her 1983 manuscript, she describes how Women's Studies theories and readings can advance a traditional curriculum; her 1990 manuscript demonstrates how theories and readings on race can advance a traditional curriculum. The latter manuscript relates to the issue of cultural diversity in more detail. Taking some liberty, I have inserted the word Psychology for History in each of the phases she delineated. The phases now become:

Phase One: All-White Psychology

Phase Two: Exceptional Minority Individuals in Psychology

Phase Three: Minority Issues, or Minority Groups as Problems, Anomalies, Absences, or Victims in Psychology

Phase Four: The Lives and Cultures of People of Color Everywhere *as* Psychology

Phase Five: Psychology Redefined and Reconstructed to Include Us All (p. 5)

A program in either Phase One or Two would probably require students to complete only a single course, as described by Copeland. Likewise, a program representative of either Phase Four or Five of McIntosh's theory would adopt an integrative approach that targets all courses in the core curriculum.

Her work critiques the patriarchical and Eurocentric worldviews, which have a dominant position in the mental health field. Hampton and Gottlieb (in this volume) consider the impact of the former perspective. I will briefly discuss how Eurocentricity impacts on the mental health field (Rowe & Grills, 1996) and family practice (McGoldrick et al., 1982).

The Eurocentric position has been called the *etic* perspective. Ridley (1995) describes the etic perspective as:

a culturally universal or generalized model of mental health. It defines behavior patterns on a fixed adjustment/maladjustment continuum. The model promotes a standard of normalcy that spans cultural, ethnic, and racial lines. The criteria for interpreting behavior always remain constant, regardless of the cultural context or personas being judged . . . respective backgrounds would not be taken into consideration. (p. 48)

This position has tremendous implications for teaching students and training practitioners to work with families. If the etic position is adopted, little variety in family structure, function, and relations is expected. There is no attention given in the classroom to culturally diverse families. If there are any readings, they are not inclusive in their orientation. In addition, having a culturally diverse educational institution is not considered and students are not expected to explore their own cultural identities in preparing for professional life (Boyd-Franklin, 1989; Giordano & Carini-Giordano, 1995; McGoldrick et al., 1991; Preli & Bernard, 1993; Sue & Sue, 1990).

Because there is no recognition of the ethnic/racial identification of families, all families are evaluated to the extent to which they have become acculturated (Casas, 1995). Based on the work of Marin (1992), Casas (1995) describes *acculturation* as "a process of attitudinal and behavioral change undergone, willingly or unwillingly, by individuals who reside in multicultural societies or who come in contact with a new culture due to colonization, invasion, or other political changes" (p. 317). Marin (1992) sees acculturation as learning another world view and as occurring at three separate levels: superficial, intermediate, and significant.

From the perspective of acculturation, psychological health is based on the extent to which the family adopts Eurocentric beliefs, values, attitudes, and norms and rejects characteristics of their racial/ethnic group, especially when they are disparate or appear to be contrary to dominant characteristics. Assuming a psychoeducational orientation, the therapist might encourage the family to become similar to the dominant culture and abandon its cultural traditions. Similarly, neither clinical supervision nor continuing education activities would be culture sensitive (Boyd-Franklin, 1993; Goodwin, 1993; Preli & Bernard, 1993).

The Eurocentric perspective encourages students to espouse this world view. Students are expected to assume what McIntosh (1990) refers to as "monoculturalism":

Monoculturalism, like all forms of single-system seeing, is blind to its own cultural specificity. It cannot see itself. It mistakes its "givens" for neutral, preconceptual ground rather than for distinctive cultural grounding. People who have been granted the most public or economic power, when thinking monoculturally about "others," often imagine that these others' lives must be constituted of "issues," "problems," and deficits relative to themselves. (p. 1)

At present, the dominant orientation continues to be monocultural, not multicultural, and classes and programs still have not made the curricular and training changes to adequately train clinicians to service a diverse clientele (Batton, 1996; Bernal & Castro, 1994; Bernal & Padilla, 1982; Dunston, 1983; Wyatt & Parham, 1985).

Another important aspect of the Eurocentric world view is how the profession deals with those identified as being culturally different. Either they are invisible, a myopic view of their problems is taken, their so-called anomalies are exaggerated, or their victim status is exploited. They are classified as outsiders, and their other status is the dominant characteristic considered.

Phases Four and Five of McIntosh's model offer some hope that the course the field has taken so far can be reversed. One of my graduate students, Denise Batton (1996), describes the fourth phase as a celebration of diversity and as an ahistorical phase that downplays past oppressions and acts of discrimination. In her view, Phase Four:

begins to exemplify the lives and cultures of people of color for their unique and valuable contributions. . . . Phase Four shows a broadening of the paradigm and a desire for the truth. Self-examination occurs and cognitive and emotional dissonance subsides. (p. 41)

In Phase Five there is a paradigm shift. Group identities are considered unique and are not compared to middle-class Eurocentric standards. To quote Batton:

The shift in paradigm is complete and diversity is accepted rather than just tolerated. Phase Five includes a vocabulary that fits a pluralistic society. The past, present, and future are recognized as being important; multiple ways of synthesizing knowledge. . . . A sense of oneness with others and the world is derived from embracing various cultural beliefs, values, and senses of spirituality. McIntosh believed that this phase to be the hardest to achieve and maintain because it demands an abandonment of the old and the development of an innovative way of doing things. (p. 42)

Sue and Sue (1990) suggest professionals question and analyze the appropriateness of traditional methods of therapy when working with those who are culturally diverse. Generic characteristics of traditional therapy need to be assessed as they apply to those coming from a culturally different background. They elaborate on the culture- and class-bound values and language variables applicable to Asian-Americans, African-Americans, Latinos/Hispanics, and American Indians as individual groups. Similarly, Rosenblum and Travis (1996) refer to racial/ethnic groups as representing what they term "master statuses" (p. 1).

Racial/ethnic grouping is just one type of master status. We live in a culture where there are other regularly recognized master statuses, in addition to race and ethnicity, such as gender, social class, and sexual orientation. All of these identity variables matter in American culture. Although the master statuses are distinct in some aspects, it is Rosenblum and Travis' position that master statuses share some "important similarities in the way these master statuses are currently constructed and in their impact on individual lives" (p. 1).

It is quite common for the salient characteristics of each master status to be considered independently. Namely, whenever a master status is discussed, the focus is on *either* race/ethnicity, gender, sexual orientation, *or* class. Absolutes are seldom given in the hope that generalizations will not lead to stereotypes or distortions "about all people who are members of a particular group" (Sue & Sue, 1990, p. 48).

What happens when the race, gender, sexual orientation, and social class identification of a person are considered? Seldom is the discourse focused on all four statuses simultaneously. Goodwin (1996) described this as follows: "When Blacks are being considered, the analysis often does not include gender. When women are being considered, the analysis often does not include race or ethnicity" (p. 185). This approach has been called the "add-on" or the "additive perspective." The mutually exclusive categories of race/ethnicity, gender, sexual orientation, and social class are analyzed separately. The interconnectedness of these statuses is overlooked; few professionals are prepared to undertake such an analysis. Such an analysis would require a shift in the paradigm, which has not occurred in family practice. Davis-Russell and Kuba (1996) have expanded the list of master statuses by taking an inclusive approach that adds religious orientation, physical disability, socioeconomic class, age, culture, national origin, and language to the four items above. So far family therapy as a recognized and organized field of study is in its infancy (Foley, 1975), and has been slow to acknowledge racial/ethnic identities (Hardy & Laszloffy, 1992), let alone gender, sexual orientation, and social class as being salient in any discussion of cultural diversity. A question we can ask ourselves is whether family practice can ever embrace multiculturalism as defined by Davis-Russell and Kuba (1996)?

A paradigm shift would involve a departure from the usual nomothetic approach to an idiographic stance (Ridley, 1995). Another name for this is the *emic* perspective. Ridley (1995) sees this model as:

a culturally sensitive or specific model of mental health. . . . This model construes mental health in terms of divergent attitudes, values, and behaviors that arise out of specific cultures. Similar overt behaviors may mean something different to people of different backgrounds. On the other hand, different behaviors could have similar meanings across various cultures. This implies that the valid interpretation of behavior rests upon a person's indigenous cultural norms. (p. 48)

He proposes five guiding principles when performing multicultural counseling:

1. Every client should be understood from his or her unique frame of reference.
2. Nomothetic, normative information does not always fit a particular client.
3. People are a dynamic blend of multiple roles and identities.
4. The idiographic perspective is compatible with the biopsychosocial model of mental health.
5. The idiographic perspective is transtheoretical. (pp. 82–83)

To quote Ridley:

Every client is unique—each one a mixture of characteristics and qualities unlike everyone else. Clients of similar background are even different from each other. Although they have much in common, their differences outweigh their similarities. When clients arrive for counseling, they bring their personal stories, and each has a different story to tell. Because everyone is unique, counselors should not attempt to counsel every client in exactly the same way. (p. 81)

This approach asks that a client not be treated as a member of a family or a member of a race, but as an individual who has multiple cultural identities and roles. Within the field of family therapy, the works of Boyd-Franklin (1989, 1993, 1995), for example, speak to this issue by offering suggestions on ways to shift the paradigm.

Boyd-Franklin made proposals that are designed to heighten cultural sensitivity in providers, such as utilizing a multisystems analysis in determining the complex interplay between a family and different systems; providing a culturally specific type of treatment; and involving trainees in classroom and supervision activities developed to extend their knowledge base and cultural sensitivity. This process might begin with the acquisition of knowledge, but it does not end there. In fact, alternative routes can produce clinicians who think with a multicultural world view and are skilled in providing culturally sensitive services (Atkinson, Morton, & Sue, 1989; Preli & Bernard, 1993; Sue & Sue, 1990). Other activities include assigning movies and videotapes of culturally diverse families in therapy.

This process becomes more salient when training programs and training sites are culturally integrated. The inclusion of faculty and students representing cultural differences facilitates the level of sensitivity and awareness evidence in a training site. Personal and professional growth in the realm of multiculturalism is facilitated when trainees are encouraged to share their own family genograms with emphasis placed on cultural identities and when they become comfortable in processing cultural transference and countertransference issues. Students are given an opportunity to uncover their cultural identities. Transference issues are processed, and students are able to develop skills that empower them to become competent, culturally skilled family practitioners.

As this review demonstrates, multiculturalism is a dominant force within counseling and psychotherapy. Cheatham, Ivey, Ivey, and Simek-Morgan (1993) refer to multicultural counseling and therapy as the fourth force of psychology, which "starts with awareness of differences among clients and the importance of the effects of family and cultural factors on the way clients view the world" (p. 94). Within the domain of family practice, the culturally effective provider is seen as a practitioner who has an understanding of how cultural differences impact both individual and family functioning. In addition, the culturally skilled provider sees him- or herself as possessing cultural identification in a way that no longer makes either the provider or the client feel uncomfortable (Boyd-Franklin, 1995; Giordano & Carini-Giordano, 1995; McGoldrick et al., 1991). Without such an awareness, the therapist runs the risk of making diagnostic errors, providing inappropriate treatment, and experiencing burnout.

Summary and Recommendations

With changing demographics in America and greater recognition of cultural identities, there is an increased demand for culturally appropriate techniques and multicultural competence. This goal is far from being achieved in family practice. There are notable problems identified above as contributing to the state of affairs, including an overemphasis on cultural knowledge to the exclusion of self-awareness, and the limitations in selection, structure, and philosophy of the curriculum and training programs. This chapter focused on curricular matters. There is much work still to be done in this area. More attention needs to be given to the limitations of the field, especially the core curriculum and how diversity issues are addressed in assigned readings.

In addition, there is a need to encourage both trainees and therapists, who are usually culturally similar, to develop an awareness of their own biases and cultural assumptions and to raise their consciousness on cultural diversity. The recognition of cultural identities (especially racial identity) of persons of European origin is paramount in eliminating the "us/them" mentality that works against an affirming view of multiculturalism.

This work has yet to be seriously undertaken in a systematic way in most settings where family practitioners receive training (e.g., Hardy & Laszloffy, 1992; Preli & Bernard, 1993). Without this paradigm shift, the competency and effectiveness of family practitioners is limited.

References

American Association for Marriage and Family Therapy. (1991). *Code of ethics*. Washington, DC: Author.

American Psychological Association. (1986a). *Accreditation handbook*. Washington, DC: Author.

American Psychological Association. (1986b). The changing face of American psychology: A report from the Committee on Employment and Human Resources. *American Psychologist, 41*, 1311–1327.

American Psychological Association. (1987). *Casebook on ethical principles of psychologists*. Washington, DC: Author.

American Psychological Association. (1992). *Ethical principles of psychologists and code of conduct*. Washington, DC: Author.

Arredondo-Dowd, P.M., & Gonsalves, J. (1980). Preparing culturally effective counselors. *Personnel and Guidance Journal, 58*, 657– 662.

Atkinson, D. R., Morton, G., & Sue, D. W. (1989). *Counseling American minorities: A cross-cultural perspective* (3rd ed.). Dubuque, IA: Brown.

Batton, D. M. S. (1996). *The inclusion of didactic materials and training experiences related to people of color in professional psychology schools and programs: An exploratory investigation*. Unpublished doctoral dissertation, Indiana University of Pennsylvania, Indiana, PA.

Bernal, M. E., & Castro, F. G. (1994). Are clinical psychologists prepared for service and research with ethnic minorities? *American Psychologist, 49*, 797–805.

Bernal, M. E., & Padilla, A. M. (1982). Status of minority curricula and training in clinical psychology. *American Psychologist, 37*, 780–787.

Bernard, J. M., & Goodyear, R. K. (1992). *Fundamentals of clinical supervision.* Needham Heights, MA: Allyn & Bacon.

Boyd-Franklin, N. (1989). *Black families in therapy: A multisystems approach.* New York: Guilford.

Boyd-Franklin, N. (1993). Race, class, and poverty. In F. Walsh (Ed.), *Normal family processes* (pp. 361–376). New York: Guilford.

Boyd-Franklin, N. (1995). Therapy with African American inner-city families. In R. H. Mikesell, D. D. Lusterman, & S. H. McDaniel (Eds.), *Integrating family therapy: Handbook of family psychology and systems theory* (pp. 357–371). Washington, DC: American Psychological Association.

Brown, A., Goodwin, B. J., Hall, B. A., & Jackson-Lowman, H. (1985). A review of psychology of women textbooks: Focus on the Afro-American woman. *Psychology of Women Quarterly, 9*, 29–38.

Casas, J. M. (1995). Counseling and psychotherapy with racial/ethnic minority groups in therapy and practice. In B. Bongar & L. E. Beutler (Eds.), *Comprehensive textbook of psychotherapy: Theory and practice* (pp. 311–335). New York: Oxford University Press.

Cheatham, H. E., Ivey, A. E., Ivey, M. B., & Simek-Morgan, L. (1993). Multicultural counseling and therapy: Changing the foundations of the field. In A. E. Ivey, M. B. Ivey, & L. Simek-Morgan (Eds.), *Counseling and psychotherapy: A multicultural perspective* (3rd ed., pp. 93–123). Boston: Allyn & Bacon.

Cheek, D. (1976). *Assertive Black . . . puzzled White.* San Luis Obispo, CA: Impact.

Copeland, E. (1982). Minority populations and traditional counseling programs: Some alternatives. *Counselor Education and Supervision, 13*, 187–193.

Corvin, S. A., & Wiggins, F. (1989). An antiracism training model for white professionals. *Journal of Multicultural Counseling and Development, 17*, 105–114.

Cyrus, V. (Ed.). (1993). *Experiencing race, class, and gender in the United States.* Mountain View, CA: Mayfield.

Davis-Russell, E. (1990). Incorporating ethnic minority issues into the curriculum: Myths and realities. In G. Stricker, E. Davis-Russell, E. Bourg, E. Duran, W. R. Hammond, J. McHolland, K. Polite, & B. E. Vaughn (Eds.), *Toward ethnic diversification in psychology education and training* (pp. 171–177). Washington, DC: American Psychological Association.

Davis-Russell, E., & Kuba, S. A. (1996, January). *Diversity integration: The next steps.* Poster session at annual meeting of the National Council of Schools and Programs of Professional Psychology, Clearwater, FL.

Dunston, P. (1983). Culturally sensitive and effective psychologists: A challenge for the 1980's. *Journal of Community Psychology, 11*, 376–382.

Foley, V. (1975). Family therapy with Black disadvantaged families: Some observations on roles, communications, and techniques. *Journal of Marriage and Family Counseling, 1*, 29–38.

Giordano, J., & Carini-Giordano, M. A. (1995). Ethnic dimensions in family treatment. In R. H. Mikesell, D. D. Lusterman, & S. H. McDaniel (Eds.), *Integrating family therapy: Handbook of family psychology and systems theory* (pp. 347–356). Washington, DC: American Psychological Association.

Goodwin, B. J. (1993). Psychotherapy supervision: Training therapists to recognize family violence. In M. Hansen & M. Harway (Eds.), *Battering and family therapy: A feminist perspective* (pp. 119–133). Newbury Park, CA: Sage.

Goodwin, B. J. (1996). The impact of popular culture on images of African American women. In J. C. Chrisler, C. Golden, & P. D. Rozee (Eds.), *Lectures on the psychology of women* (pp. 183–197). New York: McGraw-Hill.

Grieger, I., & Ponterotto, J. G. (1995). A framework for assessment in multicultural counseling. In J. G. Ponterotto, J. M. Casas, L. A. Suzuki, & C. M. Alexander (Eds.), *Handbook of multicultural counseling* (pp. 357–374). Thousand Oaks, CA: Sage.

Hampton, B. R., & Gottlieb, M. C. (1997, this volume).

Hardiman, R. (1982). White identity development: A process-oriented model for describing the racial consciousness of White Americans. *Dissertation Abstracts International, 43,* 104A. (University Microfilms No. 82–10330)

Hardy, K. V., & Laszloffy, T. A. (1992). *Families in Society, 73,* 364–370.

Helms, J. E. (1984). Toward a theoretical model of the effects of race on counseling: A black and white model. *The Counseling Psychologist, 12,* 153–165.

Hines, P. M. (1988). The family life cycle of poor Black families. In B. Carter & M. McGoldrick (Eds.), *The changing family cycle: A framework for family therapy* (2nd ed., pp. 513–542). New York: Gardner.

Ho, M. K. (1987). *Family therapy with ethnic minorities.* Newbury Park, CA: Sage.

Ivey, A. E., Ivey, M. B., & Simek-Morgan, L. (1993). *Counseling and psychotherapy: A multicultural perspective* (3rd ed.). Boston: Allyn & Bacon.

Katz, J. H. (1985). The sociopolitical nature of counseling. *The Counseling Psychologist, 13,* 615–624.

Katz, J. H., & Ivey, A. (1977). White awareness: The frontier of racism awareness training. *Personnel and Guidance Journal, 55,* 485–489.

Manual on accreditation. (1988). Washington, DC: Commission on Accreditation for Marriage and Family Therapy Education.

Marin, G. (1992). Issues in the measurement of acculturation among Hispanics. In K. F. Geisinger (Ed.), *Psychological testing of Hispanics* (pp. 235–251). Washington, DC: American Psychological Association.

McGoldrick, M. (1993). Ethnicity, cultural diversity, and normality. In F. Walsh (Ed.), *Normal family processes* (pp. 331–360). New York: Guilford.

McGoldrick, M., Pearce, J. K., & Giordano, J. (1982). *Ethnicity and family therapy.* New York: Guilford.

McGoldrick, M., Preto, N. G., Hines, P. M., & Lee, E. (1991). Ethnicity and family therapy. In A. S. Gurman & D. P. Kniskern (Eds.), *Handbook of family therapy* (Vol. 2, pp. 546–582). New York: Brunner/Mazel.

McIntosh, P. (1983). *Interactive phases of curricular re-vision: A feminist perspective* (Working Paper No. 124). Wellesley, MA: Wellesley College, Center for Research on Women.

McIntosh, P. (1990). *Interactive phases of curricular and personal revision with regard to race* (Working Paper No. 219). Wellesley, MA: Wellesley College, Center for Research on Women.

Okun, B. (1992). Object relations and self-psychology: Overview and feminist perspective. In L. Brown & M. Ballou (Eds.), *Theories of personality and psychopathology: Feminist reappraisals* (pp. 20–45). New York: Guilford.

Ottavi, T. M., Pope-Davis, D. B., & Dings, J. G. (1994). Relationship between white racial identity attitudes and self-reported multicultural counseling competencies. *Journal of Counseling Psychology, 41,* 149–154.

Pedersen, P. (1987). Ten frequent assumptions of cultural bias in counseling. *Journal of Multicultural Counseling and Development, 15,* 16–24.

Ponterotto, J. G. (1988). Racial consciousness development among White counselor trainees: A stage model. *Journal of Multicultural Counseling and Development, 16,* 146–156.

Pope-Davis, D. B., Menefee, L. A., & Ottavi, T. M. (1993). The comparison of white racial identity attitudes among faculty and students: Implications for professional psychologists. *Professional Psychology: Research and Practice, 24,* 443–449.

Pope-Davis, D. B., Reynolds, A. L., Dings, J. G., & Ottavi, T. M. (1994). Multicultural competencies of doctoral interns at university counseling centers: An exploratory investigation. *Professional Psychology: Research and Practice, 25,* 466–470.

Preli, R., & Bernard, J. M. (1993). Making multiculturalism relevant for majority culture graduate students. *Journal of Marital and Family Therapy, 19,* 5–16.

Ridley, C. R. (1995). *Overcoming unintentional racism in counseling and therapy: A practitioner's guide to intentional intervention.* Thousand Oaks, CA: Sage.

Rogers, M. F. (1996). *Multicultural experiences, multicultural theories.* New York: McGraw-Hill.

Rosenblum, K. E., & Travis, T.-M. C. (1996). *The meaning of difference: American constructions of race, sex and gender, social class, and sexual orientation.* New York: McGraw-Hill.

Rowe, D. M., & Grills, C. N. (1996, January). Eurocentric foundations of psychology: Implications for the future. In *Innovations in professional psychology and practice: Preparing for the new millennium* (pp. 13–32). Washington, DC: National Council of Schools and Programs of Professional Psychology.

Saba, G. W., Karrar, B. M., & Hardy, K. V. (Eds.). (1990). *Minorities and family therapy.* New York: Haworth

Sabnani, H. B., Ponterotto, J. G., & Borodovsky, L. G. (1991). White racial identity development and cross-cultural counselor training: A stage model. *The Counseling Psychologist, 19,* 76–102.

Sue, D., Bernier, J., Durran, A., Feinberg, L., Pedersen, P., Smith, E., & Vasquez-Nuttal, E. (1982). Position paper: Cross-cultural counseling competencies. *The Counseling Psychologist, 10,* 45–52.

Sue, D. W. (1978). Counseling across cultures. *Personnel and Guidance Journal, 56,* 458–462.

Sue, D. W., & Sue, D. (1990). *Counseling the culturally different: Theory and practice* (2nd ed.). New York: Wiley.

Troy, W. G. (1990). Ethnic and cultural diversity and the professional psychology training curriculum. In G. Stricker, E. Davis-Russell, E. Bourg, E. Duran, W. R. Hammond, J. McHolland, K. Polite, & B. E. Vaughn (Eds.), *Toward ethnic diversification in psychology education and training* (pp. 179–187). Washington, DC: American Psychological Association.

Wyatt, G., & Parham, W. (1985). The inclusion of culturally sensitive course materials in graduate school and training programs. *Psychotherapy, 22,* 461–468.

PART TWO

Professional Practice with Specific Populations

CHAPTER 5

Ethical Dilemmas in Working with Children and Adolescents

RACHEL GOLDBERG

In this chapter, I will discuss some ethical issues I have encountered as a member of the Ethics Committee of the Pennsylvania Psychological Association and as a private practitioner who works with children, adolescents, and their families. When I started in private practice, I went to every meeting on ethical issues I could find, and left each one feeling that I was a little crazy to embark on independent work. It seemed to me there were so many rules and guidelines that I would inevitably slip up and that the consequences would be disastrous. Nevertheless, I began working with my very first patient, a 7-year-old girl named Lila (all names are fictitious), who was not listening to her "very mean mother."

This will be easy, I thought. It was not hard for me to be nurturing and supportive, and in fact, over the next two months Lila began to brighten. When she felt noticeably better, her mother precipitously pulled her out of treatment. I was furious. "Why did her mother do this?" I asked myself. Only later did I realize that my relationship with Lila had threatened her mother. This was not an ethical issue, really, but it certainly was not the best treatment. Our ethical code requires that we work to contribute to the welfare of others (beneficence) and to avoid doing harm (nonmaleficence). Did my work benefit Lila by exposing her to a different kind of adult or did it harm her by encouraging her to attach to me, only to suddenly lose the relationship? Was there something different I could have done? Since the disheartening end of my work with Lila, I have become convinced that in almost all circumstances it is better for everyone concerned to be involved in the treatment process.

Now, as part of my informed consent statement, I tell parents (especially mothers of adolescent girls) that their daughters may seem to prefer me at times and may use this as a weapon against them. I reassure parents that this is a normal part of treatment and that my goal is to help build stronger family ties wherever possible. Since those early days, I have had many other ethical challenges, yet I no longer feel quite so vulnerable. I know that I can avoid most risks by using sound clinical practices and by consulting with colleagues when in doubt. It is difficult to gain mastery over ethical information when the information is changing so quickly. Nevertheless, practitioners need to be knowledgeable about their codes of ethics and about applicable federal and state law.

In this chapter, I focus on eight issues that are likely to arise in professional practice with children and adolescents. These include child abuse, custody evaluation, separation and divorce, confidentiality, treatment of minors, informed consent to treatment, psychological assessment in school settings, and informed consent to research.

Issue 1: Child Abuse

Several years ago, I volunteered in a community-base service unit, where I spoke with a mother who told me her 3-year-old son, Bobby, was not eating. Based on her comments, I was concerned that she was not feeding her son. I made a home visit and found Bobby eating dog food from the floor. Was I required to report my concerns?

The Child Protective Services Law (CPSL) of my home state of Pennsylvania was revised by the state legislature in 1994 (see Berman, 1997). The law requires a professional who has had professional contact with a child to report suspected child abuse. Specifically, the law requires that persons:

in the course of their employment, occupation, or practice of their profession, [who] come into contact with children shall report or cause a report to be made . . . when they have reasonable cause to suspect on the basis of their medical, professional or other training and experience, that a child coming before them in their professional or official capacity is an abused child. (CPSL, 1994, p. 1297)

This law may vary from state to state. The Pennsylvania law does not require professionals to report child abuse if they see only the perpetrator in therapy and the child is not in immediate danger. In fact, the state legislature wanted to change this requirement to mandate the reporting of information regarding abuse that is acquired from any source, including the alleged abuser. On the surface, this might seem quite sensible. But if the goals of treatment are to help perpetrators change and to better protect children, this mandate is counterproductive. Potential clients might be reluctant to involve themselves in treatment if they were aware they would be reported. The rate of abusers who referred themselves to therapy dropped to zero when the "abuse from any source" ruling was implemented in other states (Knapp & Tepper, 1995).

In some cases, practitioners may be uncertain whether a child is out of danger even if they are working with the perpetrator. If a child is in immediate and identifiable danger, professionals may be legally bound by their duty to protect the child by reporting their concern to a third party. Even if the child has not been abused in the past, practitioners who believe abuse might occur imminently are required to take steps to protect the child, which might mean contacting their state's children and youth services agency or the nonabusive parent. This duty may put professionals in the ethical, rather than legal dilemma of breaching confidentiality with clients who are perpetrators, because the law in Pennsylvania does not require that they do so. Even so, if the courts were to rule, they would probably decide that the duty to protect the child outweighs the perpetrator's right to confidentiality.

An individual who has inflicted abuse is defined as the perpetrator only if he or she is the child's parent, a person responsible for the child's welfare, an individual living in the same house as the child, or a paramour of the parent of the child. For example, a person responsible for the child's welfare may be an individual who has temporary or permanent care of the child, such as a regular babysitter or an employee of a residence or sheltered home, a day care center, or a psychiatric unit of a hospital.

Child abuse in Pennsylvania is classified according to four categories: emotional abuse, sexual abuse or exploitation, neglect, and nonaccidental physical injury. Emotional abuse is quite difficult to determine and is generally pursued only under extreme circumstances. Sexual abuse or exploitation includes direct sexual contact with children, prostitution that is encouraged by adults, and using children for pornographic purposes (Eviatar, 1995).

Neglect is the failure to provide necessary supervision, clothing, housing, adequate nutrition, or medical care, the absence of which could endanger the life or development of the child. Failure-to-thrive babies would also come under this category. When the parent is unable to provide for these essentials because of environmental conditions beyond his or her control, however, the issue of abuse would not apply. Likewise, abuse would not apply to Seventh Day Adventists and other religious groups that do not believe in the use of medication. If a child is in medical need, the county agency can intervene for the child and the court can order medical treatment. Finally, nonaccidental physical injury refers to assaults to a child that involve the risk of death, impairment, or injury to the body. Based on 1993 statistics from the Pennsylvania Office of Children, Youth and Families (1994), the proportion of each form of child abuse is: sexual abuse and exploitation (56%); nonaccidental injury (39%); neglect (4%); and emotional abuse (1%).

The 1994 revision defines child abuse as "a serious mental or physical injury which is not explained by the child's medical history as being accidental," or as "sexual abuse or exploitation; or physical neglect of a child under 18" (CPSL, 1994, p. 1293). In addition, the new amendments expand the definition of child abuse to include "any recent act, failure to act or series of such acts or failures to act by a perpetrator which creates an imminent risk or serious physical injury, sexual abuse or sexual exploitation or a child under 18 years of age" (p. 1296). "Recent act" refers to the last two years (p. 1295.) The law no longer requires that children who were abused through nonaccidental injuries more than two years ago be reported as child abuse victims because the perpetrator might not have had contact with the child for several years (Knapp & Tepper, 1995). This is the exception, however, and mandated reporting of sexual abuse or exploitation, emotional abuse, or neglect is still required, regardless of when the abuse occurred.

A psychologist, Janet, works at a private school. Twelve-year-old Ted was behaving quite aggressively, which was unusual for him. During Janet's interview with Ted, she discovered that he had been physically abused. When she told Ted that she would have to contact his mother, Ted yelled, "They'll beat the hell out of me if you do that." Janet did not want to betray the child and put him in more jeopardy, nor could she fail to report the abuse. What could Janet do? Eventually Janet convinced Ted that she would call his parents and ask them to come in. All of them met together. Ted's father admitted that he had been violent with him on several occasions. The family agreed to become involved in family therapy, and the school administrator reported the abuse.

When practitioners choose not to report suspected child abuse they may be criminally prosecuted for not complying with the law. The first conviction is a summary offense; subsequent convictions are misdemeanors that usually include a fine, with incremental charges for additional convictions. In some states, mandated reporters have immunity from criminal and civil liability (Eviatar, 1995). Professionals who are unsure whether to report in a particular case can consult their local children and youth services agency for feedback, presenting the actual issues without disclosing the identity of the family.

The CPSL does not cover all situations involving abuse. For example, the law applies only to children under 18. Moreover, it does not provide protection for instances of abuse when the perpetrator is not the child's caretaker, such as a visiting friend of the family or a relative or person working in the house for other than child care reasons (Knapp & Tepper, 1995).

Let us return to my earlier description of Bobby, whose mother fed him dog food. I ultimately decided to report Bobby's mother for child abuse, because I believed she would continue to give Bobby dog food, which placed him in imminent and foreseeable danger.

Issue 2: Custody Evaluation

Given the high incidence of divorce, practitioners are likely to be asked at some point to conduct a custody evaluation, which may present a range of ethical dilemmas. For example, how does one promote the welfare of the "client" when there are multiple family members whose interests may conflict, as in the case of a custody evaluation? For psychologists, the answer is clear: As specified in the APA guidelines on custody evaluation (American Psychological Association, 1994), the most important factor in an evaluation is to determine what is in the best interest of the child.

A second concern is whether practitioners can serve in the dual roles of therapist and evaluator for the same family. From an ethical perspective, if a practitioner is treating a child or several members of the family, it is unwise to conduct such an evaluation. Even when it is possible for a therapist to conduct an evaluation in an objective and impartial manner, there may be the illusion of bias, which poses risks for all parties, including the risk that the practitioner may become the target of parental anger and frustration. If appropriate releases are signed, a treating professional can serve as a factual witness who provides notes or testimony to the court regarding the client's history, presenting problems, diagnosis, treatment, and prognosis. In contrast, professionals who perform custody evaluations usually have specialized training and are often appointed by the court. As expert witnesses, evaluators can render an opinion on the psycholegal issues, such as custody and visitation. Thus, the roles of therapist and evaluator differ in some important respects.

The following vignette illustrates some risks professionals may incur when they serve in the dual roles of therapist and evaluator. Dr. Jeff was approached by the family and asked to conduct an evaluation and to make recommendations regarding custody and visitation. He interviewed and tested everyone in the family, and decided that the children's mother would be the best custodial parent. After the divorce was final and custody arrangements were formalized, the mother approached Dr. Jeff and asked if he would be willing to work with her children in therapy. He agreed. After 3 months of treatment, however, Dr. Jeff realized that his original recommendation had been mistaken, because the mother was much more disturbed than he originally believed. At this point, Dr. Jeff faced a dilemma with no simple resolution. If he approached the judge he might look incompetent. The family might be enraged. Either parent might sue him. The children might face further disruption. How could anyone trust Dr. Jeff again—or any other professional?

All of these are significant risks; and all could have been avoided if Dr. Jeff had declined to serve as the treating professional after he had conducted his evaluation. Indeed, as specified in the APA guidelines on child custody evaluations (APA, 1994), a treating psychologist should usually decline the role of an expert witness who gives a professional opinion regarding custody and visitation issues unless so ordered by the court. In most circumstances, practitioners should avoid performing multiple and potentially conflicting roles in forensic cases that involve both evaluation and treatment (see Mannarino, 1997).

Issue 3: Separation and Divorce

Many years ago, I worked with a 10-year-old boy whose parents were just separated. The mother initiated treatment. The father was furious at his wife for leaving. He would not consider therapy with her choice of therapist and made an appointment just to tell me that. I believed that he was concerned that if the custody issue were to go to trial, I would be partial to his wife. He could not be reassured that I would not take part in that process. The father found his own therapist to treat his son, and his wife thought it would be better to go along with her husband's plans. I agreed and mother and son left—along with their unpaid bill.

I always try to get both parents to agree to treatment before I begin with their youngster, especially if they are separated, or divorced and sharing custody, or if one parent is paying the bill, or they both live in the same geographic area. Sometimes I meet with separated or divorced parents jointly, if they are not too angry. Otherwise, I meet with them separately in the hope of reassuring each of them about my care of their child. If one parent is opposed to treatment, the therapy could be jeopardized at any point, and the therapist faced with the possibility of a law suit.

The following vignette illustrates some of these issues. A therapist was treating Nora, a 14-year-old fragile adolescent, and referred her to another psychologist for a psychological evaluation. The parents were divorced with joint legal custody. The father lived with another woman; Nora lived with her mother, who paid the bill. Because the parents did not want to meet together, my colleague thought it would be in Nora's best interest to meet separately with her mother and with her father and his girlfriend. She asked Nora's mother to sign a release so that her exhusband and his girlfriend could participate in the feedback session. The mother would not comply and got very angry. What are the ethical issues in this case?

In fact, the issue is not who was paying the bill. What mattered here was who had legal custody. Since the parents shared legal custody, they were both entitled to feedback regarding results of the evaluation. The practitioner working in a divorce situation should be wary of sharing private material with a person who does not have legal custody. If the mother had sole legal custody, she alone would be entitled to the testing information, even if the father was paying the bill. If the practitioner shared the results of assessment with the father's girlfriend, there would be the risk of a lawsuit.

Issue 4: Confidentiality

Because children in the private sector usually need parental consent to initiate and authorize treatment, parents have the right to obtain information from their child's therapist about that treatment. In this situation, confidentiality, in the strictest sense, cannot be promised to a child or adolescent patient, which poses challenges for clinicians who are attempting to establish a therapeutic alliance. Can we promise an adolescent that what she tells us will remain private? If she thinks her parents will be informed about what she confides to her therapist, will she still share it? I do not know. Along with many other practitioners who work with children and adolescents, I generally believe it is best to discuss the issue of confidentiality at the first session with the child and parents together, and to encourage the parents to respect their child's need for privacy. I always reassure them that I will inform them if there is imminent risk of harm to their child or to someone else.

Many clinicians believe that the right to a confidential therapeutic relationship should apply to children as well as adults, unless there is a risk to the safety and well-being of the child, as in cases of child abuse, danger to self, or danger to others. Other professionals maintain that children between ages 12 and 15 are able to understand the implications and consequences of being involved in treatment. For example, the Model Law of Confidentiality developed by the American Psychiatric Association stipulates the age of 12 as being in the best interest of the child for purposes of confidentiality (Gustafson & McNamara, 1987, p. 194).

The law specifies certain exceptions to the requirement of parental consent when a child is under age 18. Parental consent may be bypassed if there is a belief that parents will jeopardize the likelihood that the minor will receive needed counseling or medical attention for sexual abuse or rape, substance abuse, pregnancy, and sexually-transmitted diseases. Exceptions to the requirement of parental consent also exist for an emancipated minor, who is legally entitled to the rights of adulthood (a married minor, for example); a high school graduate under 18; and a child who needs emergency treatment. In the third instance the adult and hospital are acting as extensions of the parents (Knapp, Tepper, & VandeCreek, 1994).

Issue 5: Treatment of Minors

The Pennsylvania Mental Health Procedures Act of 1970 states that anyone age 14 or over can seek inpatient treatment if they understand the process of therapy and the concept of inpatient care. If the child is under 18, the facility must notify the parents, who, if they wish, can contest the admission. Involuntary treatment does not require the consent of the parents or the child. In the case of inpatient or involuntary treatment, mental health/mental retardation administrators have some discretion in interpreting the act, although many exercise caution in accepting minors between ages 14 and 18 without parental consent. In a memo concerned with parental notification and voluntary outpatient treatment of persons aged 14 to 18 (Dellmuth, personal communication, February 3, 1993), the Pennsylvania Office of Mental Health ruled that county facilities may decide to treat children over 14 without parental consent if the child objects to notifying the parent, the child does not need medication as part of treatment, and the fee can be waived. Anyone can be admitted to a drug and alcohol facility at any time with or without parental consent.

Consider the following vignette. Fourteen-year-old Lois approached her school counselor believing that she might have AIDS because she had intercourse with a drug user. Lois did not want to tell her parents about her concerns. Moreover, following her discussion with Lois, the counselor was concerned that Lois might be at risk for abuse if she shared her concerns with her parents. The counselor suggested that Lois pursue counseling with the local mental health agency. Lois did contact a caseworker, and they agreed to meet three times before making a decision about informing her parents. After three weeks Lois and the caseworker worked out a plan to bring the more receptive parent in first, with the caseworker acting on Lois' behalf. Fortunately, Lois had not contracted AIDS, nor was she pregnant.

Issue 6: Informed Consent to Treatment

Many clinicians believe that children, as well as adults, should be encouraged to make an informed choice regarding their participation in treatment. But how are children to know what they are agreeing to (Everstine et al., 1980; Hare-Mustin, Maracek, Kaplan, & Liss-Levinson, 1979)? Professionals should be sensitive to the cognitive limitations of children, provide information about therapy to children in an age-appropriate manner, and ensure that young clients are able to understand the information. In addition to information about the nature, purpose, and procedures of treatment, children should also be informed that the sessions are not always comfortable, that change is often painful, that significant benefits can result from their treatment, that they might change even without therapy, and that therapy is not the only way to help a person feel better. Informed consent also implies that a child can withdraw his or her consent to continue in the therapy or testing situation. Children also need to be encouraged to ask questions at any point.

Eight-year-old Andrew came into therapy with his mother because he was struggling with severe learning disabilities. From the beginning, he did not want to be in treatment. He felt that being in therapy made him look and feel crazy. I asked him to come for four weeks. If after that time he still felt it was worse to come than to give up the support he seemed to need, I would tell his mother that I respected his desire not to be in treatment. Andrew agreed. This was discussed in our first session.

Our second session focused on learning disabilities: what they were and how they affected each person. He asked me if I could see his disabilities and I said no (because he was a handsome child with no visible symptoms). I told him that having a learning disability did not mean he was stupid. I drew pictures of the brain. He seemed to feel better. In the third session he continued asking questions and expressed a good deal of hostility toward himself.

When Andrew and his mother arrived for the fourth session, he refused to come into my office. I talked to Andrew in the waiting room; he was angry and embarrassed. The whole idea of therapy was too much for him. Although I felt I had helped him and could continue to offer assistance, my concern about the risk of harm took precedence. As we had agreed during the first session, I had to let him go. His distress outweighed the potential benefits of therapy, at least for the present.

Issue 7: Psychological Assessment in School Settings

Practitioners sometimes encounter conflicts between their ethical responsibilities and the demands of the organizations with whom they are affiliated (APA, 1992, Section 8.03). For example, a psychologist who works for a private school in conducting admissions testing might experience a conflict of interest between the needs of the school and the needs of a child who is evaluated. Following admissions testing, for instance, perhaps the practitioner concludes that a given child would not do well in the school. On the other hand, the school administrator wants to see the child admitted because the school is in financial need. If this potential conflict has not been discussed in advance, both the administrator and the parents may assume that the practitioner is committed to meeting their needs. Such a conflict can be avoided by informing the parents at the outset that the professional is an employee of the school and may not be able to be completely impartial.

Many practitioners believe that it is their job to look out for the needs of the child regardless of the circumstances. In this situation, for example, the psychologist might decide to tell the parents that other schools might better serve the needs of their child. This would be a reflection of the individual's personal ethics, but not an obligation of the ethical code. At the same time, the APA ethical code encourages the psychologist to discuss a dilemma such as this with a supervisor or administrator, who might not agree with this policy. Nevertheless, the practitioner has fulfilled his or her ethical responsibility by raising the matter for discussion.

In another situation, a group of practitioners receives all the referrals from a private school to conduct evaluations of children attending the school. Many parents are very protective of confidentiality and may be reluctant to sign a release for practitioners to talk to school personnel regarding test results. At the same time, because the group has substantial contact with the school, the teachers want and expect information about the children they teach. If the group has not discussed this potential conflict at the beginning of such an arrangement, teachers can perceive them as withholding important information, which could ultimately jeopardize their work with the school. Thus, it is important for the group to inform the teaching staff that they cannot disclose anything about a student without a signed release from his or her parents. They also need to explain to the staff that without a signed release they would be vulnerable to a lawsuit and also committing an ethical violation (APA, 1992, Sections 5.02 and 5.05b).

The use of computerized psychological tests can also be problematic for practitioners. For example, when using test scoring and interpretation services, psychologists are obliged to retain appropriate responsibility for the appropriate application, interpretation, and use of assessment instruments, whether they score and interpret such tests themselves or use automated or other services (APA, 1992, Section 2.08). Under these circumstances, psychologists need to select scoring and interpretation services on the basis of evidence of the validity of the program and other relevant considerations. They also need to determine whether the test results are valid for a particular child.

In another situation, the administrator of a private school for children with disabilities was required to submit psychological reports in order to secure funding for summer programs for the students. To save

time, the administrator asked the consulting psychologists to incorporate results from previous testing in their current evaluations. At least
one psychologist refused, choosing to sign her name only to the portion
that included her own observations and recommendations. The administrator was so irate that she wrote a letter to the psychologist's supervisor criticizing the psychologist for doing an inadequate job.

Although this was highly stressful for the consultant, she nevertheless held to her position and refused to work with them again. Should
she have compromised and written the report as requested, especially
if she agreed with the prior psychological evaluations and did not want
to jeopardize the needed programs? In fact, as I indicated earlier, psychologists are obliged to retain appropriate responsibility for the results
of their evaluations. If the prior report appeared to be satisfactory, the
psychologist might have included portions in her own report under a
section labeled "results of prior evaluation," thus distinguishing between prior and current evaluations. On the other hand, it would be
unethical to present an earlier evaluation as one's own or to incorporate portions of an earlier report that appeared questionable or invalid.

Issue 8: Informed Consent to Research

Parents or guardians are responsible for giving permission for children to participate in research projects. Many child advocates believe
that minors should also have the right to make informed choices regarding their participation in research. Children should be informed in
an age-appropriate manner, about the purpose of the research, the reasons for their participation, potential benefits and risks, and possible
outcomes.

Actually, the case for granting children a right to make an informed choice about participating in research is similar to the case
for informed consent to therapy. In both cases, proponents of child
rights argue that these rights belong to clients, who in this case are
children (and their parents). If practitioners are willing to accord
children the rights to informed consent and confidentiality in therapy (barring legal and ethical exceptions), surely there is an equally
compelling case for respecting their right to informed consent to research. Children who participate in research may incur some risks,
such as exposure to research questions or tasks that are inappropriate, intrusive, or upsetting. It is not a matter of replacing parental

decisions or involvement but of also empowering children to make decisions regarding their own participation.

Conclusion

I have discussed eight ethical issues that may arise in professional practice with children and adolescents. Occasionally, however, practitioners may confront situations that involve several of these issues.

Consider the following vignette. I was working with an adolescent who was 1 month shy of her 18th birthday. Rose had frequent fights with her mother about her choice of boyfriends. One incident resulted in her mother beating her with an umbrella. Her school counselor saw the bruises and reported the abuse to the local children and youth service agency; they in turn recommended therapy. The family was quite chaotic, and Rose frequently paged me in the middle of the night when there was a family blow-up and she was worried about her own anger. She overdosed twice on medication. Her mother brought her to the emergency room each time, where she remained overnight.

One night Rose called from a pay phone. She was with her boyfriend. Her mother was threatening to kill her, and she did not feel she could go home. I suggested a relative or a youth shelter, but Rose chose to stay with her boyfriend's family. Rose's mother paged me several times between 2 A.M. and 7 A.M. wanting to know if I knew where Rose was staying. I did not tell her but I was not sure I was right. Her mother was furious with me; because Rose was still a minor, she thought she was entitled to be informed.

Ultimately, her mother called the police and Rose was picked up at her boyfriend's home. When the police delivered Rose to her mother, they agreed to a truce. Since Rose was almost 18, the children and youth services agency did not want to get involved. This case caused me great anxiety. Did I have an obligation to tell Rose's mother? In reality, my decision to protect Rose from a mother with a history of violence was ultimately the ethical thing to do. As it turns out, the outcome was positive in this case. I received a Christmas card from Rose along with her high school graduation picture, reporting that she hoped to go to college and was dating someone her mother really liked.

Although this case ended well, I learned that some things never change. Nearly 15 years ago I began my career with Lila's mother pulling her out of treatment presumably because I did not involve her mother in therapy. This year another mother abruptly terminated treatment for her 8-year-old son, Jimmy. He was charming, sensitive, expressive, and gifted. Jimmy was also depressed, a child who struggled with unseen disabilities and attention deficit disorder with hyperactivity. He moved from an upwardly mobile private school to a school for children with disabilities. The assault to his self-esteem was tremendous.

Over a four-month period Jimmy shared his world with me through play, expression of feelings, war stories, and enactments of his depression. When he was sad and did not want to go to school, he beeped me on my pager. I would talk to him about how his day might go, and he would call me when he got home from school to tell me how it went. As he became increasingly more depressed, I suggested to his parents that it might be time to consider an evaluation for medication. Because of my concern about Jimmy's depression, I had already spoken with his parents a number of times about the possibility of medication. But this time I felt he was really slipping into a more serious depression. Both ethically and clinically, I felt the use of medication should be considered.

Unfortunately, his parents never brought Jimmy back after that discussion. I offered to see him one final time without charge, but they refused, promising that they would be back in touch. They never were. I never had a chance to say good-bye to this child nor he to me. I learned later that after seeing several physicians, the parents finally found one who said their son did not need medication. As much as we try to support and protect children, it is sometimes impossible to do so.

In professional practice with children and adolescents, we cannot always guarantee a positive clinical outcome. As we confront the ethical dilemmas that inevitably arise in our work, however, we can take a number of steps to ensure that we are practicing in the most ethical manner. For example, practitioners should be knowledgeable about their professional codes of ethics and applicable federal and state law. When in doubt, they should consult with knowledgeable colleagues and with the ethics committees of their state or national professional organizations. Practitioners should also strive to communicate effectively about ethical matters with clients and their families, and with other relevant parties, such as school personnel.

Working with children can be both exceptionally gratifying and very challenging. I have come to believe that despite our permissive society, children have very few rights. Children usually do not choose to participate in therapy; that choice is reserved for others, usually their parents. Many children perceive a therapist as an extension of their parents, and thus may be reluctant to take the initiative in treatment. When families have significant problems, it is children who are often left to live with the damage, which shapes their self-esteem, their capacity to problem solve, and their choice of future relationships.

In my practice, where I see both adults and children, I always look out for the children, whether they are in treatment or not. I think it is important that we speak for the children's best interests with our own voices, as theirs are much too quiet.

References

American Psychological Association. (1992). Ethical principles and code of conduct. *American Psychologist, 47,* 1597–1611.

American Psychological Association. (1994). Guidelines for child custody evaluation in divorce proceedings. *American Psychologist, 49,* 677–680.

Berman, P. S. (1997, this volume).

Child Protective Service Law, 11 Pa. Con. Stat. Ann., 2201 *et seq.* (1994).

Everstine, L., Everstine, D., Heymann, G., Homma True, R., Frey, D., Johnson, H., & Seiden, R. (1980). Privacy and confidentiality in psychotherapy. In D. B. Bersoff (Ed.), *Ethical conflicts in psychology* (pp. 151–156). Washington, DC: American Psychological Association.

Eviatar, D. (1995). *Child abuse and the law* (5th ed.). Philadelphia, PA: Juvenile Law Center.

Gustafson, K., & McNamara, R. (1987). Confidentiality in minor clients: Issues and guidelines for therapists. In D. B. Bersoff (Ed.), *Ethical conflicts in psychology* (pp. 193–197). Washington, DC: American Psychological Association.

Hare-Mustin, R., Maracek, J., Kaplan, A., & Liss-Levinson, N. (1979). Rights of clients, responsibilities of therapists. In D. B. Bersoff (Ed.), *Ethical conflicts in psychology* (pp. 305–310). Washington, DC: American Psychological Association.

Knapp, S., & Tepper, A. (1995). Revised child protective services law: What are the implications for psychologists? *Pennsylvania Psychologist Quarterly, 55,* 20–22.

Knapp, S., Tepper, A., & VandeCreek, L. (1994). Treatment of minors. *Pennsylvania Psychologist Quarterly, 54,* 20–21.

Mannarino, A. P. (1997, this volume).

Pennsylvania Office of Children, Youth and Families. (1994). *1993 child abuse.* Harrisburg, PA: Pennsylvania Department of Public Welfare.

CHAPTER 6

Ethical Issues in Couple Therapy

Therapist Competence and Values

RICHARD D. MAGEE

Couple therapy* is now a credible and significant area of clinical practice. Having evolved historically from a diverse mix of professional disciplines, ranging from psychoanalysis to pastoral counseling, marital therapy (or marriage counseling) was long considered to be a somewhat peripheral activity. However, according to Gurman and Jacobson (1995), "Psychotherapy with couples, rather than being the hodgepodge it used to be, now includes some of the most significant conceptual, clinical, and empirical advances of the last twenty years in any branch of the world of psychotherapy" (p. 2). What has led to the dramatic elevation in the professional status of couple therapy?

First, the profession of marriage counseling merged with the dynamically growing family therapy movement. Although losing the advantage of a separate organizational and professional identity, the field was energized with the infusion of a new and powerful systemic paradigm. The skirmishes over differences between the two forms of therapy have subsided, and there is general recognition that marital and family therapy occupy a common ground. The American Association

---

*Following the lead of recent publications in the field (Dym, 1995; Jacobson & Gurman, 1995), the term *couple therapy* will be used in place of the traditional *marital therapy*. *Couple* is a more universally descriptive word that encompasses same-sex and heterosexual couples regardless of marital status. The traditional term, however, does appear throughout the text, reflecting its past and present use by other authors.

for Marital and Family Therapy (AAMFT) has become a major organization of mental health providers, establishing standards for professional training in the field and securing licensing for practitioners in many states (Gurman & Jacobson, 1995).

Second, over the past two decades, behaviorally-based theories and methods have been applied to the treatment of couples (e.g., Jacobson & Margolin, 1979). Behavioral marital therapy has now been the subject of more than 20 controlled clinical trials that have demonstrated its efficacy (Alexander, Holtzworth-Munroe, & Jameson, 1994); indeed, behavioral marital therapy has been recently identified as one of several well-established "empirically validated treatments" by the Division of Clinical Psychology of the American Psychological Association (APA; Chambless et al., 1996). Research on the efficacy of therapy with couples has become a vigorous enterprise, now encompassing controlled studies of cognitive-behavioral marital therapy (Baucom & Epstein, 1990); emotionally focused couple therapy (Greenberg & Johnson, 1988); insight-oriented marital therapy (Snyder, Wills, & Grady-Fletcher, 1991); preventive interventions with couples (Stanley, Markman, St. Peters, & Leber, 1995); and the application of couple therapy in the treatment of such common psychiatric disorders as depression, alcoholism, and anxiety (Gurman & Jacobson, 1995). Couple therapy is now a full-fledged member of the scientifically-based mental health establishment.

A third major factor contributing to the increasing significance of couple therapy are social and economic changes that have produced severe strains in the traditional institution of marriage. The United States has the highest divorce rate of all major industrialized nations, with at least half of marriages ending in divorce (O'Leary & Smith, 1991). Although the outcomes of divorce and even some forms of marital conflict are not uniformly negative, they do have a major impact on individual and family functioning (Bray & Jouriles, 1995). Marital distress is associated with a plethora of individual and family difficulties, including depression, physical illness, alcoholism, impaired work performance, and emotional and behavioral disorders in children (Gottman, 1994). The prevalence of marital instability and its coexistence with a host of other problems have led to sharply increasing demands on mental health professionals to provide treatment for marital distress (O'Leary & Smith, 1991). Regardless of professional identification or specialty, therapists practicing in the 1990s will inevitably encounter clients presenting problems of distressed marital relationships.

A fourth contributor to the increasing acceptance of couple therapy, and one that will inevitably become more significant, is the move toward a managed care delivery of mental health services. The focused and brief methods characteristic of most approaches to couple therapy "are consistent with the projected economic constraints of the psychotherapeutic marketplace circa the year 2000" (Gurman & Jacobson, 1995, p. 2).

The importance of couple therapy is matched by the special challenges it presents to the therapist. As a therapeutic modality, couple therapy may be more difficult to practice than individual therapy or family therapy involving parents and children (Magee, 1994). Unlike individual therapy, where therapists can focus their listening and intervention skills on one person, couple therapy requires therapists to respond to two persons who typically have conflicting views of the presenting problem, different reasons for coming to therapy, unequal commitments to change, and the option of "solving" their problem by leaving the relationship (Shoham, Rohrbaugh, & Patterson, 1995). The escape option is not open to individual clients presenting such complaints as anxiety or depression or to families focusing on problems of children. Given the difficulties of working with couples, it is not surprising that marriage counselors received lower grades than other mental health professionals in the highly-publicized *Consumer Reports* survey of client satisfaction with psychotherapy (Mental health: Does therapy help?, 1995).

The therapeutic challenges of couple therapy necessarily involve complex ethical questions. What determines clinical competence in couple therapy? How does the therapist's explicit and implicit constellation of attitudes, beliefs, and values about marriage and family relationships influence the conduct of therapy? To what extent does the therapist have an obligation to address such larger system issues as gender-related inequalities in social power and economic opportunity? How should the therapist balance work on the needs of the relationship with the needs of the individual partners? Of what treatment risks should couples be informed? What rules of confidentiality and privilege should prevail? And, perhaps most important of all, who is the client?

The ethical codes of the AAMFT (1991) and the APA (1992) address in a general fashion a few of the questions raised by multiperson therapy. For example, the APA code (Section 4.03) stipulates that therapists working with couples or families should clarify at the outset which individuals are clients and the relationship the psychologist will have with each person (APA, 1992). Most therapists, however, find the broad principles contained in ethical codes insufficient guides to the ethical complexities faced in their practices.

Fortunately, several articles and books are available that go beyond the generalities of the ethical codes to consider the specific ethical issues of multiperson therapy, encompassing, of course, couple therapy. Among these publications, some of the most useful to the couple therapist are Gottlieb (1996), Huber and Baruth (1987), Lakin (1994), and Margolin (1982, 1986). All of these publications offer comprehensive discussions of common ethical dilemmas faced by couple therapists, including the problems of defining and diagnosing the client(s), obtaining informed consent from client partners who might be differentially affected by treatment, and establishing rules for handling the confidences of the individual partners. Several chapters in this volume also make contributions to the ethics literature with special relevance to couple therapy (Gottlieb, Hampton & Gottlieb, Mannarino, all in this volume).

In this chapter, I focus on two ethical considerations related to the person of the therapist, namely the therapist's competence in couple therapy and the therapist's constellation of attitudes, beliefs, and values relevant to couple relationships. These therapist variables form the bedrock for clinical judgments, which, in practice, are always an integral part of ethical decision making (Gottlieb, this volume). Profound changes in society are affecting the nature of couple relationships; and rapid advances in clinical theory and research are requiring new approaches to the practice of couple therapy. Given these near revolutionary developments, ethical couple therapists need to engage in a continuous monitoring of their professional competence and personal values. Complacency about one's competence or undisturbed comfort regarding one's values are not consistent with ethical couple therapy.

Therapist Competence

Practicing within the boundaries of one's professional competence is a guiding principle of ethical codes of conduct (APA, 1992), but as Margolin (1986) points out in her discussion of therapist competence in couple therapy, "the difficulty lies in defining areas of competence, the way competence is demonstrated, and methods for measuring competence" (p. 622). Margolin (1986) traces the historic development of standards of competence in couple therapy from the initial stage in which therapists defined themselves as marital therapists simply by starting to treat couples; through a period when competence was obtained through apprenticeships, workshops, and training at family therapy institutes; to competence defined by the educational and supervised experience requirements set by the AAMFT Commission on Accreditation.

Couple therapy, however, is practiced by therapists of many disciplines—psychiatry, psychology, social work, nursing, and counseling—not just the marital and family therapists who have completed AAMFT-approved programs and have met the requirements for AAMFT clinical membership. AAMFT views family therapy (of which couple or marital therapy is a subset) as a separate discipline requiring course work in such areas as systems theory, family sociology, developmental theory, and family therapy methods, as well as many hours of supervised experience with couples and families. Other professions, including psychology, consider couple and family therapy not a separate discipline, but a specialty area. Given these professional differences and variations in state licensing laws regarding scope of practice, Patterson (1995) is correct in asserting that a "severe discrepancy exists within the mental health professions over the inconsistent standards, training, and definitions that have arisen within the family field" (p. 18).

Putting this interprofessional confusion aside, I will focus on competence in couple therapy within the practice of clinical psychology. This therapeutic modality has developed beyond the point where a clinical psychologist, without special preparation in couple therapy, should just start seeing couples because of personal interest or client request. The APA ethical standards present a broad, and somewhat lenient, basis for competence—"education, training, supervised experience, or appropriate professional experience" (APA, 1992, Section 1.04). Although attending a day-long workshop or reading a book might be "appropriate" to establish competence in some limited areas of clinical practice, these would not be sufficient preparation to do couple therapy.

Competent couple therapists of the 1990s have obtained specialty training and supervision in couple work. They have acquired the knowledge and skills required to work conjointly with a couple in the assessment and treatment of relational problems. This specialty knowledge base should include current work on adult attachment, gender, systems theories, communication styles, conflict resolution, marital violence, separation and divorce, cultural and ethnic variations, gay and lesbian relationships, and some acquaintance with principles of family law. Knowledge in these areas is not only essential for the explicit operations involved in assessment and intervention in couple therapy; it shapes the underlying beliefs and values that inevitably, and often covertly, influence the therapist's judgment.

The fundamental skills required are those associated with one or more of the models of couple therapy with demonstrated efficacy. For example, couple therapists should be skilled in creating a safe venue for clients, where unbridled anger, attack, and blame are not sanctioned (Heitler, 1990). They should be able to forge a working relationship with one partner without alienating the other, not by taking a position of indifferent neutrality, but by an ethical commitment to fairness and "multidirected partiality" (Boszormenyi-Nagy & Krasner, 1986). Couple therapists should know how to engender the hope and collaborative set that clients need to engage productively in the hard work of therapy (Jacobson & Margolin, 1979). They should be able to model and teach skills in communication, problem solving, conflict management, and self-soothing of intense emotional arousal (Gottman, 1994; Gottman, Notarius, Gonso, & Markman, 1976). They should be able to detect and intervene in marital violence (Holtzworth-Munroe, Beatty, & Anglin, 1995). They should be able to identify and modify the dysfunctional cognitions that contribute to couple distress (Baucom & Epstein, 1990). And competent couple therapists should be able to track negative patterns of repetitive interaction (e.g., attack/defend, pursue/withdraw) and foster the expression of "softer" emotions (Greenberg & Johnson, 1988). These are core skills common to most of the methods of couple therapy that, according to current research findings, work best, and, therefore, belong in the repertoire of the competent (and ethical) therapist.

In addition to the knowledge and skills comprising the specialty of couple therapy, the competent couple therapist needs the clinical breadth required for both family and individual work. Individual, family, and couple issues are interwoven, so a therapist must be able to make informed decisions about the suitable focus of treatment. As Margolin (1986) correctly points out, "Without this broad perspective, the clinician is likely to offer a therapeutic intervention with which she or he is most familiar and most comfortable, regardless of its appropriateness" (p. 623).

The research literature in couple therapy gives increasing attention to the issues involved in dealing with individual pathology. For example, in an introduction to a special series of papers dealing with the interaction of individual and dyadic concerns, Baucom (1994) reviews clinical questions regarding treatment selection:

Many individuals seeking psychotherapy present with individual diagnosable conditions. Yet they live in larger social units, one of the most important for many adults is marriage. Should these persons be treated in individual therapy, or should the partner be included in some manner to take important contextual and environmental factors into account? On the other hand, the majority of couples seeking marital therapy present to clinics with one or both persons having individual diagnosable disorders as well. How are such couples to be assisted? Is some form of marital therapy the intervention of choice, is individual therapy most appropriate, or should the two be combined in some manner? (p. 341)

Another example of the current interest in relating couple therapy to individual problems is found in a recently published handbook on couple therapy (Jacobson & Gurman, 1995), in which a major section concerns the use of couple therapy in treating the common individual psychiatric problems of alcoholism, anxiety, depression, eating disorders, and even personality disorders. Couple therapists should be able to recognize these and other common individual disorders, and, with the use of consultative and referral resources, provide clients with appropriate treatment. The knowledge base for this domain of competence is available, for as Gurman and Jacobson (1995) conclude, "these disorders have recently come to comprise one of the most scientifically based areas of clinical practice in the entire couple/family therapy field" (p. 5).

Competence in couple therapy, thus, consists not only of the special knowledge and skills required to work in a dyadic format; it also includes background in the basics of psychopathology, personality theory, human development, and individual assessment and treatment (Margolin, 1986). Unfortunately, even as some clinical psychologists, with grounding in the basics, venture into couple work without adequate training in this specialty area, there are others providing couple therapy (primarily belonging to other professional groups) who are well trained in the specialty but are deficient in the basics (Patterson, 1995). Where either type of deficiency exists, it should be met by additional training.

Such training should reflect current empirical developments in the field (Liddle, 1991). No longer may brief workshop exposure to the videotaped magic of a master therapist be considered adequate training. Jacobson (Anderson, Jacobson, & Wolfe, 1996) has criticized couple and family therapists for not being sufficiently skeptical of charismatic therapeutic innovations supported only by anecdotal evidence. It is indeed encouraging that additional criteria are being proposed for the ethics section of the APA continuing education sponsor-approval system. These criteria would require an APA-approved sponsor to review all proposed programs to insure that research and/or scholarly support exists for each program and this support and its limitations be presented to continuing education participants (APA, 1996).

The foundation of ethical practice with couples is professional competence, which includes both basic and specialized clinical knowledge and skills. Furthermore, the requisite knowledge and skills must be current and empirically based.

Therapist Values

In addition to competence, the ethical practice of couple therapy requires an awareness and understanding of one's own system of values that may influence clients and affect clinical judgment. In this discussion, "value" will be used in a broad sense to refer to "the cherished beliefs and preferences that guide human decisions" (Doherty & Boss, 1991, p. 609).

The issue of values is addressed indirectly in the APA ethics code (APA, 1992, Section 1.15), which cautions psychologists to be "alert and guard against personal, financial, social, organizational, or political factors that might lead to a misuse of their influence." As with insuring therapist competence, here, too, the devil is in the details. Each of the factors identified in Section 1.15 embodies a set of values—varying in the degree to which they are acknowledged and expressed by the holder. Some of the values held by the therapist may go unnoticed because they are shared by clients and/or the mainstream cultural group (e.g., staying in a marriage is preferable to getting a divorce). Other values are salient because they may be idiosyncratic with the therapist, or, at least, representative of a minority viewpoint (e.g., open marriages work). Regardless of the level of awareness the therapist has regarding her or his values, they likely will be expressed in some form, along with those of the clients, in the process of couple therapy. In addressing this issue, Margolin (1986) observes that,

Values affect almost every dimension of how a couple choose to live their lives together. As Framo (1968) poignantly illustrates, the values that surface in marital and family therapy are the same values that cause therapists most anguish and concern in their lives. Thus, therapists' value systems, as well as the individual and collective value systems of the couple, are part and parcel of the decisions made and the actions taken in the marital therapy session. (pp. 631–632)

Complicating the matter of value influence even further is the long-overdue realization that, even if therapists could totally mask their own values, value neutrality would not be achieved. Thanks largely to the feminist critique of family therapy (Nichols & Schwartz, 1995), we now understand that an unquestioning acceptance of clients' values is tantamount to endorsement. Doherty and Boss (1991) are right in asserting, "As of the early 1990s, the myth of value neutrality is dead" (p. 610).

Values concerning couple and family relationships are in a state of unprecedented flux and have become the focal point of heated ideological debate. Ethical couple therapists must seek knowledge that helps them understand their own values and the values of their clients. Specific areas requiring value reflection include gender, partner abuse, ethnicity, gay and lesbian relationships, and separation and divorce. Beyond these specific areas, ethical couple therapists should consider how their own values and sense of moral obligation should inform the therapeutic discourse (Doherty, 1995; Doherty & Boss, 1991).

Gender is by far the most critical area in which the couple therapist needs to examine personal values. Over the past 30 years, nothing less than a revolution has taken place regarding our awareness of gender-related social inequities—and, particularly, the ways these inequities are inherently a part of traditional marriages. The well-founded feminist critique of the institution of marriage focuses on the power differential that has benefitted men at the expense of women (Hampton & Gottlieb, this volume). Ethical couple therapists should take stock of their personal socialization experiences that might lead to a facile acceptance of clients' asymmetrical marital role arrangements. Moreover, they must be cautious of a mechanical application of a professionally endorsed systems theory (based on concepts of complementarity and circular causality), which obscures real differences in privilege between the wife and husband (Rampage, 1995).

In an illuminating retrospective on the Women's Project in Family Therapy (Carter, Papp, Silverstein, & Walters, 1996), the founders of the Project traced the evolution of the values they applied to couple therapy, from 1977, when the Project was introduced, to the present. The panelists described the paradigm shift in values that occurred when they began to "see" couple relationships through the lens of gender inequality. It wasn't until later, however, that they developed ways of translating the new values into new methods of clinical practice. These four master therapists reported past errors in clinical judgment that reflected an old and, for them, no longer tenable value system. These errors included assumptions that (a) therapists could and should be neutral regarding gender inequality; (b) all problems were based on reciprocal interactions and all parts of the "system" were interchangeable; (c) process considerations were more important than the content issues that reflected the realities of life; and (d) the burden of relationship change should be given to the wife rather than the husband (e.g., the pursuer should stop pursuing rather than the distancer stop distancing). The new value system—based on the belief that only equal partners can truly negotiate—led the panelists to modify their clinical practices. These modifications included raising questions with couples about income disparity and the use of time—questions aimed at making explicit the fact that, even in modern marriages, men and women are rarely equals. The leaders of the Women's Project, thus, traced a personal journey that commenced with a reconsideration of their own values, and led to the development of clinically sensitive methods of engaging clients in a values discourse. The result of this process was to expand the ethical dimensions of couple therapy.

The paradigm shift exemplified in the Women's Project inevitably stirred controversy and criticism. Rampage (1995), in her discussion of gendered aspects of marital therapy, addresses the charges that promoting feminist values in couple therapy is unethical and alienates men. She correctly points out that the introduction of feminist values does in fact enlarge the scope of therapeutic discussion to rightly include the societal pressures and constraints that couples need to consider in working to improve their relationship. The larger systems view offers the advantages of externalizing the problem, diminishing blame, enhancing empathy, and giving couples a realistic view of the potential social costs of modifications of their respective roles.

Joining the leaders of the Women's Project, Rampage (1995) considers the impact of values concerning gender on clinical practice with couples. She argues against both silence (which implicitly sanctions the status quo) and proselytizing. Rather, she recommends that couple therapists take a position that "acknowledges the impossibility of our being objective about gender, declares a willingness to participate with clients in a dialogue about the meaning and experience of maleness and femaleness—a conversation in which the ideals of equality, mutual respect, and curiosity about the other's experience would be embodied in both the goal and process of the work" (p. 272).

Related to the fundamental issue of gender inequality in couple therapy is the specific problem of partner abuse. Dealing with abuse is an unavoidable part of couple therapy. Physical aggression occurs in over half of the couples seeking treatment, but only a minority of these couples volunteer this information (O'Leary, 1995). Moreover, even when the information concerning violence is reported, it is not incorporated by many therapists into case conceptualization and treatment planning

(Hansen, Harway, & Cervantes, 1991). Because confronting violence and abuse is difficult, involving risk of harm and intense emotions, it is not surprising that violence is minimized or not mentioned at all by clients and frequently "overlooked" by therapists. In order to provide ethical treatment of violence, couple therapists first need to examine their own beliefs about partner abuse (Holtzworth-Munroe et al., 1995). At the very least, therapists need to address the following issues: What constitutes abuse? What's the difference between male and female perpetrated violence? How is violence an expression of male dominance and control? When should the conjoint treatment format be changed to some other form of intervention? Should the primary goal of therapy be to improve the relationship or end the violence?

The beliefs and values reflected in the answers to these and other questions should be informed by consultations with professionals providing service to the victims of violence (e.g., women's shelters) and treatment programs for abusers (e.g., batterers' groups). This specialized education should also include a continuing review of the newly emerging research literature on the assessment and treatment of violence.

Despite differences in emphasis among those working on couple violence, there is consensus that the fundamental problem is that men abuse women. Both men and women engage in physical aggression, but it is women who are hurt and afraid. Couple therapists should always assess for the occurrence and severity of abuse and give the highest priority to protecting the woman and stopping the violence. A broad range of interventions should be considered, including working with the legal system, referral of the woman to a shelter, referral of the man to a treatment program for batterers, and, where the woman is safe and not intimidated, couple therapy aimed at stopping the violence (Holtzworth-Munroe et al., 1995; O'Leary, 1995). Most important of all is the understanding that partner abuse is a social problem of epidemic proportions, requiring, in its prevention and treatment, a network of community resources.

Other issues in which couple therapists' values play a prominent role concern matters of relational diversity. Therapists' personal and professional socialization affect their attitudes towards cultural variations in marriage, gay and lesbian relationships, and separation and divorce. Ethical therapists need to examine their beliefs and preferences regarding these additional contextual and situational factors that have direct bearing on the nature of couple relationships.

As American society increases in cultural diversity, therapists' caseloads will include more couples with cultural backgrounds different from their own and more couples in cross-cultural relationships (Falicov, 1995). Ethical therapists should engage couples in an appreciative discussion of their cultural backgrounds, and attempt to sort out relational processes that are dysfunctional from those that are just culturally different (Margolin, 1986). Similarly, ethical couple therapists treating same-sex couples need to educate themselves regarding lesbian and gay experience, including the negative ecosystemic factors of homophobia, heterosexism, and legal systems that do not sanction their relationships (Brown, 1995; Scrivner, this volume; Scrivner & Eldridge, 1995). When treating culturally different and same-sex couples, therapists must honestly confront their own ignorance and biases, which could be manifested in a variety of nontherapeutic attitudes, ranging from hostile rejection to overglamorization of the clients' experience. Willingness to admit one's limitations in the understanding of clients who pose differences, taking action to address these limitations through open dialogue with clients, consultation with more experienced colleagues, and appropriate referral are all hallmarks of the value-sensitive and ethical couple therapist.

Perhaps the most common and vexing problem brought by couples to therapy is whether to maintain the relationship. Although requesting help to "save the marriage," at least one partner is typically ambivalent about this treatment goal. This ambivalence may be openly expressed (e.g., "help me/us decide what to do") or an unspoken agenda that the therapist must find ways to put on the table. Ambivalence about the future of the relationship arises from multiple and conflicting value considerations, including general beliefs about marriage and divorce, a desire be happy and "true to one's self," loyalty to one's partner, concern about the welfare of children, and obligations to the extended family. These value issues are grist for the therapeutic mill. Clients must struggle with these issues, and therapists, while respecting the right of clients to make their own decisions, should help them to understand the full range of alternatives open to them and the consequences of the actions they may take. Thus, the therapist plays an active role in making value considerations explicit.

The subject of values has become a vital part of the general psychotherapy literature. One of the most provocative contributions to this literature has been made by Doherty (1995), who convincingly argues that traditional psychotherapy, far from being value-free, actually promotes individual self-interest, giving short shrift to family and community responsibilities. He calls for the intentional "inclusion of moral discourse in the practice of psychotherapy and the cultivation in therapists of the virtues and skills needed to be moral consultants to their clients in a pluralistic and morally opaque world" (pp. 7–8). Doherty's description of the range of interventions useful in sharpening clients' moral sensibilities has much to offer the therapist grappling with the dilemmas of couple relationships.

Conclusion

Couple therapy is now a significant method of treatment for both relational and individual disorders. It offers the therapist daunting challenges in matters of clinical judgment and method. The ethical practice of couple therapy requires competence in the specialized techniques of conjoint therapy as well as in the broader skills of psychological assessment and intervention. This competence should be based on current empirical findings regarding the nature of couple distress and effective methods of treatment. Ethical practice also requires therapists to address their personal values, and a willingness to understand, and sometimes confront, the values of their clients.

References

Alexander, J. F., Holtzworth-Munroe, A., & Jameson, P. B. (1994). The process and outcome of marital and family research: Research review and evaluation. In A. E. Bergin & S. L. Garfield (Eds.), *Handbook of psychotherapy and behavior change* (4th ed., pp. 595–630). New York: Wiley.

American Association for Marriage and Family Therapy. (1991). *AAMFT Code of Ethics*. Washington, DC: Author.

American Psychological Association. (1992). Ethical principles of psychologists and code of conduct. *American Psychologist, 42,* 1597–1611.

American Psychological Association, Committee for the Approval of CE Sponsors. (1996, March). *Proposed changes to criteria of the sponsor approval system*. Washington, DC: American Psychological Association.

Anderson, C. M, Jacobson, N. S., & Wolfe, B. (1996, March). *The backlash against psychotherapy: What can we do?* Panel discussion presented at Family Therapy Networker Symposium, Washington, DC.

Baucom, D. H. (1994). Introduction to the special series: The person and marriage: Attending to individual and dyadic concerns. *Behavior Therapy, 25,* 341–344.

Baucom, D. H., & Epstein, N. (1990). *Cognitive behavioral marital therapy*. New York: Brunner/Mazel.

Boszormenyi-Nagy, I., & Krasner, B. R. (1986). *Between give and take: A clinical guide to contextual therapy*. New York: Brunner/Mazel.

Bray, J. H., & Jouriles, E. N. (1995). Treatment of marital conflict and prevention of divorce. *Journal of Marital and Family Therapy, 21*(4), 461–473.

Brown, L. (1995). Therapy with same-sex couples: An introduction. In N. S. Jacobson & A. S. Gurman (Eds.), *Clinical handbook of couple therapy* (pp. 274–291). New York: Guilford.

Carter, B., Papp, P., Silverstein, O., & Walters, M. (1996, March). *Couples, now and then.* Panel discussion presented at Family Therapy Networker Symposium, Washington, DC.

Chambless, D. L., Sanderson, W. C., Shoham, V., Johnson, S. B., Pope, K. S., Crits-Christopher, P., Baker, M., Johnson, B., Woody, S. R., Sue, S., Beutler, L., Williams, D. A., & McCurry, S. (1996). An update on empirically validated therapies. *The Clinical Psychologist, 49*(2), 5–22.

Doherty, W. J. (1995). *Soul searching.* New York: Basic Books.

Doherty, W. J., & Boss, P. G. (1991). Values and ethics in family therapy. In A. S. Gurman & D. P. Kniskern (Eds.), *Handbook of family therapy* (Vol. 2, pp. 606–637). New York: Brunner/Mazel.

Dym, B. (1995). *Readiness and change in couple therapy.* New York: Basic Books.

Falicov, C. J. (1995). Cross-cultural marriages. In N. S. Jacobson & A. S. Gurman (Eds.), *Clinical handbook of couple therapy* (pp. 231–246). New York: Guilford.

Gottlieb, M. C. (1996). Some ethical implications of relational diagnoses. In F. W. Kaslow (Ed.), *Handbook of relational diagnosis and dysfunctional family patterns* (pp. 19–34). New York: Wiley.

Gottlieb, M. C. (1997, this volume).

Gottman, J. (1994). *What predicts divorce?* Hillsdale, NJ: Erlbaum.

Gottman, J., Notarius, C., Gonso, J., & Markman, H. (1976). *A couple's guide to communication.* Champaign, IL: Research Press.

Greenberg, L. S., & Johnson, S. M. (1988). *Emotionally focused therapy for couples.* New York: Guilford.

Gurman, A. S., & Jacobson, N. S. (1995). Therapy with couples: A coming of age. In N. S. Jacobson & A. S. Gurman (Eds.), *Clinical handbook of couple therapy* (pp. 1–6). New York: Guilford.

Hampton, B. R., & Gottlieb, M. C. (1997, this volume).

Hansen, M., Harway, M., & Cervantes, N. (1991). Therapists' perceptions of severity in cases of family violence. *Violence and Victims, 6*, 225–234.

Heitler, S. M. (1990). *From conflict to resolution: Skills and strategies for individual, couple, and family therapy.* New York: Norton.

Holtzworth-Munroe, A., Beatty, S. B., & Anglin, K. (1995). The assessment and treatment of marital violence: An introduction for the marital therapist. In N. S. Jacobson & A. S. Gurman (Eds.), *Clinical handbook of couple therapy* (pp. 317–339). New York: Guilford.

Huber, C. H., & Baruth, L. G. (1987). *Ethical, legal and professional issues in the practice of marriage and family therapy.* Columbus, OH: Merrill.

Jacobson, N. S., & Gurman, A. S. (Eds.). (1995). *Clinical handbook of couple therapy.* New York: Guilford.

Jacobson, N. S., & Margolin, G. (1979). *Marital therapy: Strategies based on social learning and behavior exchange principles.* New York: Brunner/Mazel.

Lakin, M. (1994). Morality in group and family therapies: Multiperson therapies in the 1992 ethics code. *Professional Psychology: Research and Practice, 25*(4), 344–348.

Liddle, H. A. (1991). Empirical values and the culture of family therapy. *Journal of Marital and Family Therapy, 17*(4), 327–348.

Magee, R. D. (1994). A marital therapy protocol. In L. VandeCreek, S. Knapp, & T. L. Jackson (Eds.), *Innovations in clinical practice: A source book* (Vol 13, pp. 359–366). Sarasota, FL: Professional Resource Press.

Mannarino, A. P. (1997, this volume).

Margolin, G. (1982). Ethical and legal considerations in marital and family therapy. *American Psychologist, 37,* 788–801.

Margolin, G. (1986). Ethical issues in marital therapy. In N. S. Jacobson & A. S. Gurman (Eds.), *Clinical handbook of marital therapy* (pp. 621–638). New York: Guilford.

Mental health: Does therapy help? (1995, November). *Consumer Reports,* 734–739.

Nichols, M. P., & Schwartz, R. C. (1995). *Family therapy: Concepts and methods* (3rd ed.). Boston: Allyn & Bacon.

O'Leary, K. D. (1995, July). Assessment and treatment of partner abuse. *Clinical Research Digest, Supplemental Bulletin 12.*

O'Leary, K. D., & Smith, D. A. (1991). Marital interactions. In M. R. Rosenzweig & L. W. Porter (Eds.), *Annual review of psychology* (Vol. 42, pp. 191–212). Palo Alto, CA: Annual Reviews.

Patterson, T. (1995). Macro-ethics: The current state of the family field. *The Family Psychologist, 11*(2), 18–20.

Rampage, C. (1995). Gendered aspects of marital therapy. In N. S. Jacobson & A. S. Gurman (Eds.), *Clinical handbook of couple therapy* (pp. 261–273). New York: Guilford.

Scrivner, R. (1997, this volume).

Scrivner, R., & Eldridge, N. S. (1995). Lesbian and gay family psychology. In R. H. Mikesell, D. D. Lusterman, & S. H. McDaniel (Eds.), *Integrating family therapy* (pp. 327–345). Washington, DC: American Psychological Association.

Shoham, V., Rohrbaugh, M., & Patterson, J. (1995). Problem- and solution-focused couple therapies: The MRI and Milwaukee models. In N. S. Jacobson & A. S. Gurman (Eds.), *Clinical handbook of couple therapy* (pp. 142–163). New York: Guilford.

Snyder, D. K., Wills, R. M., & Grady-Fletcher, A. (1991). Long-term effectiveness of behavioral versus insight-oriented marital therapy. *Journal of Consulting and Clinical Psychology, 59,* 138–141.

Stanley, S. M., Markman, H. J., St. Peters, M., & Leber, B. D. (1995). Strengthening marriages and preventing divorce: New directions in prevention research. *Family Relations, 44,* 392–401.

CHAPTER 7

Working with Families with Custody and Visitation Problems

ANTHONY P. MANNARINO

Although recent statistics have suggested that the divorce rate in American society has begun to level off, nearly one in two marriages still end in divorce (National Center for Health Statistics, 1985). As a result, numerous children in this country are being raised in families in which the parents are no longer living together because of a legal break-up. Divorce inevitably creates issues related to custody and visitation for both parents and their children. When confronted by these problems, parents have traditionally consulted attorneys for guidance. However, in recent years, mental health professionals have increasingly been called upon to become involved in custody and visitation matters. Professional roles have included child custody evaluator, divorce consultant or mediator, and therapist.

It is well-known to clinicians that divorce is a painful experience for children. Research supports this clinical perspective by demonstrating that for many children, divorce results in significant, long-term negative consequences (Hetherington, Cox, & Cox, 1985; Wallerstein, 1985). In addition to the separation, children may experience a difficult time dealing with other issues, including visitation arrangements; changes in residence, schools, or economic circumstances; or the reduced availability of the noncustodial parent. In this regard, mental health professionals are frequently asked to evaluate the clinical significance of any problems or symptoms that these children present and to provide therapy to the children, parents, or family.

In this chapter, I will address some of the ethical and professional issues that clinicians encounter when working with families having custody and visitation problems. The chapter will be divided into three sections. The first section will focus specifically on definitional issues (e.g., legal vs. physical custody; partial custody) and how local and regional standards impact on clinical practice. The next section will focus on role definition and professional boundaries for mental health professionals who become involved with families having custody and visitation problems. This section will include a brief review of recommended guidelines and procedures recently promulgated by the American Psychological Association and other organizations with respect to professional roles in these cases. I will specifically address the potential conflicts involved in taking on multiple professional roles. The final section will be clinically oriented to assist the practitioner in dealing with a number of practical issues that arise when working with these families.

Definitional Issues

Mental health professionals typically do not receive legal training and should refrain from providing legal consultation when working with families with custody and visitation problems. Nonetheless, familiarity with basic legal terminology related to divorce and custody, and with local practices regarding custody and visitation enables the clinician to better understand the problems that families confront in this area.

GENERAL DEFINITIONS

Legal custody is awarded to one or both parents and pertains to which party has the right to make important decisions about a child's life, such as medical care, school, and so on. When one parent has sole legal custody, she* has the right to make these important decisions about a child's life. With joint legal custody, both parents have the right to participate in making these decisions. Local practices will vary widely from county to county and state to state regarding whether sole or joint legal custody is most commonly awarded by the courts.

Physical custody is awarded to one or both parents and pertains to where the child lives. If one parent has primary physical custody, then a child lives with that parent for the great majority of the time. With

---

*For the sake of simplicity, the pronoun *she* will be used throughout the chapter when referring to the custodial parent and *he* when referring to the noncustodial parent.

joint physical custody, a child spends approximately equal amounts of time with both parents. In 1975, only one state had laws permitting joint physical custody as a judicial alternative (Felner & Terre, 1987). However, over the past two decades, most states have passed statutes pertaining to joint custody. Again, local practices vary widely regarding whether the courts typically award physical custody to one parent or jointly to both parents.

Given that legal and physical custody are not the same, they are typically addressed in separate parts of a given court order. Moreover, there are a number of different ways that these two types of custody are awarded. Thus, one parent may obtain sole legal and physical custody, or both parents may share joint legal and physical custody. Alternatively, although parents may share joint legal custody, it is quite possible that physical custody will be awarded primarily to one parent.

Partial custody refers to the noncustodial parent's right to have visitation with his child in the absence of the custodial parent. Partial custody may be as brief as two or three hours, or as long as an entire weekend. In some instances, family courts may award partial custody to the noncustodial parent for one or two weeks at a time, particularly during the holiday season or summer. Familiarity with local practices regarding partial custody will help the mental health professional better understand what families are likely to encounter when this issue is addressed by the court system.

PROBLEMS RELATED TO DEFINITIONAL ISSUES

Perhaps the biggest problem that mental health professionals face is parental confusion or misunderstanding related to the terms of a custody order. Court orders are typically written in technical terms that make comprehension difficult. Moreover, there may be some circumstances when a parent may purposely distort the terms of a custody order to access services that they may not be entitled to pursue.

Misunderstanding and confusion are common with respect to the differences between legal and physical custody. In this regard, I have encountered numerous clinical situations in which one parent had primary physical custody of a child and mistakenly believed that the other parent had no right to participate in important decisions about the child's life, despite a court order specifying joint legal custody. In a different scenario, a parent may have partial custody of a child for weekends and believe that he should be able to provide input about the child's schooling or medical care; however, this may not be the case if the other parent has sole legal custody.

Appropriate resolution of these custody matters is critical in determining which parent can bring a child to a mental health professional for services. If a parent has sole legal custody, she can certainly call a clinician to access services. If joint legal custody exists, then either party can do so. In either case, it is strongly recommended that the professional obtain a copy of the custody order from the parent to insure that one is practicing within the constraints of the law.

In joint legal custody situations, it is further recommended that the parent bringing the child to a mental health professional inform the other parent of this decision. The parent may be reluctant to do this because she believes that the other parent would not be supportive of mental health involvement or might even actively undermine it with the child. Although these may be legitimate concerns, the clinician should advise the parent that the other parent will likely find out anyway, possibly by something the child might accidentally say. Then the other parent may feel angry about having been excluded from this process and could petition the court to prevent further mental health services or to have the child see a different clinician. In such a scenario, a child's therapeutic relationship could be abruptly terminated and the child may be faced with the stress of having to develop a new relationship with a different professional.

It is often useful for the professional to contact the other parent, even if the parent bringing the child for services agrees to inform the other parent of this decision. It has been my clinical experience that such contact helps the other parent feel included in the decision making and less threatened that the clinician will be biased against this parent. Furthermore, the most optimal situation would be to have this parent join the clinical process and actually participate in an evaluation or treatment. Both parents would then ideally perceive the clinician as a neutral party who is striving to pursue goals that would be in the child's best interests.

I have occasionally confronted situations in which a parent has partial custody of a child but no legal custody, and will purposely distort the terms of a custody order to access mental health services for the child. This can occur when a parent is dissatisfied with the current custody arrangements and wants to enlist a mental health professional to be on his side. Alternatively, a parent may feel that the other parent, who has legal custody, may be harming the child in some way or causing the child to turn against him.

Whether a parent has legitimate concerns about the welfare of his child or has a hidden agenda, that parent cannot access the services of a mental health professional for the child if he does not have legal custody. Moreover, if a professional provides services to a child at the request of a parent who does not have legal custody, then the professional would be practicing outside the constraints of the law. To prevent such an occurrence, the clinician should insist that the parent provide a copy of the existing custody order. If the parent then acknowledges that he does not have legal custody but is concerned about possible abuse or other harm to the child, the professional should not see the child but inform the parent that such issues can be appropriately investigated by the child protective services system or similar agency.

The key to resolving any issues as to whether a parent can bring her child to a mental health professional is for the professional to determine from the outset who has custody. Although a parent may be mildly offended by the clinician's desire to see a copy of the custody order, the professional's insistence in this regard will possibly prevent subsequent difficulties or complications. The worst case scenario for the child would be to begin services with a professional that are later abruptly terminated because the parent accessing these services does not have legal custody. There is potential liability for the professional in such a situation as well.

Role and Professional Boundaries

Clarification of professional roles and boundaries is important throughout the clinical practice of a mental health professional but becomes even more critical when working with families in which the parents are divorced. In particular, taking on multiple professional roles with the same family is a potential hazard, especially if the parents or their attorneys are placing pressure on the professional to do so. This section will address the issue of role boundaries with divorced families and review recent guidelines and standards that suggest that multiple roles be avoided in these cases.

CUSTODY EVALUATOR VERSUS THERAPIST

The two most common roles that the mental health professional may play with divorced or divorcing families are those of custody evaluator and therapist. In the former, the professional conducts a formal assessment to assist the court in determining which parent should have custody of their child. Alternatively, if one parent already has legal and primary physical custody of a child, a professional may be called upon to assess the issue of partial custody for the noncustodial parent. In either circumstance, the professional may be court-appointed to conduct such an evaluation, may do so at the request of one or both parents' attorneys, or may be asked by one parent who is dissatisfied with the current custody arrangements. The key element in a custody evaluator's role is the attempt to generate a set of information or data that may potentially be used by the legal system to determine primary or partial custody arrangements.

In contrast, a therapist working with divorced or divorcing families is a helping agent. The goals of therapy in these cases can be multifaceted but may include assisting the children and parents to better deal with the painful feelings generated by the separation, addressing the children's emotional or behavioral difficulties, helping with parenting issues, and working with the family to resolve practical problems related to schedules, pick-ups and drop-offs, and so on.

The roles of custody evaluator and therapist also differ along a number of other significant dimensions. (See Mannarino & Cohen, 1992, for a similar discussion regarding forensic versus treatment roles in child sexual abuse cases.)

Confidentiality

If a custody evaluator is court-appointed, it is presumed that there will not be any confidentiality and that findings will be disseminated to the judge and attorneys. Even in the absence of a court appointment, attorneys expect to receive a copy of the professional's report, which may subsequently be used in legal proceedings. (Parents may not always understand the limits of confidentiality in these scenarios. It is certainly the professional's obligation to explain and clarify this issue at the outset of the evaluation.) In contrast, the hallmark of psychotherapy is confidentiality. All of the major mental health disciplines have ethical principles governing confidentiality in therapeutic practice. There is little doubt that confidentiality is a key element in helping children and parents disclose their most private and painful feelings during therapy.

It is easy to see how taking on the multiple roles of custody evaluator and therapist with divorced or divorcing families poses an inherent conflict related to confidentiality. For example, both children and parents in treatment would be most reluctant to discuss private feelings or conflictual parent-child interactions if they believed that the therapist, acting as custody evaluator, would be sharing this information with attorneys or the court. On the other hand, professionals who play both roles may be highly ambivalent about giving information to attorneys or the court that children and parents have divulged in private. The overriding issue here is that children and parents from divorced or divorcing families require confirmation from the outset of any professional contact that confidentiality either does or does not exist. (Even in therapy, there are circumstances, such as disclosure of child abuse, when confidentiality can be ethically violated.) When the professional plays the multiple roles of custody evaluator and therapist, the limits of confidentiality can never be fully clarified.

Neutrality

A custody evaluation is a forensically-related assessment because any findings will potentially be used to assist the court in its decision-making process. In this regard, the evaluator's neutrality is the hallmark of any valid forensic assessment. Since the custody evaluator's task is to gather information about parenting issues, parent-child relationships, and so on, subjective biases could compromise the impartial collection of data. For example, biases such as a belief that young children should always live with their mother, or that joint custody is always the best solution can impact how the evaluator interprets any information provided by the parents or children. Custody evaluators need to be aware of potential prejudices and make every attempt to conduct an impartial assessment.

A therapist has a much different position with respect to the issue of neutrality. Specifically, a therapeutic alliance with children or their parents is not neutral or impartial. Caring, empathy, and acceptance are critical to the therapeutic relationship and often result in mutually positive feelings between the therapist and adult or child client (Mannarino & Cohen, 1992).

Parallel to the issue of confidentiality, playing multiple roles of custody evaluator and therapist with divorced or divorcing families also creates serious dilemmas with respect to impartiality. To illustrate, if a professional has a caring, therapeutic relationship with a mother and child, it would be extremely difficult for that professional not to be biased in favor of the mother if the court requested an evaluation of specific custody issues. Moreover, the mother in this scenario may well expect the professional-therapist to perceive her viewpoint regarding custody issues as being more valid than the father's. If the professional subsequently draws conclusions about custody issues that are more consistent with the father's perspective, the mother could potentially feel very angry and betrayed. It is also easy to understand how a professional taking on the multiple roles of custody evaluator and therapist may not convey the necessary therapeutic caring and positive regard to a child or parent while at the same time attempting to remain neutral or impartial as an evaluator. Thus, taking on multiple roles with divorced or divorcing families generates inherent conflicts related to professional neutrality.

Court Testimony

Mental health professionals who conduct custody evaluations are often appointed by the court. Alternatively, in the absence of formal litigation, the attorneys representing divorced or divorcing parents may request a custody evaluation to assist the mother and father in resolving custody issues out of court. In either case, the designated professional would certainly be expected to have appropriate qualifications and clinical experience to conduct a custody evaluation, including knowledge of local and state laws pertaining to custody and specific competencies related to forensic assessments. Moreover, if this professional testifies in court about the evaluation, it is highly probable that the professional would be considered an expert witness. Although it remains controversial as to whether an expert witness should be permitted to render an opinion regarding the ultimate issue before the court (i.e., the question of who should have custody), in many jurisdictions, the professional is expected to do so (Grisso, 1990; Melton, Petrila, Poythress, & Slobogin, 1987).

A therapist who testifies in a custody proceeding as the treating professional for a child or parent would not be an expert witness but a factual witness. In this capacity, the therapist would provide factual information to the court about the client's treatment, including diagnosis, therapeutic progress, and prognosis. However, a treating therapist would not render an opinion about custody matters, even if pressured to do so by a parent or attorney.

As with the issues of professional neutrality and confidentiality, taking on the multiple roles of custody evaluator and therapist with the same family also creates conflicts for the professional as a court witness. In particular, whether the professional could render an opinion about custody matters would be unclear. Moreover, in light of these multiple roles, the parents, attorneys, and judge may all have different expectations about the scope of the professional's testimony. Under these circumstances, it would be highly improbable, if not impossible, for the professional to establish appropriate role boundaries.

RECENT GUIDELINES AND STANDARDS

In addition to the clinical complexity of working with divorced or divorcing families, it is widely recognized that dealing with custody issues places the mental health professional at increased risk in terms of professional liability. In fact, there have been a growing number of ethical complaints against psychologists who have been involved in custody cases (American Psychological Association Ethics Committee, 1985). To address ethical concerns, but also to provide practice guidelines in what has been an area with few if any professional standards, professional organizations have recently promulgated guidelines relevant to working with families with custody problems. These guidelines will not be reviewed in their entirety. Consistent with the preceding discussion, only those sections related to the issue of multiple roles will be addressed.

One of the first attempts to establish practice guidelines was a regional task force initiated by the Greater Pittsburgh Psychological Association. This task force focused on a variety of critical issues related to custody evaluations, including the issue of dual relationships (Greater Pittsburgh Psychological Association, 1991). The final report of this task force strongly discouraged professionals from being both custody evaluator and therapist with divorced or divorcing families because of inherent conflicts posed by this dual relationship. The pioneering efforts of this task force have been duly recognized in the Pittsburgh area for promoting innovative professional standards that have contributed, in part, to a major decline in ethical complaints against psychologists related to custody cases (Allegheny County Custody Evaluation Advisory Committee, personal communication, May 15, 1994).

The American Psychological Association has recently developed *Guidelines for Child Custody Evaluations in Divorce Proceedings* (American Psychological Association [APA], 1994). Similar to the Pittsburgh task force report, the APA guidelines address a broad array of clinical and ethical issues related to custody evaluations. Pertinent to the current discussion, one suggested guideline is that "the psychologist avoids multiple relationships" (p. 6). Specifically, this document suggests that undertaking a custody evaluation is not appropriate if the psychologist has been the therapist for the child or someone in the family.

These APA guidelines subsequently suggest that "therapeutic contact with the child or involved participants following a child custody evaluation is undertaken with caution" (p. 6). I am somewhat surprised that a stronger stand is not taken regarding this issue. For family members, it may be unclear when the professional's role of evaluator stops and the role of therapist begins. Moreover, the issue of what information is confidential and what is not would certainly be confusing for the child and parents and perhaps for the professional as well.

It is also quite common for the courts to order re-evaluation of custody and visitation problems, particularly if a significant new issue emerges, such as one parent seeking to relocate, or a child's learning problems requiring a special education program that exists only in the noncustodial parent's school district. In these circumstances, the professional who conducted the original custody evaluation would likely be asked or ordered to conduct the re-evaluation. However, this would not be possible if the original evaluator now has a therapeutic relationship with a family member. A new evaluator would therefore be necessary. Unfortunately, this new professional would not have direct access to the original evaluation data or familiarity with the parties, likely resulting in a lengthier and perhaps more costly re-evaluation. In light of these ethical and procedural concerns, it is strongly discouraged that a professional undertake a therapeutic role with the child or a family member following a custody evaluation.

The revised *Ethical Principles of Psychologists and Code of Conduct* (APA, 1992) for the first time includes a section on forensic assessments. Relevant to the matter at hand, this document suggests that "psychologists avoid performing multiple and potentially conflicting roles in forensic matters" (Ethical Standard 7.03). Although custody evaluations are not specifically addressed, playing the multiple roles of custody evaluator and therapist with the same family would appear to be inappropriate under this standard.

Practical Suggestions for Clinicians

This final section focuses on clinical practice. Although a clinician may understand the different types of custody and be aware of evolving guidelines pertaining to multiple professional roles, unique problems may continue to arise when working with families with custody and visitation problems. This last section provides some practical suggestions to assist the clinician in dealing with these problems and following existing legal and ethical standards.

Clarifying the nature of one's professional role prior to any clinical contact with a given family is perhaps the most important guideline for a clinician to follow. Accomplishing this goal may not be as easy as it sounds. For example, an attorney may call a professional, requesting help for a mother and child experiencing custody or visitation problems. However, it may be unclear as to whether the attorney is requesting treatment, a court-related evaluation, or both. Additionally, attorneys may be unaware that it would be inappropriate for a clinician to play multiple roles in these cases. It is up to clinicians to clarify this issue and to be explicit about what they can or cannot do. Ideally, this would be perceived as educational by attorneys.

Even if this issue is explained clearly, attorneys may still pressure professionals by suggesting special circumstances (e.g., the family cannot afford the fees of more than one professional) or through flattery (e.g., "you're the best in the business"). Although a professional may be sympathetic to an attorney's perspective, remember that the primary role of attorneys is to protect their client's best interests. This could include persuading a professional to do something that may be marginal from a legal or ethical point of view.

A parent may call a professional directly about custody or visitation problems and also be unclear about what is being requested. Again, it is the clinician's job to clarify role boundaries, be explicit about specific tasks that can or cannot be performed, and resist any pressure to practice outside of existing standards. Despite this role clarification, a parent may subsequently ask a professional who has become the child's therapist for custody recommendations, perhaps because the child now resists visiting the other parent, or returns home emotionally distraught after visits. In these situations, the clinician can remind the parent of the previously agreed upon professional role and perhaps suggest a forensic evaluation. Although the parent may be disappointed by the clinician's unwillingness to take on dual roles, the clinician has maintained professional integrity by being consistent with the original clinical contract.

Pressure to take on multiple roles may be particularly strong in some communities, such as in rural areas, where there are limited professional resources. In these situations, it would be most practical if the professional from the community became involved therapeutically with the child and family, as there would be multiple appointments over time at the clinician's local office. This arrangement would be convenient for the family. Perhaps a forensic expert from another community could be called on a short-term, more limited basis if a court-related evaluation is necessary.

In some circumstances in which there has been a highly contentious separation or divorce, parents may try continually to drag a therapist into the middle of custody proceedings, no matter how explicitly or often the clinician has clarified role boundaries. These situations may require additional measures. On a number of occasions when I have been a therapist for a child from divorced parents, I have required the parents to sign a document indicating that they understood the limits of the therapeutic role and that under no circumstances would I testify in court. In one case of court-ordered treatment for the child, this signed document was sent to the judge and attorneys representing both parents. Although it is not clear how such a document would hold up in court if legally challenged, parents have generally responded well to it and have not seemed offended. Most importantly, when such a document has been used, it has clearly resulted in parents pressuring the therapist less frequently and intensely to take on inappropriate roles.

I would like to end this section and chapter with two additional points that we are perhaps all aware of, but do not typically focus on. First, although mental health professionals certainly try diligently to be objective in their own work, we certainly can be subject to the same biases as the average lay person, particularly with respect to emotionally-laden issues like custody and divorce. Such biases could stem from the professional's own personal history or from one-sided professional experience, such as having worked as a therapist exclusively with divorced fathers or mothers. Professionals need to be aware of their values and potential biases regarding custody and divorce issues. In some instances, professionals may decide that they cannot engage in this area of clinical practice because they cannot separate their own values and biases from clinical decision making.

The second point relates to the many challenges that divorcing or divorced parents present to clinicians. These families undergo great changes and must contend with a legal system that is not always responsive to their needs. They will likely communicate their anger, hurt, and disappointment to mental health professionals who are involved therapeutically or in another professional capacity. Occasionally, professionals may temporarily become the object of their frustration, particularly if they resist the pressure to take on multiple roles. Demands on the professional's time may also be significant. Given the high level of stress that is typically involved in these cases, professionals should not hesitate to confer with colleagues on a regular basis regarding specific clinical or forensic issues in order to reduce their own frustration, to obtain collegial support, and possibly to prevent burnout.

References

American Psychological Association. (1992). *Ethical principles of psychologists and code of conduct.* Washington, DC: Author.

American Psychological Association. (1994). *Guidelines for child custody evaluations in divorce proceedings.* Washington, DC: Author.

American Psychological Association Ethics Committee. (1985). *Annual report of the American Psychological Association Ethics Committee.* Washington, DC: Author.

Felner, R.D., & Terre, L. (1987). Child custody dispositions and children's adaptation following divorce. In L.A. Weithorn (Ed.), *Psychology and child custody determinations: Knowledge, roles, and expertise* (pp. 106–153). Lincoln: University of Nebraska Press.

Greater Pittsburgh Psychological Association. (1991). *Report of the task force on child custody evaluation.* Pittsburgh, PA: Author.

Grisso, T. (1990). Evolving guidelines for divorce/custody evaluations. *Family and Conciliation Courts Review, 28,* 35–41.

Hetherington, E.M., Cox, M., & Cox, R. (1985). Long-term effects of divorce and remarriage on the adjustment of children. *Journal of the American Academy of Child and Adolescent Psychiatry, 24,* 518–530.

Mannarino, A.P., & Cohen, J.A. (1992). Forensic versus treatment roles in cases of child sexual abuse. *Protective Services Quarterly, 7,* 1–6.

Melton, G.B., Petrila, J., Poythress, N.G., & Slobogin, C. (1987). *Psychological evaluations for the courts: A handbook for mental health professionals and lawyers.* New York: Guilford.

National Center for Health Statistics. (1985). *Advance report of final divorce statistics* (Vol. 33, No. 11) (DHHS Publication No. PH-85-1120). Washington, DC: U.S. Department of Health and Human Services.

Wallerstein, J. (1985). Children of divorce. *Journal of the American Academy of Child and Adolescent Psychiatry, 24,* 545–553.

CHAPTER 8

Ethical and Legal Issues in Lesbian, Gay, and Bisexual Family Therapy

ROY SCRIVNER

T his chapter explores ethical issues that may arise in the practice of lesbian, gay, and bisexual family therapy. Two ethical issues unique to working with lesbians, gays, and bisexuals are identified, and issues of dual relationships that are more probable with therapists in small communities are discussed. Cases reflecting generic ethical issues are presented, and the dominant ethical issue, clinical competence, is illustrated in cases presented. Legal issues are introduced.

Background

In this chapter, the designation *affectional orientation*, rather than *sexual orientation,* is used. Affectional orientation refers to the gender of an individual's love object: The love object of a gay or lesbian is someone of the same gender; the love objects of a bisexual are both genders; and the love object of a heterosexual is someone of the other gender. Sexual

I appreciate Michael Gottlieb for his long-standing support and collaboration in my addressing family therapy ethical issues; Natalie Eldridge for further educating me about feminist ethics; and the following individuals for their comments on an earlier paper (Scrivner, 1995), which contributed to the evolvement of this chapter: Anthony D'Augelli, David Greenan, Suzanne Iasenza, Larry Kurdek, April Martin, and Bianca Cody Murphy.

orientation defines persons in terms of their sexual relations and con-tributes toward people thinking of homosexuals and bisexuals only in terms of how they have sex. Affectional orientation relates to the affec-tional and love relations of lesbians, gays, and bisexuals, and these re-lations are the predominant focus of lesbian, gay, and bisexual family psychology and therapy.

Lesbian, gay, and bisexual family psychology is that body of knowl-edge about lesbians, gays, and bisexuals; lesbian, gay, and bisexual family therapy is the use of family therapy interventions that may in-clude a psychoeducational component of information from lesbian, gay, and bisexual family psychology (L'Abate, 1992).

Clinical Competence

The first ethical issue considered in the area of lesbian, gay, and bisex-ual family therapy is clinical competence in family therapy. This may be more difficult to gain for some mental health professionals than others. The profession of psychology, with its historical focus on the individual, did not have a Division of Family Psychology until 1984. Although psychology graduate programs and internships are increas-ingly offering training in family therapy, such training is not available to all students. Many students who want training in family therapy will have to seek postgraduate family therapy training through various continuing education endeavors.

In addition, training in lesbian, gay, and bisexual family therapy is typically not a part of family therapy programs. Even rarer are lesbian, gay, and bisexual family therapists and educators who are open about their affectional orientation and who can be role models for lesbian, gay, and bisexual students and therapists. Lesbian, gay, and bisexual therapists report that the heterosexism in some family training pro-grams creates discomfort to such a degree that they either do not enter such training or withdraw from it. Heterosexism in family research is well documented (Scrivner, 1996).

A prerequisite for becoming clinically competent in lesbian, gay, and bisexual family therapy is competence in individual therapy with lesbian, gay, and bisexual individuals and a knowledge of related ethi-cal issues (American Psychological Association Committee on Lesbian and Gay Concerns, 1991; Brown, 1996; Davison, 1991; Dworkin, 1992; Gartrell, 1991; Gonsiorek, 1994; Murphy, 1991; Rigby & Sophie, 1990). Competence in lesbian, gay, and bisexual family therapy includes a knowledge of lesbian and gay family psychology (Scrivner & Eldridge, 1995) and bisexual family psychology (Firestein, 1996; Fox, 1996; Scrivner, 1995). Lesbian and gay family psychology is defined as the study of lesbian and gay individuals; couples; their children; their families of origin and extended biologically-related family members; and their extended nonbiologically-related family members of choice.

It may include current or former spouses in heterosexual marriages and any children from these marriages. The recently established area of bisexual family psychology is the study of bisexual individuals and their partners, their children, and their family of origin members and extended biological family members.

Some general resources are available for professionals who wish to enhance their competency in lesbian, gay, and bisexual family psychology (Cabaj & Stein, 1996; D'Augelli & Patterson, 1995; Laird & Green, 1996; Savin-Williams & Cohen, 1996; Scrivner & Eldridge, 1995). In addition, an edited book by McGoldrick, Giordano, and Pearce (1996) is highly recommended for a better understanding of the lesbian, gay, and bisexual members of 48 ethnic groups (also see Goodwin, this volume). Finally, a resource that focuses on lesbian and gay parenting was developed by the American Psychological Association Committee on Women in Psychology; the Committee on Lesbian, Gay, and Bisexual Concerns; and the Committee on Children Youth and Families (1995).

Ethical Issues

Two additional ethical issues arise in professional practice with lesbians, gays, and bisexuals: disclosure of the therapist's affectional orientation and conflicting ethical guidelines.

DISCLOSURE OF AFFECTIONAL ORIENTATION

Disclosure of the therapist's affectional orientation is an informed consent issue for those clients specifically wanting to see only lesbian, gay, or bisexual therapists, and for those therapists who are sensitive to feminist ethics about self-disclosure (Mahalik, Simi, & Van Ormer, 1996). As Gottlieb (this volume) noted, it can be difficult to separate some ethical issues from clinical issues; self-disclosure is an example of this difficulty.

For instance if a therapist's self-disclosed affectional orientation is the same as that of a client who strongly disapproves of the orientation, the client may develop a strong dislike of the therapist. Working through this dislike may not be possible, and referral to another therapist may be appropriate. However, self-disclosure of a same-gender or bi-gender affectional orientation can help establish rapport and trust with clients who are comfortable with their and the therapist's common affectional orientation.

A second ethical issue unique to lesbian, gay, and bisexual family therapy is whether a therapist should disclose the same-gender affectional orientation of a family member to other family members (see Case 3).

CONFLICTING ETHICAL GUIDELINES

Another ethical issue that may be encountered in working with lesbians, gays, and bisexuals is the conflict between ethical guidelines and legal requirements. Principle F of the ethical code for psychologists reads: "Psychologists comply with the law and encourage the development of law and social policy that serve the interest of their patients and clients and the public;" Ethical Standard 1.02 reads: "If psychologists' ethical responsibilities conflict with law, psychologists make known their commitment to the Ethics Code and take steps to resolve the conflict in a responsible manner" (American Psychological Association, 1992).

There are statutes in 25 states and the District of Columbia that prohibit same-gender sexual relations (National Gay & Lesbian Task Force Policy Institute, 1993); similar statutes exist on local levels. Therapists and educators who address lesbian, gay, and bisexual issues can be seen as encouraging the violation of these statutes (Masters & Johnson, 1980; Masters, Johnson, & Kolodny, 1977). In one such state, a psychologist worked with the state psychological association in preparing and filing a brief in a court case challenging the law; the law was upheld.

The same psychologist worked with the state association in an attempt to include sexual orientation in the nondiscriminatory clause in legislation related to the psychology licensing act; the state legislature would not pass the proposed licensing act unless sexual orientation was removed. Subsequently, the state board included sexual orientation in the nondiscriminatory clause in its rules and regulations. A state legislator, who opposed including sexual orientation in the licensing act, accused the board of promoting homosexuality by including sexual orientation in the board's nondiscriminatory clause in its rules and regulations.

Case Studies

As an openly gay family psychologist and therapist, I have often been consulted on lesbian, gay, and bisexual family therapy cases. A question I am frequently asked is, "What are the special techniques to use in working with lesbian, gay, and bisexual families?" There are no interventions that have been developed specifically for work in this area. Rather, one needs to be competent in one's intervention(s) of choice. For example, in using analytic approaches, one needs to be familiar with those writings that are affirmative of lesbians, gays, and bisexuals (Friedman, 1988; Glassgold & Iasenza, 1995; Lewes, 1988). Most other questions reflect difficulty in identifying the generic family therapy ethical principles that apply to a given case due to a lack of clinical competence in lesbian, gay, and bisexual family psychology. Some illustrative cases are presented. These cases are hypothetical composites based on actual cases I have been consulted on or that I have seen in therapy.

Case 1

Dan was a 35-year-old professor who consulted a therapist about a number of issues. The client had some awareness of his same-gender affectional and sexual feelings prior to marriage. However, (a) he personally wanted to be a father; (b) as the only son of an only son, his family had high expectations of his marrying and having children, particularly a son, to carry on the paternal family name, the lineage of which could be traced to ancestors who came to America on the Mayflower; and (c) he was concerned that being gay would preclude his becoming successful professionally. He had married a woman with a very similar background, and both of their families had been highly supportive of their marrying.

When he entered therapy, Dan had realized early career success and had a 9-year-old son. He had experienced a few one-time sexual encounters with men, always practicing safe sex, and was occasionally seeing one specific individual. Dan was learning contemporary information about lesbians and gays. He reported to the therapist that he was thinking of divorcing his wife and "coming out," but had a number of concerns. His concerns included (a) the effect of a divorce on his 9-year-old son; (b) the effect of disclosure of his same-gender affectional orientation on his son and wife; (c) fears of leaving his wife, who sometimes abused alcohol on the weekend, to care for his son; and (d) fear of losing the new acquaintance he had been seeing, who wanted to spend more time with him.

Dan assumed the major responsibility for parenting his son, and he was concerned about gaining custody or visitation rights, should he get a divorce. His therapist consulted a colleague familiar with gay parenting issues, who suggested Dan see a local attorney familiar with legal issues of lesbian, gay, and bisexual parents and their children. The attorney told Dan that it would be very difficult for him, as a man, to gain custody of his son, even if his wife were certified as alcohol dependent, and that it would be impossible for him to gain custody if his affectional orientation were known.

The consultant suggested that Dan's therapist explore whether his thoughts of "coming out" might be separation and individuation issues. Dan confirmed this for the therapist, reporting that following his disagreement with his parents regarding their views about gays and lesbians, he began to differ with his parents on other issues. He added that his wife often followed his lead and began differing with her parents. Another issue Dan was struggling with was his parents' triangulating him into their marital conflicts. After further consultation, Dan's therapist gained additional information about Dan's marriage and the families of origin of Dan and his wife.

The therapist came to the following conclusions and presented them to Dan:

1. Dan was in the process of further individuating and separating from his family of origin, and his wife seemed to be following his lead. If he refused to be triangulated into his parents' marital conflicts, they might seek marital counseling, get a divorce, or both.

2. The wife's alcohol abuse had worsened during the last few months, presumably due to the stress associated with her working to gain tenure as a professor in two years. Her abuse might lessen after gaining tenure.

3. A divorce at this time could exacerbate her stress and contribute toward a more serious alcohol problem, resulting in reduced capabilities to parent her son.

4. The son would be less likely to experience any negative effects from a divorce after he reached adolescence, rather than at his current age of nine.

5. In general, the younger children are when they learn about a parents' same-gender affectional orientation, the easier it is for them to deal with this issue. No long-term negative effects on children related to a parent's same-gender affectional orientation have been found (Patterson, 1995).

6. The son was exposed to diversity. He met a male colleague of his father who had a physical disability and a female colleague of his mother from an ethnic minority background, as well as both of their families. Though the son had not been exposed to gays and lesbians, such exposure would be consistent with the son's previous experiences with diversity. If Dan waited for some time prior to disclosing

his affectional orientation to his son, he would have some opportunity to expose his son to positive, accurate information about gays and lesbians.

7. Dan might consider attending a group for gay fathers in heterosexual marriages.

8. The father's new acquaintance might not continue seeing him if the father remained in the marriage.

9. Dan had been living as a heterosexual for 35 years; he was tired of living a lie and of being lonely without much contact with other gay men.

After attending more therapy sessions and the support group, Dan decided to remain in the marriage for the time being. The therapist, as a part of a psychoeducational component to therapy, explained to Dan typical stages in the development of positive lesbian and gay identities: sensitization, identity confusion, identity comparison, identity tolerance, identity acceptance, first relationships, identity commitment and pride, and identity synthesis (Scrivner & Eldridge, 1995). He explained that in the acceptance stage Dan would be in his gay adolescence and might find himself acting and thinking in some ways typical of an adolescent.

The therapist also discussed typical stages his parents might go through in response to learning about his affectional orientation (Scrivner & Eldridge, 1995). He cautioned that it was taking Dan some time to accept his affectional orientation, and that he would need to give his family members, friends, and colleagues some time to adjust to learning that Dan was gay. The therapist explained to Dan that he would need to be prepared to educate his family members, friends, and colleagues about gay and lesbian issues, and recommended some books and pamphlets for them. Therapy was terminated.

Four years afterward, when his son was 13, Dan returned to the therapist. After his wife gained tenure, she reduced her alcohol abuse, and the marital relationship improved. Both Dan and his wife became more differentiated from their families of origin. Dan stopped becoming triangulated into his parents' marital conflicts, which had escalated seriously. The son had good peer relationships and a good academic record. Dan arranged for his son to be exposed to positive information about gays, lesbians, and bisexuals.

What precipitated the father returning to therapy at this time was his first experience of falling in love with another gay man, whom he had been seeing for seven months. Dan explored his ambivalent feelings about leaving the marriage and "coming out," and decided to do so. He saw the therapist for ten months, during which time he addressed his grief over the end of a heterosexual life and, particularly, his marriage.

His wife was shocked and surprised at his disclosure; she felt both angry and sad about losing a husband who had provided her with a lot of support. She began attending a support group for heterosexuals with current or former spouses or partners who were gay, lesbian, or bisexual (Buxton, 1994).

After the father came out to his son, the two discussed the father's orientation only briefly. In time, the son became comfortable being with his father and his father's new male partner.

DISCUSSION

This case illustrates several issues, including the need for competence in lesbian, gay, and bisexual family therapy and related legal concerns; the value of a psychoeducational component in therapy; the importance of viewing "coming out" as a possible part of and contributing factor in individuation and separation processes; the significance of the family-of-origin response to these processes; and the need for competence or consultation in the area of divorce and its effects on children.

The case also demonstrates how changes in an individual or system can create changes in other systems (Fox, 1991; Scrivner, 1993). As Dan differentiated more from his family of origin, his wife followed his lead, differentiating more from her family. When Dan stopped being triangulated into his parents' marital conflicts, the conflicts escalated. Without seeing persons who are not included in family therapy, the therapist cannot offer a professional opinion about these individuals; however, the therapist can offer systemic perspectives about the possible responses to changes in how a client relates to these other individuals.

Case 2

A British-American lesbian, Beth, made an appointment to see a lesbian therapist who was well-known in the local gay and lesbian community. During the first session, the therapist addressed dual relationship issues (Biaggio & Greene, 1995). Namely, she asked how Beth would prefer to handle the situation if she and the therapist were in a context together outside of therapy. The therapist noted that some clients of hers were comfortable being seen socially with her, whereas others were not, fearing other people would infer that they were in therapy with her. Beth asked that the decision be left up to her in any such circumstances.

Beth told the therapist that she had an African-American partner, Roberta. The therapist then explained that often she would see someone in individual therapy who had a partner and that later the client would ask that the partner come in for couple therapy (Gottlieb, 1995). For these cases the therapist adopted a policy of not keeping confidential any information that was discussed in the individual sessions if it were relevant in the couple therapy sessions. Beth agreed to this policy.

During the first two sessions, Beth complained of depression. Some of it was related to her job, and some to her relationship with her partner, which did not seem as good as it used to be. The therapist suggested that she and her partner come in for couple therapy, and explained that the state law provided for privileged communication in individual therapy, but not family therapy (Fulero & VandeCreek, 1990; Watkins, 1979). She added that this lack of privileged communication had never been a serious issue in her previous family work. Beth decided to ask her partner to come in.

Roberta was unwilling to participate. The therapist then explored with Beth the possibility of the therapist sending Roberta a letter. In the letter, the therapist would explain that individual therapy was more likely than couple therapy to have a negative impact on a couple relationship (Wilcoxon & Fennell, 1986). Beth supported this idea, and the therapist sent the letter; Roberta agreed to come in. When Roberta attended the first therapy session, the therapist discussed the lack of privileged communication and the agreement she had with Beth about therapist-client contacts outside of therapy. Roberta agreed to these decisions.

After two sessions, the therapist made an assessment that therapy was not progressing. The following weekend, Beth went out of state on business and the therapist went to another state to attend a lesbian and gay film festival. At the festival, she observed Roberta with another woman and inferred that the two had a rather close relationship. The therapist thought that perhaps Roberta was having an affair, which could be precluding progress in therapy.

At the next session, the therapist explained that she found it helpful to sometimes meet individually with partners and explained her policy of "no secrets" (see Scrivner, 1995, pp. 3–7), meaning the therapist would not keep secret any information gained in the individual sessions that was relevant to the couple sessions. The partners agreed to meet with her individually and to accept her policy. In the individual session, Roberta complained of Beth putting her job before her; she did not say anything about another significant relationship. In her individual session, Beth complained that Roberta was too dependent on her family.

After these sessions, the therapist consulted another therapist more experienced with ethnicity who might help her decide what to do with the information the therapist had about seeing Roberta with another woman. The consulting therapist explained how some problems between the partners were a reflection of their respective ethnic backgrounds; the consultant also noted that sometimes a partner having a significant relationship with someone outside of a primary relationship helps maintain the systemic balance of a couple system.

In order to gain a more comprehensive understanding of the couple, the consultant suggested that the therapist assess the relationships between each partner and her family of origin and extended family members, and also assess the contextual (ecological) factors (Marsh, 1997) in the dominant culture that might have a negative impact on the couple.

The therapist learned that Beth's parents supported her in becoming independent and in assuming individual responsibility for her problems. She was working as a chief accountant in a private firm and was well respected and well paid. However, she occasionally overheard sexist, racist, and heterosexist remarks.

Fearful of losing her good position, she never confronted these remarks, but worked harder, with typical British-American stoicism. She hoped that, should her orientation become known to her employer, her excellent work record would overcome any difficulties about her lesbianism. However, she was typically very tired at the end of the week, and devoted much of the weekend to resting. When Beth rested on weekends, Roberta often visited her family of origin members. Roberta was also socialized by her parents to be competent and independent, and, unlike Beth, to maintain close family ties.

At times the partners felt discriminated against by others in their neighborhood for both their affectional orientation and Roberta's ethnicity. During the past year, Roberta successfully filed an EEO complaint at her place of employment, and felt no ill feelings from anyone at the agency. However, the experience had been stressful for the couple.

The therapist assessed that the couple's four-year relationship was very strong and was weakened by negative contextual factors. She reviewed the stages of lesbian couple formation and development: prerelationship, romance, conflict, acceptance, commitment, and collaboration (Scrivner & Eldridge, 1995). After this review she assessed that the couple was between the conflict and acceptance stages.

Following consultation, the therapist decided to apply guidelines for ethical decision making in determining how to use the information she had gained by seeing Roberta with another woman outside of therapy. These guidelines were developed for use when existing ethical codes do not address a given issue (Keith-Spiegel & Koocher, 1985). Following her analysis, the therapist resolved not to confront Roberta at that time.

The therapist decided to share her overall assessment of Beth and Roberta's stage in lesbian couple development and of their systemic and contextual issues, including a discussion of partner problems related to their different ethnic backgrounds. The therapist assessed that the couple relationship was strong enough to work through the issue of another woman, should the issue arise.

Both partners reported feeling that their relationship was very validated by the therapist's assessment. Afterward, Beth indicated she had been thinking of getting a job in a government agency where a lesbian friend of hers worked. She acknowledged that she was more depressed than she realized, and apologized to Roberta for not being more available to her. Roberta told Beth that what she said meant a lot to her, as she was beginning to question how much Beth cared for her.

Later, Roberta disclosed that she occasionally dated another lesbian who met some needs that Beth and her family members could not meet. The therapist never confronted Roberta about having seen her with another woman at the film festival. During subsequent therapy sessions Beth terminated her employment and accepted a position at the agency where her friend worked. The couple moved to a neighborhood where other lesbians, gays, and African-Americans lived without discrimination.

Four years later, Roberta came back to see the therapist. Roberta reported she had a friendship of many years with a co-worker who was a heterosexual man. Recently, she became aware of being sexually attracted to him though she was not in love with him. With further explorations in therapy, Roberta came to the realization that she was bisexual (Firestein, 1996; Fox, 1996).

DISCUSSION

This case illustrates how therapists in small communities may be more likely to encounter dual relationship issues and how one therapist addressed these concerns. My own experience has been that dual relationships with clients in individual therapy, particularly long-term therapy, can be more problematic than with clients in couple or family therapy. In individual therapy, the relationship between the therapist and client may be much more intimate and have a stronger emotional connection than the relationships between the therapist and clients in couple or family therapy.

In addition, a common problem is addressed in this case: how to reach a decision about an ethical issue in the absence of any existing ethical guidelines on the issue. The decision in this case was whether to use in therapy sessions information about the client gained outside of therapy. This issue may be more common among therapists in small communities. Moreover, the case illustrates the need to use consultation.

Also illustrated in this case is the importance of a contextual (ecological) assessment (see Marsh, 1997). My experience in working with minority members is that they have often become accustomed to—and sometimes numbed by—contextual stress and may not report it, unless the therapist assesses this issue. Even when there are no specific issues, the therapist can validate minority individuals and families for their strength in living in a dominant culture that often discriminates against them.

Finally, the case reflects that some individuals who identify themselves as lesbian, gay, or heterosexual may later come to a realization that they are bisexual.

Case 3

Sam and Barbara were married and joint partners in a business. They were having some problems with boundaries at work and saw John, a therapist. They mentioned that their two children, Naomi and David, especially David, were not as close to them as they used to be. The therapist suggested seeing all family members. During the therapy session, it was evident that all family members cared for one another. The parents discussed their pride in David's and Naomi's academic achievements and extracurricular activities, as well as their wish to be closer to their children.

David and Naomi said that they complained to their parents about their tendency to share the children's private information with the grandparents on both sides of the family. When their parents continued to do so, David and Naomi quit discussing their concerns with them.

John said that he had a policy of meeting individually with adolescents in families. He explained that if issues discussed in the individual sessions were relevant to overall family functioning, these issues would be discussed in a session with the parents. All family members agreed to this policy. He first met separately with David, then with Naomi.

During the first part of the individual session, David did not say very much. Later in the session, he began talking more and disclosed that he was gay. He asked John to keep this information a secret from his family. David said he had heard his parents make negative comments about gays and anticipated that they would be very upset. He added that whenever his parents were upset about any issue, they typically consulted their own parents. David was concerned that if his grandparents knew this information, it might be leaked to other family members and, eventually, to his peers at school. He reported that there were no openly gay or lesbian students at school and that students thought to be gay or lesbian were sometimes harassed.

David, now age 15, related that at the age of 11 he became aware of being sexually attracted to other boys and experienced unreciprocated love for two of his male peers. Though he was very active in school and knew a lot of people, he had withdrawn from close emotional relationships. He was afraid that if people got to know him, they might discover his secret. He occasionally went to a nearby large city and participated in anonymous gay sex, always practicing safe sex. These sexual encounters were significant in helping him reduce his emotional isolation, though on a temporary basis.

John had some knowledge of gay issues, but had never had a family member bring this up as an issue and request that the information not be shared with other family members. John was concerned that he and the son shared a secret, and that this secret alliance could impede family therapy. Thus, John consulted another therapist more experienced in lesbian and gay issues.

They reviewed an article by Sobocinski (1990) and concluded that David was competent to make a decision about his affectional orientation. He had been dealing with this issue, alone, for four years and was coping well, given the family system and the ecological issues (see Marsh, 1997). David was also being responsible in practicing safe sex. Other material that the therapists read indicated that many lesbian, gay, and bisexual adolescents do not reveal their orientation to their parents (Savin-Williams & Cohen, 1996, pp. 133–139).

John also learned that parents typically go through a five-stage grief process (shock, denial, guilt, anger, and acceptance) in coming to accept the same-gender affectional orientation of a child (Scrivner & Eldridge, 1995), and that some parents never reach an acceptance (Sohier, 1993). He and the consultant were concerned that if David's parents knew of his orientation, they would likely seek support from the grandparents. David's secret could reach his peers.

The therapist decided not to tell David's parents about his orientation. Instead, John would try to work out an agreement between the parents and the children that the children would be more disclosing if the parents would honor their wishes to keep some information secret from the grandparents and other family members.

At the next family therapy session, John was able to get all of the family members to agree to his proposal. John then met individually with David; he told him he would not share his secret and gave him the names of some references on lesbian and gay issues. David was appreciative of this. However, he said he did not feel he needed to see the therapist again. Subsequently, John met only with the parents for a few sessions.

Discussion

This case presents another ethical issue unique to lesbian, gay, and family therapy: whether a therapist should disclose the same-gender affectional orientation of a family member to other family members. Disclosure of affectional orientation can be both an ethical and a clinical issue. Some could argue from an ethical and legal perspective that the therapist should have told David's parents about their son's orientation. However, there is increasing support for the idea that minors may be entitled to the same rights of confidentiality as adults, and increasing evidence that minors can effectively participate in treatment decisions (Gustafson & McNamara, 1995; also see Goldberg, 1997). In this case, the clinical and contextual assessment supported the therapist's decision to keep the orientation confidential.

Other situations in which a therapist may decide to disclose the affectional orientation of a client, if the client is unwilling to do so, are those cases involving a gay or bisexual male partner and a female partner. The therapist may consider it a "duty to warn" the woman about her partner's orientation and the possibility of his being exposed to HIV by not practicing safe sex with gay and bisexual men (see the section on AIDS).

Case 4

Linda was the third child in a Latin-American family. Her mother had always dominated her and did not help her develop competence. After high school graduation, Linda married her high school sweetheart, who dominated the relationship. The couple had two children. Her husband's mother was always supportive of Linda, helping her develop competence in many areas, and helping Linda with her children. As the children grew older, Linda was very good at loving them and meeting most of their needs, except their need for discipline. Her husband did most of the disciplining.

When the daughter was 13 and the son 14, the two children began to refuse to do what Linda asked of them. Her husband would exhort her to take a firmer stand with the children, and other marital disagreements were escalating.

During this time, Linda fell in love with Maria, a divorced mother with a daughter, age 14, and a son, age 15. No one knew about their lesbian relationship. Linda and her husband agreed to separate, and Linda moved in with Maria, expecting Maria to discipline her children as her husband had. This did not happen, and all the children were unhappy with the new arrangement. Linda and Maria sought help at a community mental health center. The therapist was not experienced in working with lesbians and gays, and sought consultation from a treatment team.

Linda and Maria told their children about their relationship without talking with the therapist; Maria's children already knew of her orientation. Linda's children were shocked and talked to their father about the issue and their unhappiness with their living situation. Soon everyone in Linda's husband's and Linda's family knew about the situation. Linda's mother wanted to take the children from her and rear them herself. Linda's mother and husband wanted to meet with the therapist. Because Linda and Maria were her clients, the therapist was uncertain whether to agree to such a meeting.

The consultation team recommended the therapist meet with Linda and her mother. In the therapy session, the mother predominantly criticized Linda. Only with skillful guidance from the therapist could the mother acknowledge some of Linda's strengths. Next, the therapist met with Linda and her husband, as the parental subsystem of their family. Her husband did not want to take the children, but did not want them living with Linda. Linda and her husband agreed that possibly his parents, with whom the children had often stayed, would take the children for a period of time. A meeting was arranged with them.

After much consultation and assessment, the following was worked out:

1. The children would stay with the paternal grandparents temporarily and continue going to the same school.
2. The therapist would teach Linda how to discipline the children more effectively when they visited on weekends.
3. Linda and her husband agreed to work together in their parenting of the children in conjunction with his parents taking care of them.
4. Being in a local chapter of Children of Lesbians and Gays Everywhere (COLAGE) was an option for the children.
5. The therapist would meet with the children periodically.
6. The children would continue attending the same Protestant church they had attended since early childhood.
7. Some towns and cities have Metropolitan Community Churches. These churches have gay or lesbian ministers and predominantly gay and lesbian congregations. Linda and Maria would be referred to this church and a local chapter of Gay and Lesbian Parents Coalition International (GLPCI).

Within a year, Linda was more effective in disciplining the children. She followed the therapist's instruction that, in a blended family, the non-biological parent should first establish a friend relationship with the children. Linda did this in time, and, in time, Maria did with Linda's children. Within a year, there began to be discussions about Linda's children going to live with her.

This case was resolved with an atypical minimum of difficulties due to the high value Linda's husband's family placed on family relationships. Also, there was a lesbian in Linda's extended family and a gay male in her husband's extended family. Thus, the issue of same-gender affectional relationships already had been introduced in both families. In addition, the church and school Linda's children attended provided ongoing support for them, and the Metropolitan Community Church Linda and Maria attended provided invaluable social and spiritual support for them (Haldeman, 1996). Linda and Maria also received valuable support from the local GLPCI chapter. All of their children benefitted from attending the local COLAGE chapter.

DISCUSSION

This case might not have seemed so complicated had the therapist imagined what she might have done if the mothers were heterosexual. A greater awareness of lesbian and gay issues can affect and improve a therapist's decision making for lesbian and gay clients on other issues. This case illustrates issues that are receiving increasing recognition and attention.

AIDS

A comprehensive discussion of the issues of AIDS in family therapy (e.g., "secrets" and "duty to warn") is beyond the scope of this chapter. The reader is referred to other sources that address these concerns (American Psychological Association Office on AIDS, 1996; Anderson, in press; Black, 1993; Friedman & Hughes, 1994; Gard, 1990; McGuire, Nieri, Abbott, Sheridan, & Fisher, 1995; Pope & Morin, 1991; Rein, 1996; Schlossberger & Hecker, 1996; Walker, 1991, Chapter 8).

Legal Issues

Clinical competence in working with lesbians, gays, and bisexuals requires knowledge of the challenging local and national legal issues that these individuals face. There are no federal statutes that provide legal protection for these persons as members of a minority group, and only a few state and local statutes. Recent discussions in the U. S. Congress about not supporting same-gender marriages and the recent history of gays in the military reflect the lack of legal protection for lesbian, gay, and bisexual individuals and families. Some significant negative effects of this lack of legal protection can include: (a) a lack of spousal benefits, such as health insurance; (b) a lack of authority to make medical decisions for a partner who is unable to make those decisions; and (c) a lack of recognition as a primary or secondary beneficiary in a partner's will.

General information about legal issues is provided by Leonard, Curry, and Clifford (1994); Purcell and Hicks (1996); and Rubenstein (1996). For assistance with specific cases, the reader is referred to the Committee on Lesbian, Gay, and Bisexual Concerns of the American Psychological Association; the Association has filed briefs in cases challenging statutes that prohibit same-gender sexual relations and in custody cases involving lesbian and gay parents. Other mental health associations might be consulted. Education and attorney referrals may be provided by the Gay and Lesbian Parents Coalition International; Parents, Families, and Friends of Lesbians and Gays (PFLAG); and the

National Gay and Lesbian Task Force (see the list of organizations following References).

Conclusion

The majority of lesbian, gay, and bisexual individuals are indistinguishable from heterosexuals. Unlike people of color, the minority status of these individuals and of the families they create is invisible. Until disclosure is made, a therapist is likely to assume that a presenting client is heterosexual. This chapter shows the similarities between the issues of lesbian, gay, and bisexual families and those of heterosexual families. Professionals can increase their understanding of the differences among the four types of families by enhancing their competence in the area of lesbian, gay, and bisexual family psychology.

This chapter does not discuss the basics of lesbian, gay, and bisexual family psychology that are necessary to be competent in this area, as this information can be gained elsewhere (see the section on Clinical Competence). For example, it is important to understand the differences among lesbian, gay, bisexual, and heterosexual couples due to gender role socialization (see Hampton & Gottlieb, 1997).

An awareness of the lack of legal protection for lesbians, gays, and bisexuals and their family members helps professionals recognize the strength of the loving and committed relationships among lesbian, gay, and bisexual family members. Developing clinical competence in working with lesbian, gay, and bisexual issues, and addressing the related ethical and legal issues will enhance one's overall competence in family therapy, especially in working with families from other minority groups.

References

American Psychological Association. (1992). Ethical principles of psychologists and code of conduct. *American Psychologists, 47,* 1597–1611.

American Psychological Association Committee on Lesbian and Gay Concerns. (1991). *Bias in psychotherapy with lesbians and gays.* Washington, DC: American Psychological Association.

American Psychological Association Committee on Women in Psychology; Committee on Lesbian, Gay, and Bisexual Concerns; and Committee on Children, Youth, and Families. (1995). *Lesbian and gay parenting: A resource for psychologists.* Washington, DC: American Psychological Association.

American Psychological Association Office on AIDS. (1996). *Training curriculum: Ethical issues and HIV/AIDS mental health services.* Washington, DC: American Psychological Association.

Anderson, J. R. (Ed.). (in press). *Ethics and HIV/AIDS: A mental health practitioners' guide.* Washington, DC: American Psychological Association.

Biaggio, M., & Greene, B. (1995). Overlapping dual relationships. In E. J. Rave & C. C. Larsen (Eds.), *Ethical decision making in therapy: Feminist perspectives* (pp. 88–123). New York: Guilford.

Black, L. W. (1993). AIDS and secrets. In E. Imber-Black (Ed.), *Secrets in families and family therapy* (pp. 355–369). New York: W. W. Norton.

Brown, L. (1996). Ethical concerns with sexual minority patients. In R. P. Cabaj & T. S. Stein (Eds.), *Textbook of homosexuality and mental health* (pp. 897–916). Washington, DC: American Psychiatric Press.

Buxton, A. (1994). *The other side of the closet: The coming-crisis for straight spouses and families.* New York: Wiley.

Cabaj, R. P., & Stein, T. S. (Eds.). (1996). *Textbook of homosexuality and mental health.* Washington, DC: American Psychiatric Press.

D'Augelli, A. R., & Patterson, C. J. (Eds.). (1995). *Lesbian and gay identities over the lifespan: Psychological perspectives on personal, relational, and community processes.* New York: Oxford University Press.

Davison, G. C. (1991). Constructionism and morality in therapy for homosexuality. In J. C. Gonsiorek & J. D. Weinrich (Eds.), *Homosexuality: Research implications for public policy* (pp. 137–148). Newbury Park, CA: Sage.

Dworkin, S. H. (1992). Some ethical considerations when counseling gay, lesbian, and bisexual clients. In S. H. Dworkin & F. J. Gutierrez (Eds.), *Counseling gay men and lesbians: Journey to the end of the rainbow* (pp. 325–334). Alexandria, VA: American Association for Counseling and Development.

Firestein, B. A. (1996). *Bisexuality: The psychology and politics of an invisible minority.* New York: Sage.

Fox, R. C. (1996). Bisexuality: An examination of theory and research. In R. P. Cabaj & T. S. Stein (Eds.), *Textbook of homosexuality and mental health* (pp. 147–171). Washington, DC: American Psychiatric Press.

Fox, R. E. (1991). Treating individuals and families together: Further thoughts from a different therapist. *The Family Psychologist, 7*(1), 13.

Friedman, A. L., & Hughes, R. B. (1994). AIDS: Legal tools helpful for mental health counseling. *Journal of Mental Health Counseling, 16,* 291–303.

Friedman, R. C. (1988). *Male homosexuality: A contemporary psychoanalytic perspective.* New Haven, CT: Yale University Press.

Fulero, S. M., & VandeCreek, L. (1990). Privilege in group, marital, and family therapy: A review of cases. *Psychotherapy Bulletin, 25*(2), 14–17.

Gard, L. H. (1990). Patient disclosure of human immunodeficiency virus (HIV) status to parents: Clinical considerations. *Professional Psychology: Research and Practice, 21,* 252–256.

Gartrell, N. K. (1991). Boundaries in lesbian therapist client relationships. In B. Green & G. M. Herek (Eds.), *Psychological perspectives on lesbian and gay issues: Vol. 1. Lesbian and gay psychology: Theory, research and clinical applications* (pp. 98–117). Thousand Oaks, CA: Sage.

Glassgold, J. M., & Iasenza, S. (1995). *Lesbians and psychoanalysis.* New York: Free Press.

Goldberg, R. (1997, this volume).

Gonsiorek, J. C. (1994). *Breach of trust: Sexual exploitation by healthcare professionals and clergy.* New York: Sage.

Goodwin, B. J. (1997, this volume).

Gottlieb, M. C. (1995). Ethical dilemmas in change of format and live supervision. In R. H. Mikesell, D.-D. Lusterman, & S. H. McDaniel (Eds.), *Integrating family therapy: Handbook of family psychology and systems therapy* (pp. 561–569). Washington, DC: American Psychological Association.

Gottlief, M. C. (1997, this volume).

Gustafson, K. E., & McNamara, J. R. (1995). Confidentiality with minor clients: Issues and guidelines for therapists. In D. N. Bersoff (Ed.), *Ethical conflicts in psychology* (pp. 193–197). Washington, DC: American Psychological Association.

Haldeman, D. C. (1996). Spirituality and religion in the lives of lesbians and gay men. In R. P. Cabaj & T. S. Stein (Eds.), *Textbook of homosexuality and mental health* (pp. 881–896). Washington, DC: American Psychiatric Press.

Hampton, B. R., & Gottlieb, M. C. (1997, this volume).

Keith-Spiegel, P., & Koocher, G. P. (1985). *Ethics in psychology: Professional standards and cases.* New York: Random House.

L'Abate, L. (1992). Family psychology and family therapy: Comparisons and contrasts. *American Journal of Family Therapy, 20,* 3–12.

Laird, J., & Green, R. J. (Eds.). (1996). *Lesbians and gays in couples and families: A handbook for therapists.* San Francisco: Jossey-Bass.

Leonard, R., Curry, H., & Clifford, D. (1994). *A legal guide for lesbian and gay couples.* Berkeley, CA: Nolo.

Lewes, K. (1988). *The psychoanalytic theory of male homosexuality.* New York: Quartet.

Mahalik, J. R., Simi, N. L., & Van Ormer, E. A. (1996, August). Self-disclosure in feminist ethics and among ethical feminists. In M. Brabeck (Chair), *Feminist theory and ethics: Challenge and response to psychological practice.* Symposium conducted at the annual meeting of the American Psychological Association, Toronto, Canada.

Marsh, D. T. (1997, this volume).

Masters, R., & Johnson, V. (1980). *Ethical issues in sex therapy and research.* Boston: Little, Brown.

Masters, R., Johnson, V., & Kolodny, R. (1977). *Ethical issues in sex therapy and research.* Boston: Little, Brown.

McGoldrick, M., Giordano, J., & Pearce, J. K. (Eds.). (1996). *Ethnicity and family therapy.* New York: Guilford.

McGuire, J., Nieri, D., Abbott, D., Sheridan, K., & Fisher, F. (1995). Do Tarasoff principles apply in AIDS-related psychotherapy? Ethical decision making and the role of therapist homophobia and perceived client dangerousness. *Professional Psychology: Research and Practice, 26,* 608–611.

Murphy, B. C. (1991). Educating mental health professionals about gay and lesbian issues [Special issue]. *Journal of Homosexuality, 22*(3/4), 229–246.

National Gay & Lesbian Task Force Policy Institute. (1993). *Privacy project fact sheet.* Washington, DC: Author.

Patterson, C. J. (1995). Lesbian mothers, gay fathers, and their children. In A. R. D'Augelli & C. J. Patterson (Eds.), *Lesbian and gay identities over the lifespan: Psychological perspectives on personal, relational, and community processes* (pp. 262–290). New York: Oxford University Press.

Pope, K. S., & Morin, S. F. (1991). AIDS and HIV infection update: New research, ethical responsibilities, evolving legal frameworks, and published resources. In A. Keller & S. R. Heyman (Eds.), *Innovations in clinical practice: A source book* (Vol. 10, pp. 443–457). Sarasota, FL: Professional Resource Press.

Purcell, D. W., & Hicks, D. W. (1996). Institutional discrimination against lesbians, gay men, and bisexuals: The courts, legislature, and the military. In R. P. Cabaj & T. S. Stein (Eds.), *Textbook of homosexuality and mental health* (pp. 763–782). Washington, DC: American Psychiatric Press.

Rein, J. A. (1996). *AIDS-related disease: "Duty to warn/duty to protect."* Unpublished manuscript, Indiana University of Pennsylvania.

Rigby, D. N., & Sophie, J. (1990). Ethical issues and client sexual preference. In H. Lerman & N. Porter (Eds.), *Feminist ethics in psychotherapy* (pp. 165–175). New York: Springer.

Rubenstein, W. B. (1996). Lesbians, gay men and the law. In R. C. Savin-Williams & K. M. Cohen (Eds.), *The lives of lesbians, gays, and bisexuals: Children to adults* (pp. 331–343). New York: A New Press.

Savin-Williams, R. C., & Cohen, K. M. (Eds.). (1996). *The lives of lesbians, gays, and bisexuals: Children to adults.* Fort Worth, TX: Harcourt Brace.

Schlossberger, E., & Hecker, L. (1996). HIV and family therapists' duty to warn: A legal and ethical analysis. *Journal of Marital and Family Therapy, 22,* 7–40.

Scrivner, R. (1993). A next review of principles of psychologists and code of conduct. *The Family Psychologist, 10,* 20.

Scrivner, R. (1995, August). *Family therapy ethical issues in working with lesbians and gays.* Paper presented at the annual meeting of the American Psychological Association, New York.

Scrivner, R. (1996). Sexual orientation: A variable in all family research. *The Family Psychologist, 13,* 13–15.

Scrivner, R., & Eldridge, N. (1995). Lesbian and gay family psychology. In R. H. Mikesell, D.-D. Lusterman, & S. H. McDaniel (Eds.), *Integrating family therapy: Handbook of family psychology and systems theory* (pp. 327–345). Washington, DC: American Psychological Association.

Sobocinski, M. R. (1990). Ethical principles in the counseling of gay and lesbian adolescents: Issues of autonomy, competence, and confidentiality. *Professional Psychology: Research and Practice, 21,* 240–247.

Sohier, R. (1993). Filial reconstruction: A theory of development through adversity. *Qualitative Health Research, 3,* 465–492.

Walker, G. (1991). *In the midst of winter: Systemic therapy with families, couples, and individuals with AIDS infection.* New York: W. W. Norton.

Watkins, S. A. (1979). Confidentiality: An ethical and legal connection for family therapists. *American Journal of Family Therapy, 17,* 291–302.

Wilcoxon, A., & Fennell, D. (1986). Linear and paradoxical letters to the nonattending spouse: A comparison of engagement rates. *Journal of Marital and Family Therapy, 12,* 191–193.

Organizations

American Psychological Association Committee on Lesbian, Gay, and Bisexual Concerns, 750 First Street, NE, Washington, DC 20002. (202) 336-5500.

Children of Lesbians and Gays Everywhere (COLAGE), 2300 Market St., Box 165, San Francisco, CA 94114. Tel: (415) 861-KIDS; Fax: (415) 255-8345; e-mail: kidsofgays@aol.com.

Gay and Lesbian Parents Coalition International (GLPCI), P. O. Box 43206, Montclair, NJ 07043. (201) 783-6204.

National Gay and Lesbian Task Force, 1734 14th Street, NW, Washington, DC 20009. (202) 332-6483.

Parents, Families, and Friends of Lesbians and Gays (PFLAG), 1101 14th St., N.W., Suite 1030, Washington, DC 20005. (202) 638-4200.

CHAPTER 9

Professional and Ethical Issues in Family-School Mental Health Interventions

JOHN P. QUIRK

P ublic education was first required to meet the educational needs of emotionally disordered children with the passage of Federal Law 94-142. Special education services, along with parent participation in program planning, were mandated for all exceptional children. Parents, for the first time, became active partners in educational decision making. The focus of school programs for these children has been primarily educational.

Involvement of the public schools in the prevention and treatment of drug and alcohol abuse established student mental health as a legitimate concern for regular education. In a national survey on attitudes toward schools, student drug abuse was seen as the most important problem facing schools (Reitz, 1987). These survey findings confirmed the need for the federal and states' commitment to the funding of school-based drug prevention programs for youth. A number of states, including Pennsylvania, adopted statewide K–12 drug and alcohol prevention programs.

A student assistance program (SAP) was also adopted in Pennsylvania to identify secondary students at risk for substance abuse. More recently, the focus of the SAP teams has been broadened to include students at risk for depression and suicide. As these programs have taken root, mental health activities have grown and mental health professionals have established a presence in the public schools. Mental health has become a concern of regular education as well as special education.

With the greater emphasis on mental health and awareness of the family's impact on the educational process, a whole new set of ethical and professional issues arise for those practicing in an educational setting or with school-related problems of children. The new roles and activities spawned by a family/school-focused approach bring into question the adequacy of the training and experience of both educators and mental health professionals. With parents being the targets and the consumers of school-related mental health services, the issue of advocacy—who is the client—can become blurred for the professional. As family and parental information is collected as part of a psychoeducational assessment or is discussed in staff meetings, the issues of confidentiality and the proper use of this sensitive data become a concern.

A systems model, when applied to the schools, changes the relationship of mental health professionals to both teachers and parents in ways that can jeopardize the assurance of a right to privacy, full disclosure, and informed consent. As more people are considered part of the problem as well as part of the solution, relationships can get complicated. Interventions based on systems thinking may threaten ethical guidelines in any setting, but are particularly at issue in schools where role relationships are more traditionally defined.

Ethical and professional issues may impact practitioners differently, depending on the mental health role they play in the schools. External consultants, such as private practice psychologists or counselors assigned by a mental health agency, may view their relationship with the school and parents differently than educational specialists, such as school psychologists or special educators. A family/parent-focused intervention can also make some issues, such as advocacy or confidentiality, more problematic than when the target is purely educational.

Parent-school consultation on a one-to-one basis is a much different process than the team problem-solving approaches commonly used to address behavior difficulties of students today. The legal mandate that parents be involved in educational decision making can lead to disputes that may require a parent-school mediational approach. Direct service to parents or families in the form of parent education or family therapy may have a place in a school setting, but traditional roles and expected parent-school relationships can significantly change as a result of these interventions.

Finally, mental health services in the schools must be viewed in a different light, depending on whether the focus of assessment and treatment is on the child alone or includes the parents and teachers as well. From a family-systems perspective, all individuals within the system are legitimate targets for change, even though in schools, there may be a reluctance on the part of adults to see themselves as part of the problem.

In the remainder of the chapter, I will discuss these issues and their implications for family practice within the schools.

Mental Health Consultants: Professional Training and Experiences

All psychologists know that ethical guidelines require them to limit their practice to areas in which they have received proper training. Unfortunately, what constitutes sufficient training is not clearly defined and is left to the discretion of institutions and the professionals providing service. In a survey of family-oriented practices in the schools, Carlson and Sincavage (1987) found that only 52 percent of school psychologists questioned had received specific training in parent-family interventions. The type of training varied from formal coursework to internship experiences and continuing education workshops.

As schools expand their involvement with parents and families, other educators, usually with less training in family work than school psychologists, are asked to participate in prereferral group activities that can focus on mental health and family-related problems. Several weeks of continuing education is seen by state and local educational administrators as sufficient to allow teachers to assess and make recommendations for addressing complex mental health and family problems. Adolescents and their families thought to be at risk for suicide or drug and alcohol abuse are identified and referred for service by groups of educators who have a minimal level of training and experience.

Based on a few guidelines for behavior that suggest risk, a team of teachers and administrators process information provided by other teachers, students, and sometimes parents in order to assess the possibility that a student is involved in substance abuse. The fact that their services are offered in groups may provide some protection against ill-advised decisions, but may also increase the probability that the evaluation and recommendations made will be at a superficial level that matches the minimal training of the participants.

INTERNAL VERSUS EXTERNAL MENTAL HEALTH CONSULTANTS

Many mental health professionals and private practitioners working with families or children include academic-related issues as part of their treatment focus. They may be in contact with the schools on a contractual basis through a mental health agency or consult periodically as private practitioners on behalf of a family. In either case, they may attempt to recommend changes in classroom procedures without having any formal training in teaching methodology or exposure to the complex environment of schools. Limited experience within schools may make them unaware of the need to take seriously certain "sacrosanct" procedures in order to insure that a school-based intervention will be accepted. For example, most teachers will not pass high school students who will not complete homework assignments even though they may have mastered the material.

Differences in training and experience can influence the expectations of external consultants as to the kinds of interventions that will be acceptable to schools. The primary goals of schools center on academic attainment, not mental health or family issues. Academic achievement and family stability often go hand in hand, but there are times when the needs or desires of a family are in direct conflict with school policy or the professional views of the teacher. The teachers' right to make the final decision as to what goes on in their classroom gets pitted against the parents' rights regarding what is in the best interest of the child. Private practitioners consulting with schools may inflame an already adversarial relationship with teachers because of a lack of sensitivity to the needs of the school. This may happen because of a lack of exposure to schools but may also be due to negative stereotypes of teachers held by some professionals. It is difficult under these conditions to take a balanced view.

Unlike clinics, schools have multiple constituents to satisfy. Maintaining group cohesion in a classroom, supporting teachers, preserving professional integrity, meeting the educational needs of the other children, and providing these services in a cost-effective way to the community are all goals that may compete with the needs of an individual child. Thus, accepting suggestions for instructional or programmatic adjustments does not just hinge on their appropriateness for a young child, but on how well they fit the needs of the teacher and the other children as well.

External consultants, ideally, can choose whether to engage in a consultative relationship with a school based on an estimate of their shared values with the institution (Schien, 1969). Once they make a commitment to consult, however, they are ethically required to accept the superintendent of schools as the final authority in making decisions and as the primary interpreter of agency goals (Gallessich, 1982). When the external consultant is a private practitioner being paid by parents rather than the school, a conflict in regard to these ethical guidelines can easily occur.

Conversely, as internal consultants—school psychologists or special educators— may find it difficult to see the legitimacy of parents participating as equals in educational decision making for their child. When deciding which point of view or which set of needs should be most influential in making an educational decision, educators often respond first to the more immediate needs of the school, the classroom, or the child, leaving the family's concerns a distant fourth.

It is easier to blame the parents for the problems of a child than to make them active participants in the solution. Parents viewed as culprits have a reduced status in the decision-making process. When schools only invite parents to participate in problem-solving meetings to comply with state and federal mandates, their full inclusion may be seen as an intrusion into the school's sphere of influence. Teachers sometimes view the activities and skills necessary to include and accommodate parent's needs as an unwanted additional professional burden.

Doherty and Colangelo (1984) suggest that schools make a fundamental error when they view problem behavior in children and the uncooperativeness of their parents as primarily an issue of control. Who has the legitimate right to make decisions obscures the real issue: the full inclusion of parents in the problem-solving process. Inclusion is defined here as the collaborative organization and bonding of constituent groups within the school setting. When there is a feeling of interpersonal connectedness between parents and schools, the concern about control tends to be diminished and collaboration becomes a possibility.

Establishing a sense of connectedness is not easily done during a time of crisis. Weiss and Edwards (1992) found that establishing a collaborative problem-solving relationship after a child has been referred for a problem is sometimes difficult. Therefore, they support the development of schoolwide programs of climate-building activities to enhance family-school relations for all children. Starting in kindergarten, parents can be actively encouraged to participate in the educational process. Thus, when problems arise, a trusting, familiar relationship already exists between teachers and parents that allows for more open collaboration. When educators understand that parent collaboration will ultimately make their jobs easier, they will fully embrace parental participation.

Advocacy: Who Is the Client?

Child advocacy is ingrained in the professional ethics of the mental health and education professions. Putting the needs and welfare of the child as the first priority is an essential guide to practice. Too often, educators and sometimes clinicians turn this strong sense of advocacy into a search for a scapegoat to explain the etiology of the problem or its resistance to treatment. Why won't this child learn or behave in my classroom? Why can't I promote change therapeutically? It is difficult for many professionals to explain their frustrations away without an explanation external to the child or themselves. Looking for external attributions for failure is normal. Schools and parents can become easy targets. Child advocacy then becomes the rationale to allow blaming to occur.

How can we handle child advocacy in a constructive fashion? Ecosystem theory could provide part of the solution. If we believe that behavior is a product of the reciprocal interaction of systems and people within these systems, advocacy in its traditional form may not be appropriate. In systems thinking, all parties are part of the problem as well as part of the solution. Making the system more functional may become the primary target of treatment, rather than a particular individual or group. Advocacy then becomes a sensitivity to and consideration of a broad range of people and organizational concerns that will probably result in the best outcome for the child.

A complicating variable to this broader definition of advocacy may be the employer-employee relationship of the educational specialist and fee-for-service relationship of the private practitioner. In both cases, specialists or clinicians may feel pressure to exclusively represent the interests of their constituency to the detriment of creating a climate of compromise. Instead, they need to be skilled in communicating to the parents or educators involved the benefits derived from a nonadversarial relationship with the other parts of the system. If the needs of all parties can be met to some degree, the outcome for the child will surely be better. Entrenched suspicions and negative expectations can become established in some family-school relationships that defy even the most deft clinical management. However, professionals need to resist being co-opted by clients or colleagues into generalizing from a few intractable family-school relationships to other families they serve.

Advocacy, Consultation, or Mediation

When the family-school relations are strained, the mental health professional may need to adopt the role of mediator for conflict resolution. Conflicts between parents and schools, particularly when special education is involved, are usually solved through due process procedures. Unfortunately, when this happens, one side generally ends up feeling like the winner and the other party like the loser, depending on the outcome of the hearing. A more helpful approach might be for the mental health professional to recognize the strained relationship early in the process and switch from a consultation-advocacy role to a mediational approach.

Mediation has become a popular strategy to resolve conflicts between students (Umbreit, 1991); between parents and students (Stern, Van Slyck, & Newland, 1992); and on occasion, between parents and schools (Hogan, 1990). The latter use of mediation may not receive as much attention because of the assumption that due process will ultimately resolve differences. But earlier conflict resolution would be more cost-effective and would strengthen long-term family-school relationships. Mediation strategies are designed to encourage win-win outcomes when resolving conflicts.

Following the simple guidelines suggested by Fisher and Ury (1991), the mental health consultant or educational specialist can begin by encouraging the separation of the people from the problem. By understanding and explicitly acknowledging differences in perceptions and emotions of school staff and parents, more open, solution-oriented communication can begin. Identifying shared interests or outcomes can be more productive than immediately focusing on solutions or programmatic differences. Generating options that in the spirit of compromise allow for meeting shared interests, as well as some individual concerns, should become the focus of problem solving.

The way Fisher and Ury (1991) recommend that mediation goals be evaluated may be difficult to apply to mental health or educational problems. The use of objective criteria for evaluating the success of a mediated solution, although desirable when engaging in behavior change strategies, may not always be possible, particularly in the short-term. Sometimes the most productive outcomes of family-school problem solving are enhanced feelings of mutual support and a sense of being able to cope better with the child's problem behaviors. These feelings do not always lend themselves to objective measurement.

The school psychologist, as an internal consultant on the mental health and behavior problems of children, can find the task of supporting parental involvement in team problem-solving meetings difficult. These meetings, which may include four or more educators, can be an intimidating experience for parents. How can they truly express how they feel? How can they openly disagree with a formidable group of professionals? Under these circumstances, the school psychologist needs to adopt the role of ombudsperson. Working to establish a relationship with parents prior to this meeting, then taking a supportive role in allowing parents full participation can offset the sense of intimidation they experience. Conflict mediation skills can also be very helpful under these circumstances.

Systems Theory, Mental Health Consultation, and Informed Consent

Mental health consultation, as originally proposed by Caplan (1970), underscores the need for a collaborative relationship and co-equal status between a consultant and consultee. Each party is seen as having some expertise to contribute to solving the problem. A good consultative relationship is considered to be the catalyst for eliciting and applying this expertise effectively. In this type of client-centered case consultation in the schools, the consultant works with the consultee to solve the problems of the child. The teachers and parents collaborate, with the help of the consultant, to design a program that meets the needs of the child. It is assumed that the solution for one child will be generalized and applied to other children when similar problems arise.

The ecosystemic consultation model, however, broadens the focus of treatment to include all members of the child's subsystems, both home and school. Parents and teachers now are viewed potentially as part of the problem. As targets of assessment and treatment, the parents and teachers can no longer fully maintain a co-equal status with a school psychologist or mental health professional. In school settings, both parents and teachers do not usually assume that they will be the target of treatment when they make a referral for a child. They see the problem as being within the child. By assuming the problem to be child-centered, parents and teachers enter the consultative relationship unaware that their role may fluctuate from collaborative partner to dysfunctional client during the course of the consultation. This kind of shifting relationship in parent and teacher consultations can have some ethical and professional implications (Quirk, Fine, & Roberts, 1992). During an ecosystemic consultation, requirements of full disclosure and informed consent to treatment may not be fully met.

The legal standard for informed consent was, for many years, the disclosure of that information normally disclosed by other professionals using the same type of treatment (*Natanson v. Kline*, 1960). However, the more recent interpretation has been the "reasonable patient or client" standard. This standard requires that disclosure of information concerning treatment should be sufficient for a reasonable client to make an informed decision about participation in treatment (*Canterbury v. Spence*, 1972). Basing the standard on reasonable parent-teacher judgment reduces the latitude of the clinician and forces greater openness.

To meet the criterion for informed consent, the consent must be voluntary, knowing, and competent (Brakal, Parry, & Weuner, 1985). When the referral of a problem child originates at a family clinic or in private practice, parents often assume that they may be the target of treatment as well as their child. The criterion of voluntary involvement and awareness of their status in the therapeutic relationship is usually met. In schools, this may not be the case. Parents do not usually come to public schools for the purpose of getting mental health services for themselves or their families. Their inclusion as targets of assessment or treatment may not be wanted.

Schools often put subtle and, in some cases, extreme pressure on parents to participate in an intervention with their child. Talk about retention, suspension, or court action is sometimes used to get parents to cooperate. Parents do not feel they can withdraw from participation easily without negative consequences for their child. The voluntary criterion of informed consent may also be compromised in that parents must work with the professionals assigned to the school where their child is located. If there is an interpersonal incompatibility between the family and the school personnel, the possibility of shifting to other staff members is usually not considered.

The voluntary participation of parents in school interventions could be enhanced if the impact of school difficulties and handicapping conditions on the emotional life of parents and families were openly discussed by educational staff. The family's reaction to and ability to cope with their child's school-based problems are not addressed in most multidisciplinary evaluations. Feedback of test results is still given in some school districts by telephone or through a mailed psychological report. Emotions are rarely discussed comfortably in parent-school consultations.

Parents are assumed to have the same objectivity as the educator. It is only when parents react negatively to school consultations that school-based professionals begin to consider relational issues. At that point it may be too late to remove the bad taste left by the negative early contacts. To openly recognize a parent's pain over his or her child's problem may be one of the best ways to solidify a collaborative relationship. Parents who feel understood are far less likely to resist the school's ideas as to the best educational plan for their child.

Full disclosure and informed consent can be even more problematic when teachers' behavior or personality variables are part of the problem. Teachers, even more than parents, resist being seen as part of the referred child's problem. They hold firmly to the concept that a child's problem is within the child or his or her family. The reciprocal nature of relationships and their effects on behavior may not be fully understood or accepted. In team meetings, even when educational colleagues recognize the part a teacher is playing in a child's problem, staff cohesion may prevent this issue from being addressed openly. Behavior problems are discussed while ignoring the significance of a teacher's functioning within the classroom, or efforts are made to change the teacher's behaviors without ever indicating that they are part of the problem. It is important to note that in an open discussion of the problem, blame should not occur, because being part of a dysfunctional system does not mean that a person is the primary cause of the problem (Quirk, 1992).

Some clinicians suggest that not being fully open as to the techniques or process of a systems intervention can be justified as long as client agreed-upon goals are achieved in a reasonable period of time (Haley, 1976; Papp, 1984). In the case of a school-based program, the teacher agreed-upon goal would be improved functioning of the child in the classroom. Hughes (1986), however, sees deceptive techniques as highly manipulative and not consistent with the collaborative relationship of consultation. Because open discussion of the teacher's part in the problem may arouse enough resistance to undermine the overall intervention, the use of nonblaming reframes to increase the willingness of people to participate becomes essential (Alexander & Parsons, 1982). But there is a fine line between therapeutic reframing and outright deception that should be considered.

Families, Mental Health Problems, and Rights of Privacy

The extension of the school-based practitioner's role into mental health and family issues requires him or her to consider the rights of privacy of those involved. When parents refer a child for help in school, they assume the focus of assessment and treatment will be educationally oriented. They may be willing to participate in the process to the extent that they contribute information about the child. They may be reluctant to have the assessment go beyond what they see as educationally relevant factors at home. Are the parents' marital problems, although impacting the child's functioning in school, legitimate topics of discussion? Do parents have the right to limit the range of issues that are considered as part of an assessment without being seen as defensive or uncooperative? The school-based practitioner does not have the right to use the coercive power of the school to get a parent to accept a broader definition of the problem (Quirk, 1992).

Respecting the client's right of privacy, whether parent or child, should mean allowing them to choose the level at which they feel comfortable in dealing with the problem. Practitioners functioning from a systems perspective need to be willing to restrict the range of their focus to the concerns of the client. It is appropriate to gently support the connections between family dysfunction and school problems; but if further discussion is avoided, the practitioner should be prepared to follow the lead of the parents. A parent's desire to limit intrusion into family affairs should not negatively color the practitioner's perceptions of the parent's desire to get the child's problem solved (Quirk, 1992).

Most of the information obtained about family dynamics as a part of school-based assessment is done through individual interviews of parents or children. The informality of this kind of assessment can allow for the collection of sensitive information in a judicious, supportive way. The lack of structure, however, may compromise the reliability, validity, and completeness of the data obtained. In community-based settings, family self-report questionnaires are commonly used as a cost-effective way of collecting comprehensive family information. These instruments could also be a time-efficient way of collecting family data in schools. At the same time, a questionnaire might be a more comfortable approach for collecting sensitive information from parents participating on problem-solving teams.

Brassard (1986) describes a comprehensive family assessment strategy that is appropriate for personality and behavior problems of children and adolescents. In addition to interviewing, she suggests a wide range of techniques for collecting demographic and interactional patterns of families. The techniques and instruments suggested, however, have all been developed in clinic settings. The issues covered and the questions included on these self-report measures were not designed to show direct relevance to educational problems or to be sensitive to the desire for privacy of parents. Parents can easily be offended when they do not see the connection between their child's problem and the information they are asked to divulge.

There is a clear need for parent-sensitive, educationally relevant, family assessment instruments. Quirk (1992) and Yesseldyke and Christenson (1993) developed self-report measures and a structured interview, respectively, that elicit family information directly relevant to school achievement. Based on a review of research literature, questions about a parent's attitude toward education, parent-child relations, and family activities that support school achievement are included to varying degrees on both instruments. The content has clear relevance to the educational success of the child but also gives the school-based practitioner an opportunity to explore overall family functioning. Once again, however, the practitioner must be sensitive to a parent's resistance to probes that go beyond educational concerns and must adjust the focus accordingly.

Confidentiality of Information in School Settings

Working with mental health problems and family issues in school settings has created a new set of ethical demands for educators. Since the passage of the Family Educational Rights and Privacy Act of 1974, school systems have developed detailed guidelines for managing written information and student files. The kinds of information that can be recorded and who has access to it has been clearly codified. But orally shared information is more difficult to control. Discussion of family and parent information can occur in many forums, some formal and others informal.

Sensitive information about student behavior also becomes more of a concern when a mental health focus is taken. Unlike mental health professionals, educators do not have a strong emphasis on the need for confidentiality as part of their preservice training. Educational problems of children are routinely shared in formal meetings and informally in the teachers' lounge as well. Student behavior is a collective concern of the entire faculty. As parent and family information is included in assessments and interventions, the rules governing the sharing of information must change. The potential for breaches of confidentiality and the political fallout that may ensue for a school district are increased if educators do not adjust to the new reality of a family orientation.

When mental health and behavior problems of students were handled individually by school psychologists or guidance counselors, there were far fewer risks to confidential information. But as team approaches to problem solving have become the norm, the number and types of school staff who have access to sensitive information increases dramatically. What kind of family information should be part of a multidisciplinary team meeting? Are the kinds of family issues discussed at team meetings different when the parents are in attendance? Do all staff have the training needed to address and discuss family issues in a professional manner rather than in the form of gossip? Should some kinds of information be withheld from team discussions? Can a school-based team be expected to collaboratively problem solve if they do not have full access to relevant information?

The standard of confidentiality developed by the American Psychological Association (APA) in its *Ethical Principles of Psychologists and Code of Conduct* (APA, 1992) suggests that psychologists have a primary obligation to respect the confidentiality of information obtained from persons in the course of their work as psychologists. Strict rules for obtaining a release prior to discussing confidential information is routinely followed in most clinic settings. Sharing information with other members of a treatment team within the clinic is common practice, because all clinic team members have the primary goal of treating the mental health problem of the family and are well versed in the need for confidentiality. But in the public schools, multidisciplinary team members, like teachers and administrators, may have multiple relationships with parents.

As previously discussed, teachers can be viewed as part of the problem as well as part of the treatment team. Parents must interact with principals and teachers on other nonproblem issues or in relation to other children they may have enrolled in the same school. Schools serve multiple functions for families, providing educational, recreational, and personal growth experiences for children and parents. The parent's relationship with team members is unlikely to be exclusively tied to his or her child's problem. Safeguarding these other relationships from the effects of embarrassing or pejorative information is essential.

This lack of clarity in role relationships confounds the principles of confidentiality and may require the psychologist to filter what is disclosed at a team meeting. As stated in *Principles for Professional Ethics* (National Association of School Psychologists, 1995), "school psychologists discuss confidential information only for professional purposes and only with persons who have a legitimate need to know" (pp. 1143–1154). In group settings, the psychologist may be required to make judgments about the appropriateness of discussing particular family information, depending on who is attending the meeting. This may not always be possible because other members of the team may have access to sensitive information and spontaneously bring it forward.

In addition to limiting the kinds of family information introduced into team meetings to only what is essential to constructively address the problem, psychologists and other practitioners should be sensitive to the need to describe parent behavior in the most positive way possible. Reframed descriptions of family behavior that make its members appear to be well-intentioned victims of circumstances should be the guideline when discussing family activities (Alexander & Parsons, 1982).

There may be no one solution to the problem of confidentiality of sensitive mental health and family information in the schools. Developing a school or district-wide policy on the kinds of information that should be collected and with whom it can be shared on a need-to-know basis may be a first step in protecting the confidentiality of oral communication. Unfortunately, school administrators tend to be very cautious when writing procedural guidelines with legal implications. Restrictive guidelines developed by administrators could hamper efforts to provide quality services to families.

A second step might be to involve the entire educational and administrative staff in an inservice program on mental health and family issues with a strong component on confidentiality of information. Such inservice training must be ongoing if it is to have any long-term impact on behavior.

A third strategy for protecting parents and families would be to make a shift in the orientation of those professionals discussing families from the traditional pathology-focused approach to a family needs and resources model (Quirk, 1992). Identifying family needs and the resources necessary to meet those needs can be a positive approach to helping families cope with children's problems (Dunst, Trivette, & Deal, 1994). Recognizing that even severely problematic families have strengths that can be enhanced and used to support a school-based intervention takes the emphasis off what's wrong with the family and redirects the conversation toward providing support in an empowering relationship.

Confidentiality and Family Treatment in the Public Schools

Extending the concern for mental health and family functioning to the public schools ultimately leads to questions about whether treatment for parenting and family problems should be undertaken in educational settings. There is evidence that recommendations for family counseling outside of school are the least likely to be followed by parents (Conti, 1975). Having therapeutic treatment offered as part of school programming could encourage more parents to participate. In rural communities, the school psychologist may be the most highly trained mental health professional available. Opportunities for quality mental health services from community agencies may be limited or available only with great inconvenience to parents. Under these circumstances, it would seem reasonable for schools to provide therapeutic services to parents and families.

Schools have offered parenting education in a wide variety of models and formats for many years. These formats can include providing child management ideas, group discussion, sharing of parenting experiences, and some skill-building activities (Fine, 1980). In some schools, the emphasis is on providing general information and parent-child interaction strategies that may be found in many of the popular prepackaged parent education programs. Under these circumstances, the risk of self-disclosure by parents and threats to confidentiality of information are minimal. However, the effectiveness of these approaches in terms of behavior change has not been well documented (Kramer, 1990). The evidence suggests that these programs can empower parents to feel more competent, which may be viewed as an equally valuable outcome.

Based on an expanding database, the most effective way to promote change is the use of parent-training strategies that are adapted to meet the needs of a particular family (Kramer, 1990). Given the workloads of both school psychologists and rural community mental health workers, time to provide parent training is at a premium (Carlson & Sincavage, 1987; Childs & Melton, 1983). Cost-effective therapy services within a school setting will probably require a group treatment approach. The application of parent-training strategies to the individual needs of families in a group format requires the disclosure and discussion of sensitive personal family information. Behavioral models, such as those described by Forehand and McMahon (1981) and by Barkley (1987) also suggest the importance of direct practice of management skills by parents with their children in the presence of the trainer. Here again, children's and parents' privacy can be jeopardized if these activities are carried out in a group. The relationships of families and schools, particularly in rural areas, are intertwined in varied ways and can involve long-standing multigenerational family connections. Maintaining anonymity or confidentiality of information shared in a group is not easily achieved under these circumstances.

As with any group format, procedures involving sensitive information, confidentiality, and the protection of privacy cannot be assumed. Parents, as well as school professionals, need to be continuously trained and reminded of the importance of treating sensitive information appropriately. What constitutes sensitive information, when and with whom it can be discussed, and the legal and personal impact of wrongful disclosure must be continuously emphasized within the group. As with other ethical standards, the issue of confidentiality in practice is never clear-cut. Professional judgment always comes into play (Parsons, 1996).

Summary and Conclusion

Whenever a new role is introduced into a traditional institution like the public schools, changes in people's relationships and professional behavior will require the re-examination of the ethical standards that guide practice. Increased school involvement with the behavioral and emotional problems of students and their families bring mental health professionals into the schools who may have a different frame of reference and dissimilar training than the teachers and administrators with whom they need to collaborate. Group problem solving, family systems thinking, and in-school family treatment strategies add complexity to the way staff, parents, and consultants work together and share sensitive information.

The impact of these changes suggests that even with good ethical intentions, a course of action may not always be clear in some situations. We need to recognize that, although some ethical obligations are mandatory, other guidelines are aspirational (Woody, LaVoie, & Epps, 1992). That is, in some situations, the code of ethics dictates behavior that if, violated, will lead to legal or professional sanctions. At other times, ethical guidelines help practitioners strive for a level of excellence in providing service. Given the multiple functions schools serve, the most desirable handling of all ethical risks and dilemmas may not be achievable.

Whether ethical guidelines provide a floor or ceiling for professional practice, an ongoing review of how they need to be interpreted in light of changing circumstances is essential. It cannot be assumed that everyone involved in addressing mental health problems in schools is aware of appropriate ethical guidelines or sees how they impact the provision of services to students and families. In their broadest sense, codes of ethics should not simply be viewed as guidelines to protect us from legal action, but rather as a way to structure relationships that will promote trust and confidence on the part of the people that we serve and to meet their needs more effectively.

References

Alexander, J., & Parsons, B. V. (1982). *Functional family therapy.* Monterey: Brooks/Cole.

American Psychological Association. (1992). Ethical principles of psychologists and code of conduct. *American Psychologist, 47,* 1597–1611.

Barkley, R. A. (1987). *Defiant children: A clinician's manual for parent training.* New York: Guilford.

Brakal, S. J., Parry, J., & Weuner, B. A. (1985). *The mentally disabled and the law.* Chicago: American Bar Foundation.

Brassard, M. R. (1986). Family assessment approaches and procedures. In H. M. Knoff (Ed.), *The assessment of child and adolescent personality* (pp. 399–449). New York: Guilford.

Canterbury v. Spence, 464 F. 2d 772 (D.C. Cir 1972).

Caplan, G. (1970). *The theory and practice of mental health consultation.* New York: Basic Books.

Carlson, C. I., & Sincavage, J. M. (1987). Family-oriented school psychology practice: Results of a national survey of the National Association of School Psychologists' members. *School Psychology Review, 16*(4), 519–526.

Childs, A. W., & Melton, G. B. (1983). *Rural psychology.* New York: Plenum.

Conti, A. P. (1975). Variables related to contacting/not contacting counseling services recommended by school psychologists. *Journal of School Psychology, 13,* 41–50.

Doherty, W. J., & Colangelo, N. (1984). The family FIRO model: A modest proposal for organizing family treatment. *Journal of Marital and Family Therapy, 10*, 19–29.

Dunst, C. J., Trivette, C. M., & Deal, A. G. (Eds.). (1994). *Supporting and strengthening families*. Cambridge, MA: Brookline Books.

Family Education Rights and Privacy Act, 20 U.S.C.A. Section 1239 with accompanying regulations set down in 45 C.F.R., part 99 (1974).

Fine, M. J. (1980). The parent education movement: An introduction. In M. J. Fine (Ed.), *Handbook of parent education* (pp. 3–26). New York: Academic Press.

Fisher, R., & Ury, W. (1991). *Getting to yes: Negotiating agreement without giving in*. New York: Penguin Books.

Forehand, R. L., & McMahon, R. J. (1981). *Helping the noncompliant child: A clinician's guide to parent training*. New York: Guilford.

Gallessich, J. (1982). *The profession and practice of consultation*. San Francisco: Jossey-Bass.

Haley, J. (1976). *Problem-solving therapy*. San Francisco: Jossey-Bass.

Hogan, J. (1990). Advocating for children: A parent's guide. *Journal of Reading, Writing, and Learning Disabilities International, 6*(1), 81–88.

Hughes, J. (1986). Ethical issues in school consultation. *School Psychology Review, 15*, 489–499.

Kramer, J. J. (1990). Training parents as behavior change agents: Successes, failures, and suggestions for school psychologists. In T. B. Guthen & C. R. Reynolds (Eds.), *The handbook of school psychology* (2nd ed., pp. 685–702). New York: Wiley.

Natanson v. Kline, 350 P. 2d 1093 (Kan 1960).

National Association of School Psychologists. (1995). Principles for professional ethics. In A. Thomas & J. Grimes (Eds.), *Best practices in school psychology III* (pp. 1143–1154). Washington, DC: Author.

Papp, P. (1984). The treatment of a child's underachievement in school using a paradoxical approach with the family. In C. E. Schaefer, J. M. Briemeister, & M. E. Fitton (Eds.), *Family therapy techniques for problem behaviors of children and teenagers* (pp. 19–22). San Francisco: Jossey-Bass.

Parsons, R. D. (1996). *The skilled consultant: A systematic approach to the theory and practice of consultation*. Boston: Allyn & Bacon.

Quirk, J. P. (1992, March). *Assessing the family's role in a child's underachievement*. Paper presented at the meeting of the National Association of School Psychologists, Nashville, TN.

Quirk, J. P., Fine, M. J., & Roberts, L. (1992). Professional and ethical issues and problems in family-school systems interventions. In M. J. Fine & C. Carlson (Eds.), *The handbook of family-school intervention: A systems perspective* (pp. 414–427). Boston: Allyn & Bacon.

Reitz, R. (1987). *Drug abuse*. Bloomington, IN: Center on Evaluation, Development, Research.

Schein, E. H. (1969). *Process consultation: Its role in organization development.* Reading, MA: Addison-Wesley.

Stern, M., Van Slyck, M. R., & Newland, L. M. (1992). Adolescent development and family dynamics: Delineating a knowledge base for family mediation. *Mediation Quarterly, 9*(4), 307–322.

Umbreit, M. S. (1991). Mediation of youth conflict: A multi-systems perspective. *Child and Adolescent Social Work Journal, 8*(2), 141–153.

Weiss, H. M., & Edwards, M. E. (1992) The family-school collaboration project: Systems interventions for school improvement. In S. L. Christenson & J. C. Conoly (Eds.), *Home-school collaboration: Enhancing children's academic and social competence* (pp. 215–243). Silver Spring, MD: National Association of School Psychologists.

Woody, R. H., LaVoie, J. C., & Epps, S. (1992). *School psychology: A developmental and social systems approach.* Boston: Allyn & Bacon.

Yesseldyke, J., & Christenson, S. (1993). *The instructional environment system: 2. A system to identify a student's instructional needs.* Longmont, CO: Sopris West.

PART THREE

Current Topics in Professional Practice

CHAPTER 10

Ethical Issues in Child Maltreatment

PEARL S. BERMAN

Anational incidence study done in 1986 reported that more than one million children in the United States had been injured as a result of maltreatment and that half a million more were estimated to be at risk for maltreatment. That year, 1,100 children died as a result of confirmed cases of abuse or neglect (U.S. Department of Health and Human Services, 1988).

On a statewide level in Pennsylvania, in 1993, 9 out of every 1,000 children were reported as victims of suspected abuse. Of these reports, 7,814 cases of abuse were substantiated. A total of 54 children died as a result of substantiated abuse (Pennsylvania Department of Public Welfare, 1993).

In an attempt to protect the welfare of children through early intervention, mandatory state reporting laws were passed. Although professionals working with children are in agreement on the need to prevent child abuse, research indicates that large numbers of clinicians either do not understand the need to report or they comply inconsistently with reporting laws (Brosig & Kalichman, 1992a, 1992b).

In this chapter, I provide guidance to clinicians for interfacing mandatory reporting into good clinical practice. First, as an example of how practitioners can come to fully understand the mandatory reporting laws of their state, I offer a detailed analysis of the Child Protective Service Law in Pennsylvania, Title 23 PA C.S.A. Chapter 63 as amended by Act 151 of 1994. Second, case examples are presented to illustrate how ethical dilemmas that arise in therapy with maltreating families can be resolved ethically and effectively.

All the names and family configurations have been altered within the case examples to protect the confidentiality of the families.

Analysis of Pennsylvania's Child Protective Service Law

WHAT IS THE LAW CONCERNING MANDATED REPORTING?

The law regarding mandated reporting consists of three components: (1) the statute as enacted by the legislature: Child Protective Service Law (CPSL); (2) the Child Protective Services Regulations promulgated by the Department of Welfare; and, (3) any case law involving either the CPSL or the regulations. Case law refers to how court cases have interpreted the CPSL and regulations when these have been cited in court cases. The CPSL was designed to provide general guidelines on reporting. The Regulations are intended to provide further clarification on how to implement the CPSL. CPSL and its accompanying regulations are always open to changes in interpretation based on case law.

To understand the law in your state, some important legal terms must be defined. If the word *shall* occurs in the wording of the law, it means you must do it. There is a legal duty to do it and if it is not done, there is legal liability. If the word *may* occurs in the wording of the law, it means there is a choice or discretion about what can be done, depending on professional judgment.

Professionals should obtain copies of the laws and regulations of their states and become part of mailing lists, such as the bulletins put out by the Pennsylvania Department of Human Services, that will provide them with updates on any case law reinterpretations and explanations of the law.

WHAT SHOULD BE REPORTED TO CHILD PROTECTIVE SERVICES (CPS)?

CPS is mandated to investigate serious injury inflicted by someone who is in a *caretaking role* for someone who is less than 18 years old. A caretaking role can be taken by a parent, paramour, person residing in the same home, or person responsible for the child's welfare. A serious injury can be physical, sexual, or mental and can be the result of acts or omissions by a caretaker. Serious physical neglect is also defined as child abuse. A physical injury must have occurred within the last two years to be covered under the law. There is no time limit for the reporting of sexual abuse. The initial report of abuse should be made to the Department of Public Welfare's ChildLine and Abuse Registry (800-932-0313). ChildLine will then contact the CPS agency that has local jurisdiction to investigate the report. Reports can also be made directly to a local CPS; the local CPS will then forward the information to ChildLine.

WHAT SHOULD BE REPORTED TO THE POLICE?

If an abuser is not in a caretaking role, abuse should be reported to the police. One area of confusion for clinicians is how to determine when a relative not living in the home is considered a caretaker. A grandfather who babysits every weekend is a caretaker. Thus, if child abuse occurs, this should be reported to CPS. However, a grandfather who abused his grandchildren on a visit is not considered a caretaker. This grandfather has committed a violation of *criminal law,* not *child protective service law.* Thus, the report should be made to the police, not to CPS.

A pedophile not living in the *home* and not related to the *child* should always be reported to the police, not CPS. The fact that a person is not a caretaker does not alleviate a professional's responsibility to take action; however, the action is to call the police, not CPS.

A second area of confusion for clinicians is sibling abuse. Siblings can be considered perpetrators of abuse if they are at least 14 years old. Sometimes CPS will consider the sibling in a caretaking role and sometimes they will not. If they determine the sibling is not a caretaker, a report can be made to the police if a parent or legal guardian wants to press charges.

A final area of confusion is if peer abuse should be reported to CPS. Peer abuse does not fall within the CPSL. However, it could be investigated by the police as a case of assault. Juvenile probation would determine if there was enough evidence to bring the case to court.

After making an oral report of suspected abuse, a written report (CY 47) is due within 48 hours to CPS. If an oral report is made directly to CPS, the CPS worker may collect all the information needed for CY 47 and thus a written report may be unnecessary.

If unsure about whether to report, consult with a CPS worker to aid in the decision. This has been found to increase reporting of appropriate cases and decrease unnecessary reporting (Brosig & Kalichman, 1992a, 1992b).

WHAT TYPE OF KNOWLEDGE OF ABUSE RESULTS IN A REPORT?

The section of the CPSL covering mandated reporters indicates that only direct knowledge of abuse results in a report. Pennsylvania case law supports the direct knowledge clause. The section of the CPSL code (Title 23 PA. C.S.A. Chapter 63, Subchapter B) is as follows:

6311. Persons required to report suspected child abuse.

(a) General rule.—Persons who, in the course of their employment, occupation or practice of their profession, come into contact with children shall report or cause a report to be made in accordance with section 6313 (relating to reporting procedure) when they have reason to believe, on the basis of their medical, professional or other training and experience, that a child coming before them in their professional or official capacity is an abused child. Except with respect to confidential communications made to an ordained member of the clergy which are protected under 42 Pa. C.S. 5943 (relating to confidential communication to clergymen) the privileged communication between any professional person required to report and the patient or client of that person shall not constitute grounds for failure to report as required by this chapter. (p. 6)

What about seemingly dangerous abuse that a professional learns about from a parent or other individual (heresay)? This moral dilemma is raised in states, such as Pennsylvania, requiring direct knowledge of abuse. The intent of the CPSL is to protect children through encouraging reporting (Section 6302, Subchapter A):

6302. Findings and purpose of chapter.

(a) Finding.—Abused children are in urgent need of an effective child protective service to prevent them from suffering further injury and impairment.

(b) Purpose.—It is the purpose of this chapter to encourage more complete reporting of suspected child abuse. (p. 1)

This intent seems at odds with the requirement for direct knowledge of the child. Heresay knowledge of abuse puts the professional in a moral dilemma. One resolution of this dilemma can be to file a report of suspected abuse as a nonmandated reporter, as this section of the law makes no discrimination between heresay and direct knowledge (Subchapter B):

6312. Persons permitted to report suspected child abuse.

In addition to those persons and officials required to report suspected child abuse, any person may make such a report if that person has reasonable cause to suspect that a child is an abused child. (p. 7)

A second, longer term resolution of this moral dilemma is to work toward improved wording of statutory reporting laws. Research suggests that clinicians base their reporting decisions on the wording of child protective statutes. Clinicians report suspected abuse less often when the statutes require them to see the child suspected of being abused. They report more frequently when the statutes only require a reasonable suspicion of abuse (Brosig & Kalichman, 1992b).

ARE MANDATED REPORTERS AT LEGAL RISK?

In the past 20 years, only three cases have been reported (published) that have had any connection to the CPSL. Both *Brozovich v. Circle C Group Homes, Inc.* (1988) and *Roman v. Appleby* (1983) concluded that the law requires professionals to immediately report suspected abuse and further stated that the urgency of prompt reporting is stressed throughout the law's provisions. In the third, *Fewell v. Besner* (1995), a mandated reporter was considered to have reported incorrectly, but was not held liable for this mistake in judgement.

WHAT IF THE ABUSE REPORTED IS UNFOUNDED?

Some practitioners fear that an improper report will put them in legal jeopardy. In Pennsylvania, there is no liability for following a legal mandate on reporting abuse if a mandated reporter is coming forward in good faith. A prosecutor/attorney would have to prove willful deception to hold a professional liable for making a report. In the three cases reported since 1975, the mandated reporter was almost immediately dropped from the lawsuit. The relevant section of the CPSL (Title 23 PA. C.S.A. Chapter 63, Subchapter B) reads as follows:

6318. Immunity from liability

(a) General rule.—A person, hospital, institution, school, facility or agency employee that participates in good faith in the making of a report, cooperating with an investigation, testifying in a proceeding arising out of an instance of suspected child abuse, the taking of photographs or removal or keeping of a

child pursuant to section 6315 (relating to taking child into protective custody), and any official or employee of a county agency who refers a report of suspected abuse to law enforcement authorities or provides services under this chapter, shall have immunity from civil and criminal liability that might otherwise result by reason of those actions.

(b) Presumption of good faith.—For the purpose of any civil or criminal proceeding, the good faith of a person required to report pursuant to section 6311 (relating to persons required to report suspected child abuse), and of any person required to make a referral to law enforcement officers under this Chapter shall be presumed. (p. 10)

If a person made a nonmandated report (as in 6312) in good faith, this person would not be held liable. The difference is that mandated reporters are presumed to be acting in good faith and nonmandated reporters have to demonstrate their good faith.

The spirit of the law was to *facilitate early reporting.* It is the job of CPS, not a *reporter,* to determine if the abuse is founded or unfounded. In Pennsylvania, there is no case law at this time suggesting lawsuits against reporters are an immediate concern. However, statistics clearly show that abuse of children is an immediate concern.

What Happens after a Report Is Made?

Within 24 hours of a report, a CPS investigation must be conducted to insure the immediate safety of the child. Within 30 to 60 days, a detailed investigation must be completed. If there is evidence that a reportable offense has occurred, CPS reports this to the police.

In Pennsylvania, the mandated reporter has the right to know if after the investigation abuse was *indicated* (clear and convincing evidence that there was maltreatment), *unfounded* (no clear and convincing evidence of maltreatment), or *founded* (court has made a ruling about the maltreatment), and if any services were provided or arranged for by the county agency.

Mandated Reporting and Ethical Clinical Practice

Ethical practice with maltreatment cases will frequently involve active consulting with colleagues and other professionals, as well as sustained coordination of service with other professionals involved with the case. In addition, building a collaborative relationship with the family and developing their competencies may be key to providing effective treatment. The following cases are concrete examples of how this can be done.

Case 1

Karen, a single mother, comes for an intake interview with her two children. She has been waiting several weeks for an appointment. Before the therapist can introduce herself, the mother erupts with information about her family and how she bit her daughter (age 3) this morning to discipline her for biting her brother (age 18 months). She then describes a week of parent-child confrontations in which she has felt out of control. She uses statements such as "I cannot control my anger. I need help. I can't be trusted around her."

There are marks on the daughter's arm. This, coupled with the mother's statements, requires the therapist, as a mandated reporter, to report Karen to CPS for an abuse investigation. However, the dilemma is how to balance this reporting mandate with professional ethics that promise confidentiality. Karen wants help and is reaching out for therapy. If reported, she may flee treatment and an opportunity to prevent further abuse will be lost. If Karen doesn't flee and is told by CPS to continue treatment, she may not want to cooperate with the therapist.

How can the therapist respond ethically to this dilemma? It is ethically appropriate to breach confidentiality in this situation. The relevant section on disclosures in the American Psychological Association ethical code (APA, 1992, Section 5.05) is as follows:

(a) Psychologists disclose confidential information without the consent of the individual only as mandated by law, or where permitted by law for a valid purpose, such as (1) to provide needed professional services to the patient or the individual or organizational client, (2) to obtain appropriate professional consultations, (3) to protect the patient or client or others from harm, or (4) to obtain payment for services, in which instance disclosure is limited to the minimum that is necessary to achieve the purpose.

(b) Psychologists also may disclose confidential information with the appropriate consent of the patient or the individual or organizational client (or of another legally authorized person on behalf of the patient or client), unless prohibited by law. (p. 1606)

Information on the limits of confidentiality should be given prior to a client having the opportunity to reveal confidential information. In

Karen's case, this has not happened. Will Karen withdraw from treatment if reported? Surveys of therapists indicate that they *fear* that reporting will destroy the therapist-client relationship and prevent constructive treatment. Studies of actual outcome indicate that trust is the important issue in keeping clients in treatment, not reporting. A study by Watson and Levine (1989) indicated that the therapeutic relationships of 76 percent of psychotherapy cases reviewed either did not change or actually improved after mandated reporting.

Karen did not withdraw from treatment. The therapist's first step was to explain the state and APA ethical guidelines to her and apologize for not reviewing this material sooner. During this process, Karen's strengths were emphasized, such as her ability to recognize that the home situation was out of control and that collaboration with a professional was needed. Legally, Karen had to be reported. However, a prompt, not an instantaneous, report was needed. Thus, the second step was to work with Karen during the session to develop a safety plan to prevent further abuse; the plan could then be shared when making the report to CPS. A search for resources was carried out. Was there a grandmother, a friend, a pastor, or someone else, who could help keep the children safe while the family worked on this problem in therapy? Were there any strategies that Karen used in the past that helped her feel in control of her anger? It took more than the traditional hour to develop a plan that both the therapist and mother had confidence in. This process encouraged Karen to view herself as collaborating with the therapist and CPS to (a) insure the safety of her children, and (b) resolve the present state of family crisis.

Once this was done, the third step was to review with Karen the procedure for filing an abuse report and encourage her to report the biting incident herself to CPS while the therapist remained with her as a source of support. After Karen reported herself, the therapist talked directly to the CPS worker about her belief in Karen's ability to carry through the safety plan. Karen was able to hear everything the therapist said to help establish trust with Karen and treat her as an active collaborator in the process of protecting her children. Finally, the therapist asked the CPS worker what steps CPS would take so that Karen could be informed and *unpleasant surprises,* such as CPS insisting the children move in with their grandmother, could be avoided. Watson and Levine (1989) found that this type of reporting, which handles the report within the context of the therapeutic relationship, is more likely to result in positive outcomes.

Case 2

The Jeffrey family came into treatment because of *founded* child sexual abuse involving five of their seven children. The court mandated therapy for the family under the supervision of CPS. All members of the Jeffrey family expressed hatred for both the court system and CPS, and indicated that unless the therapist had no dealings with these agencies, they would refuse to cooperate with treatment. CPS was paying for all treatment services.

The ethical dilemmas facing this therapist included resolving who is the client (CPS, Court, Jeffrey family), what, if any, confidentiality can be offered to the Jeffrey family, and how to establish trust between the therapy agency and the clients after they have established such active distrust of CPS and the court system. The APA ethical code (APA, 1992, Section 1.21) addresses third party requests for services and is directly relevant to these dilemmas:

(a) When a psychologist agrees to provide services to a person or entity at the request of a third party, the psychologist clarifies to the extent feasible, at the outset of the service, the nature of the relationship with each party. This clarification includes the role of the psychologist (such as therapist, consultant, organizational consultant, diagnostician, or expert witness), the probable uses of the services provided or the information obtained, and the fact that there may be limits to confidentiality.

(b) If there is a foreseeable risk of the psychologist's being called upon to perform conflicting roles because of the involvement of a third party, the psychologist clarifies the nature and direction of his or her responsibilities, keeps all parties appropriately informed as matters develop and, resolves the situation in accordance with this Ethics Code. (p. 1602)

How were these conflicting roles negotiated with the Jeffrey family? First, the limits of confidentiality and laws regarding mandatory reporting were reviewed with the family prior to discussion of any other issues. Family members tried to interrupt this with their complaints about the system. Firmly, but with respect, the therapist stated that building trust was extremely important and the family would not be expected to share any information at all within this therapeutic agency until they understood the legal rules the therapist was obligated to follow.

Second, the family's right to be angry both with the information just imparted and with the manner in which the courts and CPS had dealt with them was validated by the therapist and their strength of family loyalty was underscored. The therapist agreed that it would be ideal to have no contact with the court or CPS but told the family that if any further abuse or neglect was revealed, the therapist would have to initiate such contact.

Third, the therapist revealed that CPS had indicated that they would be requiring regular reports on the family and that a prior treatment setting had been terminated because such reports had not been forthcoming.

Fourth, the therapist suggested that the family take control of this snooping by developing a contract about what types of information would be shared. At first, the family objected to any sharing with CPS. The therapist agreed to contact CPS and only discuss with them the family's request to not share any information and find out if there were any potential negative consequences to this refusal to share. The therapist made the call with the family in the room so that they could hear exactly what the therapist said to the CPS worker.

The CPS worker stated that without therapist assurance that the children were safe, they would be removed from the home. The therapist negotiated with CPS exactly what information they would have to have to prevent such an extreme step. The therapist then discussed this information with the family and a contract was developed. On a biweekly basis, CPS would be called and the following information would be shared: whether there was any suspicion from the therapy sessions of ongoing abuse or neglect; whether the family had or had not attended the therapy sessions; what the family goals for therapy were; and, if the family was making no, a little, moderate, or a great deal of progress in achieving each of these goals.

No content from the sessions would be shared beyond the statement about progress or the lack of it. CPS would share with the therapist its plans with regard to monitoring the family so that the therapist could keep the Jeffreys clearly informed. This biweekly report would be made by phone subsequent to a therapy appointment and the therapist would first review with the family exactly what information was to be shared in this phone call. At the next therapy session, the therapist would review any information from this phone contact with the family.

Child Protective Service workers face their own ethical dilemmas when trying to collaborate with therapists. The following examples were provided by Tina Semon, the Director of Indiana County Children and Youth Services (personal communication, October 6, 1994). In Example 1, a therapist puts a child referred by CPS for individual treatment into a group. The dilemma for the caseworker is to determine if this was a therapeutic decision for the child or just a default choice because the therapist had no individual appointments currently available.

Example 2 involves a child who may be facing immediate consequences for maladaptive behaviors related to the abuse experience, such as school expulsion, or disruptions within the family or peer relationships, and the therapist is not directly addressing these behaviors. The dilemma for the caseworker is, while the therapist indicates that no progress can be made on these behaviors until the child has dealt constructively with the abuse experiences, the caseworker is very aware of the real and potentially traumatic immediate consequences facing the child.

Example 3 involves a situation where, in the CPS worker's opinion, the therapist is trying to make a child progress too quickly through a treatment protocol. In all of these examples, the CPS worker has the social and legal responsibility for the child and must determine who has the greatest expertise for deciding what needs to be done. Open and direct collaboration among all professionals involved can minimize the occurrence of these dilemmas and enhance their resolution when they do arise.

Case 3

The Calvins have five children between ages 3 and 12. The family was referred for treatment by Child Protective Services due to physical abuse of the 12-year-old son by his father and because of the 12-year-old's physical abuse of his 10-year-old sister. CPS continues to monitor the family through home visits and monthly contacts with the therapist. The family attends family sessions, the parents attend marital sessions, and the son attends individual sessions. Within family and marital treatment, progress consisted of gaining the trust of the mother and father, but no changes in parenting behavior had occurred at this time. The son made significant improvement in learning anger control strategies within individual therapy sessions. The therapist began to encourage the boy to use these new anger management strategies at home. A new incident of abuse occurred over the weekend when the son said to his father, "I'm mad at you because . . ." Mr. Calvin exploded and said, "Don't tell me you are mad." An emergency family session was initiated. The father said to the therapist, "How dare he tell me that he was angry with me."

The therapist is faced with having to report the father for this incident of abuse. Furthermore, this case illustrates the dilemma of how to determine when it is safe to institute therapy interventions with various members of a violent family. Everyone in the Calvin family was attending treatment regularly. The possible consequences of the son making faster progress than his father and mother in dealing with anger was not thought through. In working with maltreating families, professionals must constantly monitor levels of dangerousness in the home environment.

To minimize the potential danger, every point in a treatment plan needs to be carefully thought through and reviewed weekly; the order of the treatment goals may be critical. There is a danger in providing multimodal treatment when parents are not informed in advance, and their approval gained, for an intervention to be made with their child. Professionals must respect the parents' right to influence treatment. A parent has more power in the family than a child. There is danger in assuming that the parent-child relationship will be improved by anyone developing clearer communication skills. Insuring the physical safety of the child is critical and must take precedence over other treatment objectives. When interventions are to be made within the home, follow-up calls can give family members the opportunity to ventilate if they found they didn't like the intervention. The therapist can also verify that the family's coping strategies are working.

Through treating the clients' wishes and feelings about interventions with respect, the therapist becomes an advocate for the family, rather than an enforcer for the system. Thus, the family is more likely to tell the therapist if tensions are building up or in fact have exploded.

The dilemma of how to assess the safety of interventions is intensified when caregivers are not cooperative with or are not participating in treatment. If only the children and not the adults are receiving or profiting from treatment, the abuse may escalate because the abusive parent may not appreciate the child's attempt to speak assertively about problems and may fear a child's disclosures to the therapist. Therapists can try to help children develop age-appropriate self-protection plans—however, adults are responsible for the safety of children. It is not realistic to expect children to protect themselves (Berman, 1993). Differential power between child and caregiver is a reality. Safety issues must be addressed before personal growth is realistic. This includes assessing whether it is physically or emotionally safe to include perpetrators of abuse within family sessions (Gruszenski, Brink, & Edleson, 1988).

Therapists cannot effectively monitor dangerousness of a family situation when having contacts only with the child. To deal with this dilemma, they can collaborate with other professionals involved with the case. For example, CPS can mandate and maintain families in therapy services and make home visits. If necessary, they can temporarily remove a child from the home. A CPS worker can also serve as a validating source of reality for the parents about the negative impact of maltreatment on their children (Berman, 1994). It is valuable to develop an effective working relationship with CPS prior to sharing a client with them.

GENERAL STRATEGIES FOR RESOLVING ETHICAL DILEMMAS

There are many other ethical dilemmas that can arise in child maltreatment cases. For example, problems may occur when the parents and therapist disagree about what types of interventions an abused child needs, when abused children and their parents disagree about what types of interventions are needed, or when a therapist has worked with a family through so many crises that the boundaries between the therapist's needs and that of the client family have become blurred. In all of these cases, the therapist can receive guidance through (a) collaboration and consultation with other professionals, (b) active collaboration with the family members through frank discussions of the issues, and (c) an effective working knowledge of their professional ethical standards and the laws governing the issues within the state.

Conclusion

Mandatory reporting laws are written in legal jargon, not psychological jargon. In addition, mechanisms for interfacing good clinical practice with laws and regulations that may be in constant modification by case law are not standard features of professional educational curricula. This dynamic and confusing process can be clarified if clinicians adhere to the following guidelines for ethical and competent practice with child maltreatment cases. First, professionals need to keep updated on state mandatory reporting laws. Second, they need to keep updated on professional ethical guidelines. Third, they should consult and collaborate with other professionals. Finally, professionals should never forget that therapeutic interventions can increase, as well as decrease, the possible incidence of child abuse.

References

American Psychological Association. (1992). Ethical principles of psychologists and code of conduct. *American Psychologist, 47,* 1597–1611.

Berman, P. (1993). Impact of abusive marital relationships on children. In M. Hansen & M. Harway (Eds.), *Battering and family therapy* (pp. 134–146). Newbury Park, CA: Sage.

Berman, P. (1994). *Therapeutic exercises for victimized and neglected girls: Applications for individual, family, & group psychotherapy.* Sarasota, FL: Professional Resource Press.

Brosig, C., & Kalichman, S. (1992a). Clinician's reporting of suspected child abuse: A review of the empirical literature. *Clinical Psychology Review, 12,* 155–168.

Brosig, C., & Kalichman, S. (1992b). Child abuse reporting decisions: Effects of statutory wording of reporting requirements. *Professional Psychology: Research and Practice, 23,* 486–492.

Brozovich v. Circle C Group Homes, Inc., 548 A.2d 698 (Pa.Cmwlth., 1988).

Child Protective Services Law, 23 Pa. C.S.A. chapter 63 (1975 & Supp. 1994).

Fewell v. Besner, 664 A.2d 577 (Pa.Super. 1995).

Gruszenski, R., Brink, J., & Edleson, J. (1988). Support and education groups for children of battered women. *Child Welfare, 67,* 431–444.

Pennsylvania Department of Public Welfare, Office of Children, Youth and Families. (1993). *Department of Public Welfare 18th annual child abuse report.* Harrisburg, PA: Author.

Roman v. Appleby, 558 F. Supp.449 (E.D.Pa., 1983).

U.S. Department of Health and Human Services, Office of Human Development Services. (1988). *Executive summary: Study of national incidence and prevalence of child abuse and neglect* (Contract 105-85-1702). Washington, DC: Clearinghouse on Child Abuse and Neglect Information.

Watson, H., & Levine, M. (1989). Psychotherapy and mandated reporting of child abuse. *American Journal of Orthopsychiatry, 59,* 246–256.

CHAPTER 11

The Recovered Memories Debate and Clinical Practice with Families

PAUL S. STRAND and MICHAEL R. NASH

F amily and individual therapists are increasingly confronted with scenarios like the following:

- In the context of a heated custody battle, a 10-year-old boy suddenly reports sexual dreams involving his noncustodial mother. After several therapy sessions arranged by his father, the boy comes to confidently (and dramatically) report that he now "remembers" having been abused at the age of 3 by his mother. He is believed by his father and stepmother.

- Two adult sisters, both over the age of 35, report in intensively regressive individual psychotherapy that they are now certain that they were brutally sexually abused by their father when they were 8 and 9 years old. These women come to "remember" that their father also involved them in bestiality, ritual torture, and multiple murders. An explosive rupture of the extended family results.

- A 20-year-old woman in psychotherapy comes to experience new and unbidden images of being sexually abused by her older brother when she was 12 and 13 years old. She understands these experiences as memories and confronts her brother, who denies the abuse. Her parents are split on the matter; and she essentially disengages from the family altogether.

It is fairly safe to assert that just 5 to 10 years ago, the sensibilities of the clinical community were such that the above reports of having been abused would have been taken at face value. Family clinicians and theorists would have disagreed about the precise legal, social, family, and individual interventions to be employed, but all approaches would have been predicated on two assumptions: (1) that the reports represent memory traces of actual abuse events; and (2) that dealing with the reality of this history is essential to getting better—for patient, for family, and for society.

As late as 1988, Bass and Davis (in *Courage to Heal*) boldly offered the following advice: "If you are unable to remember any specific instances . . . but still have a feeling that something abusive happened to you, it probably did" (p. 21). And "if you think you were abused and your life shows symptoms, then you were" (p. 22). It is, in fact, now abundantly clear that neither of the above assertions is at all secure. In fact, the havoc wrought on thousands of families by false accusations of abuse is now well documented (American Medical Association, 1995; Tavris, 1993). The problem resides jointly in a misunderstanding of the purpose of clinical intervention and the relationship between memory and historical event. And we, as therapists, are culpable—put bluntly, we must come to understand the difference between telling a story and telling the truth.

Social Constructivism and Family Therapy

The idea of telling a story is a popular notion in psychotherapy today. What is referred to as the *narrative approach* grew out of *social constructivism*, a philosophy that maintains that meaning arises from social interaction and is shaped and constrained by language. It holds that truth does not exist in an objective sense and is, therefore, not discoverable. Rather, our realities are created and perpetuated in the form of the stories we generate and live by.

In one sense, social constructivism appears to be useful to the clinician. After all, differential reactions of people exposed to similar traumatic events tell us that what happens to people in a historical sense does not dictate their response. Rather, in the case of experienced trauma, some people cope well; others do not. The nature of coping has been shown to be related to the nature of how each individual makes sense of the past event (Kushner, Riggs, Foa, & Miller 1992; Miklulineen & Solomon, 1988; Solomon, Mikulincev, & Flum 1988). Also important to the outcome is the input of significant others with whom the victim processes the event (Perry, Difede, Musngi, Frances, & Jacobsberg, 1992). Understanding the mental constructions that follow traumatic events and their role in dictating the impact of the trauma may point to useful clinical strategies for helping victims cope. For instance, it may be clinically useful to guide people having difficulty recovering from trauma to think about, or narrate, the traumatic events in ways similar to those who are coping well. This is a potentially fruitful area for clinical research.

On the other hand, it is possible that social constructivist thinking could be taken too far. In its extreme form, social constructivism argues that facts do not exist, only stories. Furthermore, the best stories are those that are most useful to the persons creating them. Once again, social constructivism appears very appealing to the clinician implicitly or explicitly charged with helping someone lead a more functional life. It is at this point, however, where social constructivism meets functionalism, that we run into an important problem. In a world characterized by humans leading vastly interconnected lives, some stories may be functional for some people and not so functional for others. This is especially the case when one's narrative implicates another person as a causative agent responsible for damage or suffering. When the stories of two such individuals diverge, whose narrative are we to live by? Social constructivism has no answer to this question.

Social constructivism has been highly influential within the ranks of family therapy and is, in part, responsible for recent changes in the metaphors used by family therapists (Zimmerman & Dickerson, 1994). The move has been away from physical and biological metaphors and toward the use of social and cultural descriptors (Newmark & Beels, 1994). The notion of shaking up a recalcitrant system through strategic interventions has given way to a collaborative stance characterized by conversation and reflection. This new narrative approach focuses on the stories people tell of themselves and how such stories govern their lives. While such narrative approaches have enjoyed much recent success, they have not been without their critics.

The 1980s saw the first wave of criticisms leveled against family therapy originating from within its own ranks (Nichols & Schwartz, 1995). The most severe, informative, and transformative of these came from feminism. The feminist critique challenged the very foundations of family therapy theory and practice by attacking its most basic assumptions. It called into question the notion that the family is the most fundamental context dictating the behavior of family members.

Feminists contend that the family is nested within, and is therefore a collusive part of, a larger sociopolitical climate fostering the unequal treatment of men and women. Additionally, family therapy writers influenced by the feminist critique have questioned the veridicality of circularity and its primary corollary, so fundamental to family systems theory, that all parts of a system are equally responsible for its present organization and functioning (Dell, 1989; Erikson, 1988; Hoffman, 1986). In support of their position, feminists documented staggering statistics on the injustices perpetrated against women in the context of intimate and family arrangements. Data suggest, for example, that one in three American women have experienced sexual abuse prior to age 18, 95 percent of which were perpetrated by a male; that every year one in six American women is abused by a man with whom she lives; and that severe, repeated violence occurs in 1 in 14 marriages, with an average of 35 incidents before it is reported (Myers Avis, 1992). It is little wonder, then, that through the eyes of feminism, any theory that does not address the unequal distribution of terror and victimization in families appears to be "a hypersophisticated version of blaming the victim and rationalizing the status quo" (Goldner, 1985, p. 33).

In addition to questioning the prize concepts deriving from systems theory, circularity, and context, feminists have also expressed concern about family therapy's enamoration with social constructivism. By questioning the existence of a true reality, social constructivism may lead to reluctance on the part of therapists to intervene at any level other than narrative discourse. Coupled with the Batesonian notion that power differences within families are nonexistent, a social constructivism that advocates remaining close to family definitions of the problem and the use of dialogue as the primary technique for altering family problems may surreptitiously create a *don't ask, don't tell* collusion between family and therapist regarding domestic violence. As Fish (1993) states, "Perpetrators of abuse almost always attempt to control information—to dictate the family story" (p. 229). This occurs within as well as outside of therapy. Therefore, it is incumbent on family therapists to actively seek out information concerning power inequalities, their repercussions, and the underlying assumptions that perpetuate them (Hare-Mustin, 1994).

Family therapists, so say feminists, must realize their front-line position in working with families that abuse and respect their duty to protect disempowered family members. They must have theories and techniques for altering injustice. These should involve identifying the abuse and the abuser, utilizing methods of social control when appropriate, and restructuring the family such that it is safe, empowering, and option-generating for the victimized (Myers Avis, 1992). These methods are active rather than narrative, and they focus on reality as experienced rather than reality as constructed.

The feminist critique of family therapy highlights many of the central dilemmas facing clinicians. These dilemmas have to do primarily with power and violence within families, and they were captured by Bograd (1992) in the following series of questions:

How do we balance a relativistic world view with values about human safety and the rights of men and women to self-determination and protection? When is the clinical utility of neutrality limited or counterproductive? When is conviction essential to the change process? How do we confront the batterer about the destructive nature of his behavior without condemning him? How strongly and passionately do we employ our values to therapeutic advantage while maintaining a caring, respectful connection with family members struggling with the trauma of violence? (pp. 248–249)

Recently the charge toward empowering the less powerful members of families has run into difficulty. The problem lies in the fact that in the case of family violence in general, and sexual abuse in particular, the distinction between victim and victimizer has been blurred. Evidence suggests that, at least in some cases, allegations of sexual abuse have been false. Such information complicates the current struggle within family therapy to come to terms, both theoretically and practically, with violence within families.

The Theoretical Implications of False Memories

As mentioned earlier, the primary theoretical framework for family therapy (family systems theory) has in the past been called into question for failing to provide the means to protect persons being mistreated within families. Dell (1989) writes, "systems theory is a very powerful conceptual tool, but it has its limitations. . . . Violence exists in the domain of human lineal experience, not in the domain of systemic explanation" (p. 11). The message is that we must realize power differences within families, identify cases of victimization, and intervene more actively on behalf of victims (Fish, 1990; Fish & Faynik, 1989; Sheinberg, 1992; Trepper & Barrett, 1986). Yet, family therapy, indeed all of psychology, continues to struggle to determine, on a case-by-case basis, whether abuse has occurred. A volley of accusations among parents, "survivors," and psychotherapists has ensued. Alleged perpetrators now claim to be the victims of an out-of-control psychotherapy industry bent on twisting the truth—and the thoughts of vulnerable consumers of psychological services—to fit a model of the world consistent with the beliefs and desires of psychotherapists. As a result, psychotherapy presently faces what is perhaps its greatest credibility crisis.

What, then, is a therapist to do? Social constructivism, although a powerful therapeutic tool for bringing about change, breaks down as a useful framework for guiding clinical work when proper conduct requires historical accuracy rather than simple narrative coherence. Some degree of historical accuracy is called for when more than one person will be affected by the stories created between client and therapist. Given that people do not live in a vacuum, this is likely to be the case more often than not. What must be remembered is that constructivism within the therapeutic setting is an active process. It not only helps people make sense of their circumstances, but it also changes those circumstances with respect to present and future functioning and relationships. Therapists bent on producing symptom-oriented change have utilized powerful techniques to help patients come to a new and sometimes more coherent understanding of their lives, but have in some cases failed to look at their clients' lives within a larger interpersonal context. Regarding the current trends in psychotherapy toward an overly symptom-focused and change-oriented approach, Madanes (1990) offered the following warning: "Co-created realities, minimalism, and local level outcomes come dangerously close to nihilism, arbitrariness, and alienation from larger ethical concerns." (p. 120). Therapists must always consider whose agenda they are working in the service of.

In the remainder of this chapter we discuss what we believe are important guidelines for dealing with the issue of repressed memories.

On Telling a Story: The Job of the Clinician

We agree with Loftus' take on the research literature:

Our representation of the past takes on a living, shifting reality; it is not fixed and immutable, not a place way back there that is preserved in stone, but a living thing that changes shape, expands, shrinks, and expands again, an amoeba-like creature with powers to make us laugh and cry, and clench our fists.

Enormous powers—powers even to make us believe in something that never happened. (Loftus & Ketcham, 1991, p. 20)

Historical facts do not reside in statue in memory, but are influenced by imagination, wishes, contemporary social factors, linguistic conventions, and cultural press. That is not to say that historical facts (events) do not exist, as some postmodernists would have it. Rather, human mental representations of the past are malleable in the present, allowing for great adaptive utility that may be harnessed toward clinical ends—but at the cost of historical accuracy (Harth, 1993).

Clinical Efficacy:
It Is Not the Truth That Sets Our Patients Free

Leaving the vexing nature of memory aside for the moment, we contend that clinical utility may have little or nothing to do with uncovering the truth. It has more to do with the patient and therapist jointly constructing a compelling story—a compelling self-narrative. As therapists, we are not in search of the truth. We are not conducting an archeological excavation of the mind, a literal exhumation of the past. We are instead proceeding much more like literary critics as we enable patients to co-construct a meaningful believed-in story that accounts for the thematic richness of a lifetime. Here we agree with the constructivists. But there is nothing new about this: Roy Schafer (1983) has been beating the hermeneutic drum within the psychoanalytic community for many years now, noting that patients get better in expressive therapies, not because they discover dark truths heretofore shrouded by repression, but because they co-construct with their therapists a believed-in story that compellingly creates and explains who they are and who they were. The problem, of course, is that therapists have a nasty tendency to believe their own propaganda, especially when the therapy has been successful. That is, they walk into courtrooms and into scientific forums contending that these stories about the past, co-constructed in the intimate atmosphere of therapy, are in fact not stories at all, but literal exhumations of past events. They believe this to be the case because when patients told such stories they did so with conviction and because they improved. But these clinicians forget: (a) that the stories were not simply told, they were co-authored—with conviction—by the therapist; and (b) that clinical efficacy in no way assures accuracy.

A simple example from the historical literature will illustrate these two points. Three hundred years ago, a young woman suffering from (what we would call) glove anesthesia might have sought help from the village priest, who construes the causative agent as demonic possession. The priest invites the young woman and her family to search their memory for relevant evidence concerning the specific nature of the demon; memories emerge of strange occurrences involving a hellish imp; an exorcism is performed with family members present; and the woman is cured. Clearly the effectiveness of the therapy in no way supports the accuracy of the woman's memory concerning the existence of imps per se.

In sum, we cannot with certainty rely on clinical efficacy to validate the mnemonic experience of our patients in therapy: For some of our successful therapy patients, narrative truth and historical truth may be almost identical; for others there may be little or no correspondence (Spence, 1982). At the very least, what we as clinicians must do is stop "inhabiting" courtrooms and scientific forums, claiming to have special access to historical truth just because we did the therapy. In some sense, nothing could be further from the truth. In addition, those who persist in conducting highly suggestive therapies should quietly contemplate the violence they may be doing to their patients, their patients' families, and society when uncorroborated narratives of abuse are embraced as unqualified truth. Be assured that the attorney of the patient's parent will consider the negative effects of such therapies routinely, and in a manner that is neither quiet nor benignly contemplative.

For instance, in a recent civil case in Napa, California (*Ramona v. Ramona*, 1994), Mr. Gary Ramona, a 50-year-old father with a $300,000-a-year corporate position was accused by his adult eating-disordered daughter, Holly, of decades-old sexual abuse, memories of which were first retrieved in intensive therapy. As a consequence, Mr. Ramona lost his family, his career, his reputation, and his home. Mr. Ramona sued the daughter's two therapists (a licensed marriage, family, and child counselor, and a psychiatrist) for malpractice, charging that these therapists had planted memories in his daughter's mind through suggestion, sodium amytal interviews, and recovered memory techniques. In a court decision that has proved exceedingly influential, the court found in favor of Mr. Ramona. This decision is important for two reasons. It is the first time in the United States that a therapist was found guilty of malpractice because of false memories. Also, it establishes that it is not only the patient who can sue a therapist for malpractice or negligence; affected nonpatients can sue as well. Note that Mr. Ramona was permitted to sue even though the patient did not believe malpractice had occurred. In an even more recent and weighty decision (*Carlson v. Humenansky*, 1996) a Minnesota woman and her family were awarded $2.5 million for injuries suffered as a result of negligent psychotherapy to recover so-called repressed memories.

On Telling the Truth:
The Job of the Investigator-Scientist

For forensic purposes, it does matter whether the abuse event happened or not. If we are ever to construct a scientifically viable theory of human psychological development, we must know what actually happened in the child's environment, and not be satisfied with retrospective report. For example, if we are ever to understand the relationship between trauma, dissociation, and psychopathology, we must know what really happened.

What can we say to our patients, communities, and court systems about the vexing issue of recovered memories: First and foremost, we must bracket off, as best we can, our personal-political agendas on the matter. Special interest polemics will get us nowhere. Second, with unfailing fidelity, we must be familiar with, rely on, and support our heritage of laboratory and clinical research on memory, psychopathology, and repression. Third, though sometimes a little embarrassing, we must firmly acknowledge that there is much we do not know. In so doing, we disabuse the courts and the public of their distressingly boundless confidence that science has all the answers. Below we briefly outline some empirically-validated points that can help orient clinicians and educate others on the issue of false memories.

THE MUTABILITY OF MEMORY: THE POST-ENCODING PROBLEM

There are at least three related research traditions that support the contention that people can report "remembering" events that never occurred: memory research, developmental psychopathology, and contemporary psychoanalytic theory. It is abundantly clear now that human memory is not immutably stored in pristine form somewhere in the brain. Indeed, organization, encoding, and recall are highly dependent on meaning structures at the time of the event and on subsequent beliefs about feeling and reality (Bradburn, Rips, & Shevell 1987; Goodman & Hahn, 1987; Loftus, Korf, & Schooler, 1989).

In addition, many contemporary psychoanalytic and developmental theorists argue that the psychic structure of a child is unalterably changed during the course of development. As a consequence, old stages, or infantile modes of functioning, are simply not "there" to be retrieved (Bruner, 1968; Erdelyi, 1985; Peterfreund, 1978; Piaget, 1973; Rubinfine, 1981; Spitz, 1965; Westin, 1989). These theorists offer persuasive evidence that humans do not passively record the events around them, thereby creating exact copies in the mind. Instead, memories and cognitive schemata appear to be transformed as the child progresses through successive stages, and thereby changed forever (Eagle, 1984; Piaget, 1973; Piaget & Inhelder, 1969). Indeed, contrary to earlier notions of psychopathology as a return to infantile phases of development, there is a growing research literature that fails to support the notion that adult psychopathology is similar to, or even properly analogous to, normal phases of child development (Donaldson & Westerman, 1986; Flavell, 1985; Harter, 1986; Harter & Buddin, 1987; Westin, 1989).

Why does it seem so natural for us to construe adult psychopathology as a manifestation of some genuinely infantile or immature mode of psychological operation? We believe that at the root of this problem is one of Freud's earliest and most appealing ideas about the lawfulness of psychopathology, the concept of temporal regression (Freud, 1917/1957). Freud based his concept of temporal regression on the assumption of an orderly pattern of human development that evolved from simpler, less organized states to more complex, advanced states. Freud (1915/1957) also maintained that these structures in human development are imperishable, that under special circumstances they may "again become the mode of expression of the forces in the mind" (p. 285), and that "the essence of mental disease lies in a return to earlier states of affective life and of functioning" (p. 286). Many psychoanalytic theorists and cognitive developmental psychologists have embraced the idea that old developmental stages remain imperishable and that psychopathology is most essentially a regression to, or eruption of, one or more of these previously abandoned modes of relating to self and others (Balint, 1968; Bion, 1977; Kohut, 1971; Langer, 1970; Stolorow & Lachman, 1980; Werner, 1948).

The notion that this kind of temporal regression is possible and that psychopathology is a lawful undoing of development is exceedingly appealing to clinicians and theorists who struggle to make sense of the seemingly random disorganization arising from pathology. A formulation based on this type of ontogenic regression defines a linear continuity between presumed etiological factors in childhood (like a trauma) and the adult symptoms themselves. It charts a sure course for treatment involving a therapeutic regression to the developmental stage in question, re-emergence of long-repressed memories and feeling states, and a gradual resumption of development from that point. But this model of human psychopathology does not, in fact, appear to be the case. Freud made revolutionary and lasting contributions to our understanding of why people suffer emotionally, and how their misery can be alleviated, but we believe that it is Freud's mistaken concept of the imperishability of psychic structures (memories, modes of relating, psychosexual stages) and his related claim that patients have access to these stages through regression, that underlies our propensity to infer that patient reports of trauma are quite literally reproductions of a historical event.

Though perhaps not the most compelling, certainly the most controversial evidence for remembering things that never happened emerges from the dramatic increase in reports of bizarre satanic ritual abuse, especially among dissociative patients. Ganaway (1991) found that up to 50 percent of dissociative-disordered patients report satanic ritualistic abuse involving heinous, even cannibalistic crimes carried out by an organized network of secret covens. These fantastic accounts, though compellingly rendered, have rarely, if ever, been confirmed by law enforcement authorities.

There are several studies that appear to document that false memories can, and do, occur under laboratory and field conditions (Abelson, Loftus, & Greenwald, 1992; Garry & Loftus, 1994; Haugaard, Reppucci, Laurd, & Nauful, 1991; Laurence & Perry, 1983; Neisser & Harsch, 1992; Piaget, 1962; Pynoos & Nader, 1989). For example, in the field, Piaget (1962) had long remembered an incident of attempted kidnapping that occurred when he was an infant. Over a decade later, his nanny, who had received a reward for the "rescue," painfully confessed that she had fabricated the entire story. Piaget (1962) surmised that, "I, therefore, must have heard as a child, the account of this story, which my parents believed, and projected into the past in the form of a visual memory" (in Loftus & Ketcham, 1991, p. 191). In another field example, Pynoos and Nader (1989) discovered that following an actual sniper attack at an elementary school, children who had no direct experience of the attack (already at home or on vacation) still reported vivid memories of gunshots, bodies, and chaos. In the laboratory, researchers have implanted compellingly believed-in false memories of being lost in a shopping mall (Loftus, 1993), loud noises at night

(Laurence & Perry, 1983), and even past-life identities (Spanos, Burgess, & Burgess, 1994).

Thus, based on the theoretical and empirical literature, it appears that at least under some circumstances, individuals can come to report memory of events that did not in fact occur. The caveat here is that no laboratory researcher has yet produced false memories of the emotional intensity and gravity of early sexual trauma. Although clinicians and researchers will undoubtedly continue to debate the ecological validity of these theories and their associated studies, no responsible investigator or clinician can simply ignore the possibility of this form of memory error.

No Distinguishing Signs

As noted in task force reports by the American Psychiatric Association (1993), the American Medical Association (1995), and the American Psychological Association (1995), there is no uniform abuse profile or methodology that distinguishes abused from nonabused patients, or reports of actual abuse from reports of imagined abuse. Clinicians who claim to be able to distinguish "real" reports of abuse are operating outside the bounds of accepted scientific practice.

Childhood Amnesia

Recent research in developmental-cognitive psychology suggests that "past the age of ten, or thereabouts, most of us find it impossible to recall anything that happened before the age of four or five" (Morton, 1990, p. 3). Further, Ceci and colleagues (Ceci, Loftus, Leichtman, & Buck, 1994) have documented empirically that "although all children are susceptible to making source misattributions, very young children may be disproportionately vulnerable to these kinds of errors" (p. 304).

Certainty and Confidence Not Related to Accuracy

The eye-witness and clinical-research literatures suggest that subjects undergoing recovered memory-type procedures will evidence an increase in confidence about previously presented information even though it is inaccurate (Loftus & Ketcham, 1991; Orne, 1979). Accordingly, an eyewitness's confidence is not a good predictor of his or her accuracy (Kassin, Ellsworth, & Smith, 1989).

THE TRAUMA-DISSOCIATION LINK

It is by no means established that dissociative pathology is causally linked to traumatic experience (Kendall-Tucker, 1993; Tillman, Nash, & Lerner, 1994). Arguing backwards from adult or child dissociative presentation to childhood trauma is not justified.

HYPNOSIS AND OTHER THERAPEUTIC MEMORY-REFRESHING TECHNIQUES

Hypnosis does increase the volume of material recalled. However this increase does not reflect an increase in the percentage of material that is accurately recalled. Hypnosis increases both accurate and inaccurate information. Use of hypnosis or other therapeutic expressive techniques may actually disqualify the patient as a witness (Nash & Nadon, in press; Perry, Orne, London, & Orne, 1996).

Working Clinically with Uncertainty

Family therapy models are developing to accommodate issues of abuse within families (e.g., Friedrich, 1990; Sheinberg, 1992), but presently fail to offer suggestions for therapists working in situations in which doubt exists concerning the veridicality of alleged abuse. Doubt concerning veridicality of past abuse may be expressed in the form of a declaration of innocence on the part of the accused, or in the form of equivocation on the part of the accuser. Equivocation may be evidenced by unclarity concerning what happened in the past, or by the recovery of experiences that had been outside of awareness for some period of time.

Currently available models of intervention that begin simply with the notion that alleged abuse occurred fail to take into account the true complexity of the problems facing clinicians. Therapists must be aware of this and be careful to follow sound clinical principles in working with repressed memory patients. They should also be aware of legal implications of their work.

Given uncertainty about what happened in the past, how should a therapist proceed with regard to allegations of sexual abuse? This issue was recently addressed by Knapp, Tepper, and VandeCreek (1995), who developed a Risk Management Checklist designed to help clinicians be more effective in their work and minimize legal liability.

Many of the suggestions that follow derive from or have been informed by these authors:

1. In light of recent legal challenges against therapists working in the area of the false-repressed memories, it is important for clinicians to be familiar with pertinent literature. This includes the literature on childhood abuse and forgotten memories of traumatic events (Briere, 1992; Herman, 1992; Terr, 1994), and research on reconstructive memory and memory implantation (Loftus, 1993). By having knowledge regarding both sides of the debate, therapists are in a better position to act appropriately and with justification.

   Furthermore, in many such cases, therapy should begin by helping patients curious about the possibility of past abuse learn what we as a discipline know about memory. We know, first, that memories are not snapshots of the past. Rather, they are constructions made in the present of past events. Information may be forgotten and then remembered, but the remembering may not be perfect, and pieces may be deleted or added in ways that do not correspond with the actual past event. Second, most people who were sexually abused as children remember all or part of what happened to them (APA, 1995). Nevertheless, it is possible (though not established) that childhood abuse may be forgotten only to emerge at a later time. As for discovering whether someone was abused in the past, it is outside of our scientific ability to help someone with this question. Therefore, therapists should not indicate that they can help a patient remember the *truth*. It should also be pointed out that as therapists, we have no known techniques for determining if the experience of a memory by a patient reflects what occurred in the past, or whether it is a *pseudomemory*—that is, a false memory (APA, 1995).

2. Therapists should utilize treatment procedures that are supported by outcome data. In cases where this is not possible, therapists should rely on sound clinical judgment that would be deemed acceptable practice by one's peers. It is also a good idea to systematically review outcomes within one's own practice. About 20 percent of mental health professionals conduct some kind of outcome research on their patients (Knapp, Tepper, & VandeCreek, 1995).

3. All treatment procedures should show concern for the long-term impact on the patient, *including future relationships with family*

members. Patients often enter therapy to re-author their lives. We must help them do so, but with respect for current interpersonal arrangements and the complexity of symptom formation.

4. One's stance toward patients should be collaborative in the establishment of treatment goals, and open to alternative hypotheses. Despite the current "faster is better" zeitgeist, therapists should not be overly directive or overly anxious to produce change. Symptom formation is a complex process, often not reducible to one particular cause or circumstance. As therapists, we must heed the words of Sheinberg, True, and Fraenkel (1994) who state, "In the emotional minefield of incest, the temptation is to reduce confusion by reducing complexity" (p. 275).

5. The therapist should be aware of and informative about the limitations of our techniques and abilities, despite the possible attribution by patients of greater power to psychotherapists than is warranted. Therapists should take care not to oversell themselves or their profession.

6. The focus of treatment should be each individual patient, as opposed to public advocacy for a particular issue.

7. Finally, Watkins (1993) makes the important point that therapists must be aware of their role in the lives of their patients. Psychotherapists are typically not lawyers, and should take care not to overstep their bounds by offering legal advice. When called upon to be a psychotherapist, one is not signing on as a detective of the past or as an advocate for legal action. Psychotherapists should perform only those services for which they are trained and licensed to practice.

Conclusion

It is at the level of the family and the individual family member that the repressed memory controversy claims its casualties. Allegations of sexual abuse often result in traumatic schisms within families. In many of these instances, seemingly healthy families are torn asunder by controversy and strife. For these reasons, no other issue has occupied and polarized the mental health field like the issue of repressed memories. The well-being of families and the integrity of our profession requires that we deal with this controversy in such a manner that we understand our potential contributions and our inherent limitations.

In this chapter, we contextualized the repressed memory debate within the field of family therapy, focusing on the role of constructivism. We pointed out the differences between telling stories and telling the truth as they apply to clinical practice. Therapists do not have a special view of reality or the truth, and they must realize this. The pull to take sides or act on incomplete information is great, but must be avoided. All effort must be made by clinicians to practice according to established standards dictated by their profession and the available knowledge-base.

References

Abelson, R. P., Loftus, E. F., & Greenwald, A. G. (1992). Attempts to improve the accuracy of self-reports of voting. In J. M. Tanur (Ed.), *Questions about survey questions: Meaning, memory, expression, and social interactions in surveys* (pp. 138–153). New York: Russell Sage Foundation.

American Medical Association. (1995). *American Medical Association Council on Scientific Affairs, Report on memories of childhood abuse.* Chicago, IL: Author.

American Psychiatric Association. (1993). *American Psychiatric Association board of trustees' statement on memories of sexual abuse.* Washington, DC: Author.

American Psychological Association. (1995). *Questions and answers about memories of childhood abuse.* Washington, DC: Author.

Balint, M. (1968). *The basic fault: Therapeutic aspects of regression.* London: Tavistock.

Bass, E., & Davis, L. (1988). *The courage to heal: A guide for women survivors of child sexual abuse.* New York: Harper & Row.

Bion, W. R. (1977). *Seven servants.* New York: Aronson.

Bograd, M. (1992). Values and conflict: Challenges to family therapists' thinking. *Journal of Marital and Family Therapy, 18,* 243–253.

Bradburn, N. M., Rips, L. J., & Shevell, S. K. (1987). Answering autobiographical questions: The impact of memory and inference on surveys. *Science, 236,* 157–161.

Briere, J. (1992). *Child abuse trauma.* Newbury Park, CA: Sage.

Bruner, J. S. (1968). *Processes of cognitive growth: Infancy.* Worcester, MA: Clark University Press.

Carlson v. Humenansky, Case No. CX-93-7260 Ramsey Co., Minnesota (January 24, 1996).

Ceci, S. J., Loftus, E. F., Leichtman, M. D., & Buck, M. (1994). The possible role of source misattributions in the creation of false beliefs among preschoolers. *International Journal of Clinical and Experimental Hypnosis, 42,* 304–320.

Dell, P. F. (1989). Violence and the systemic view: The problem of power. *Family Process, 28,* 1–14.

Donaldson, S. K., & Westerman, M. A. (1986). Development of children's understanding of ambivalence and causal theories of emotion. *Developmental Psychology, 22,* 655–662.

Eagle, M. N. (1984). *Recent developments in psychoanalysis: A critical evaluation.* New York: McGraw-Hill.

Erdelyi, M. H. (1985). *Psychoanalysis: Freud's cognitive psychology.* New York: Freeman.

Fish, V. (1990). Introducing causality and power into family therapy theory: A correction to the systemic paradigm. *Journal of Marital and Family Therapy, 16,* 21–37.

Fish, V. (1993). Poststructuralism in family therapy: Interrogating the narrative/conversational mode. *Journal of Marital and Family Therapy, 19,* 223–232.

Fish V., & Faynik, C. (1989). Treatment of incest families with the father temporarily removed: A structural approach. *Journal of Strategic and Systemic Therapies, 8,* 53–63.

Flavell, J. (1985). *Cognitive development* (2nd ed.). Englewood Cliffs, NJ: Prentice-Hall.

Freud, S. (1957). A metapsychological supplement to the theory of dreams. In J. Strachey (Ed. and Trans.), *The standard edition of the complete works of Sigmund Freud* (Vol. 14, pp. 222–235). London: Hogarth Press. (Original work published 1917)

Freud, S. (1957). Thoughts for the times on war & death. In J. Strachey (Ed. and Trans.), *The standard edition of the complete works of Sigmund Freud* (Vol. 14, pp. 275–300). London: Hogarth Press. (Original work published 1915)

Friedrich, W. N. (1990). *Psychotherapy of sexually abused children and their families.* New York: Norton.

Ganaway, G. (1991, August). *Alternative hypotheses regarding satanic ritual abuse memories.* Paper presented at the annual meeting of the American Psychological Association, San Francisco.

Garry, M., & Loftus, E. (1994). Pseudomemories without hypnosis. *International Journal of Clinical and Experimental Hypnosis, 42,* 363–378.

Goldner, V. (1985). Feminism and family therapy. *Family Process, 24,* 31–47.

Goodman, G. S., & Hahn, A. (1987). Evaluating eyewitness testimony. In I. B. Weiner & A. K. Hess (Eds.), *Handbook of forensic psychology* (pp. 258–292). New York: Wiley.

Hare-Mustin, R. T. (1994). Discourses in the mirrored room: A postmodern analysis of therapy. *Family Process, 33,* 19–35.

Harter, S. (1986). Cognitive-developmental process in the integration of concepts about emotions and the self. *Social Cognition, 4,* 119–151.

Harter, S., & Buddin, B. J. (1987). Children's understanding of the simultaneity of two emotions: A five-stage developmental acquisition sequence. *Developmental Psychology, 23,* 388–399.

Harth, E. (1993). *The creative loop: How the brain makes a mind.* New York: Addison-Wesley.

Haugaard, J. J., Reppucci, N. D., Laurd, J., & Nauful, T. (1991). Children's definitions of the truth and their competency as witnesses in legal proceedings. *Law and Human Behavior, 15,* 253–272.

Herman, J. L. (1992). *Trauma and recovery.* New York: Basic Books.

Hoffman, L. (1986). Beyond power and control. *Family Systems Medicine, 3,* 381–396.

Kassin, S. M., Ellsworth, P. C., & Smith, V. L. (1989). The "general acceptance" of psychological research on eyewitness testimony. *American Psychologist, 44,* 1089–1098.

Kendall-Tackett, K. A., Williams, L. M., & Finkelhor, D. (1993). Impact of sexual abuse on children: A review and synthesis of recent empirical studies. *Psychological Bulletin, 113,* 164–180.

Knapp, S., Tepper, A. M., & VandeCreek, L. (1995). Recovered truth or implanted fabrication? Risk management issues in the false memory debate. *Psychotherapy Bulletin, 30,* 69–73.

Kohut, H. (1971). *The analysis of the self: A systematic approach to the psychoanalytic treatment of narcissistic personality disorders.* New York: International Universities Press.

Kushner, M. G., Riggs, D. S., Foa, E. B., & Miller, S. M. (1992). Perceived controllability and the development of posttraumatic stress disorder (PTSD) in crime victims. *Behaviour Research and Therapy, 31,* 105–110.

Langer, J. (1970). Werner's comparative organismic theory. In P. H. Mussen (Ed.), *Carmichael's manual of child psychology* (3rd ed.) (Vol. 1, pp. 733–771). New York: Wiley.

Laurence, J. R., & Perry, C. (1983). Hypnotically created memory among highly hypnotizable subjects. *Science, 222,* 523–524.

Loftus, E. F. (1993). The reality of repressed memories. *American Psychologist, 48,* 518–537.

Loftus, E. F., & Ketcham, K. (1991). *Witness for the defense.* New York: St. Martin's Press.

Loftus, E. F., Korf, N. L., & Schooler, J. W. (1989). Misguided memories: Sincere distortions of reality. In J. C. Yuille (Ed.), *Credibility assessment* (pp. 155–174). Dordrecht, The Netherlands: Kluwer Academic Publishers.

Madanes, C. (1990). *Sex, love, and violence: Strategies for transformation.* New York: Norton.

Miklulineen, M., & Solomon, Z. (1988). Attributional style and posttraumatic stress disorder. *Journal of Abnormal Psychology, 97,* 308–313.

Morton, J. (1990). The development of event memory. *The Psychologist, 1,* 3–10.

Myers Avis, J. (1992). Where are all the family therapists? Abuse and violence within families and family therapy's response. *Journal of Marital and Family Therapy, 18,* 225–232.

Nash, M. R., & Nadon, R. (in press). The scientific status of hypnosis in the courts. In D. Faigman, D. Kaye, M. Saks, & J. Sanders (Eds.), *Scientific evidence reference manual.*

Neisser, U., & Harsch, N. (1992). Phantom flashbulbs: False recollections of hearing the news about Challenger. In E. Winograd & U. Neisser (Eds.), *Affect and accuracy in recall: Studies of "flashbulb" memories* (pp. 9–31). New York: Cambridge University Press.

Newmark, M., & Beels, C. (1994). The misuse of science in family therapy. *Family Process, 33,* 3–17.

Nichols, M. P., & Schwartz, R. C. (1995). *Family therapy: Concepts and methods* (3rd ed.). Boston: Allyn & Bacon.

Perry, C., Orne, M. T., London, R. W., & Orne, E. C. (1996). Rethinking per se exclusions of hypnotically elicited recall as legal testimony. *International Journal of Clinical and Experimental Hypnosis, 44,* 66–81.

Perry, S., Difede, J., Musngi, G., Frances, A. J., & Jacobsberg, L. (1992). Predictors of posttraumatic stress disorder after burn injury. *American Journal of Psychiatry, 149,* 931–935.

Peterfreund, E. (1978). Some critical comments on psychoanalytic conceptualizations of infancy. *International Journal of Psychoanalysis, 59,* 427–441.

Piaget, J. (1962). *Plays, dreams, and imitation in childhood.* New York: Norton.

Piaget, J. (1973). *The child and reality: Problems of genetic psychology* (A. Rosin, Trans.). New York: Grossman.

Piaget, J., & Inhelder, B. (1969). *The psychology of the child.* New York: Basic Books.

Pynoos, R. S., & Nader, K. (1989). Children's memory and proximity to violence. *Journal of the American Academy of Child and Adolescent Psychiatry, 28,* 236–241.

Ramona v. Ramona, Case No. 1898 Cal.Supr.Ct (1994).

Rubinfine, D. L. (1981). Reconstruction revisited: The question of the reconstruction of mental functioning during the earliest months of life. In S. Tuttman, C. Kaye, & M. Zimmerman (Eds.), *Object and self: A developmental approach: Essays in honor of Edith Jacobson* (pp. 383–395). New York: International Universities Press.

Schafer, R. (1983). *The analytic attitude.* New York: Basic Books.

Sheinberg, M. (1992). Navigating treatment impasses at the disclosure of incest: Combining ideas from feminism and social constructionism. *Family Process, 31,* 201–216.

Sheinberg, M., True, F., & Fraenkel, P. (1994). Treating the sexually abused child: A recursive, multimodal program. *Family Process, 33,* 263–276.

Solomon, Z., Mikulincev, M., & Flum, H. (1988). Negative life events, coping response, and combat-related psychopathology: A prospective study. *Journal of Abnormal Psychology, 97,* 302–307.

Spanos, N., Burgess, C., & Burgess, M. (1994). Past-life identities, UFO abductions, and satanic ritual abuse: The social construction of memories. *International Journal of Clinical and Experimental Hypnosis, 43,* 433–446.

Spence, D. P. (1982). *Narrative truth and historical truth.* New York: Norton.

Spitz, R. A. (1965). *The first year of life: A psychoanalytic study of normal and deviant development of object relations.* New York: International Universities Press.

Stolorow, R. D., & Lachmann, F. M. (1980). *Psychoanalysis of developmental arrests: Theory and treatment.* New York: International Universities Press.

Tavris, C. (1993, January 3). Beware the incest-survivor machine. *New York Times Book Review,* p. 1.

Terr, L. (1994). *Unchained memories.* New York: Basic.

Tillman, J. G., Nash, M. R., & Lerner, P. M. (1994). Does trauma cause dissociative pathology? In S. Lynn & J. Rhue (Eds.), *Dissociation: Clinical and theoretical perspectives* (pp. 395–414). New York: Guilford Press.

Trepper, T. S., & Barrett, M. J. (1986). *Treating incest: A multiple systems perspective.* New York: Haworth.

Watkins, J. G. (1993). Dealing with the problem of "false memory" in clinic and court. *Journal of Psychiatry and Law, 21,* 297–317.

Werner, H. (1948). *Comparative psychology of mental development.* Chicago: Follett.

Westin, D. (1989). Are "primitive" object relations really preoedipal? *American Journal of Orthopsychiatry, 59,* 331–345.

Zimmerman, J. L., & Dickerson, V. C. (1994). Using a narrative metaphor: Implications for theory and clinical practice. *Family Process, 33,* 233–245.

CHAPTER 12

Serious Mental Illness

Ethical Issues in Working with Families

DIANE T. MARSH

In Chapter 1, I offered an overview of the ethical issues that arise in professional practice with families and presented a model for ethical decision making that can be used to resolve ethical dilemmas. In this chapter, I will examine those issues from the perspective of practice with families that include a member who has serious mental illness, such as schizophrenia, bipolar disorder, or major depression. Because these disorders are often severe and persistent, professionals are likely to have many opportunities to meet the needs of family members themselves and to assist them in supporting their relative's treatment, rehabilitation, and recovery. At the same time, a number of ethical issues may pose particular problems in professional practice with these families.

Applying the model of ethical decision making developed by Kitchner (1984, 1986), I will consider selected ethical issues that may arise at each of the three hierarchically-tiered levels: ethical rules, such as those included in professional codes of ethics and in other sets of rules or laws; ethical principles, which are enduring beliefs and specific modes of conduct that protect the interests and welfare of all involved; and ethical theories, which offer a metalevel of analysis that can be used to resolve conflicts between ethical rules or principles.

Consider a practitioner at a university medical center whose responsibilities include working with the families of college students who have been hospitalized at the center. A recent case involves an 18-year-old freshman who is currently a patient in the psychiatric unit, with an admitting diagnosis of schizophrenia. Although the student had been experiencing psychotic symptoms with increasing frequency during the past year, this is his initial hospitalization. Following a course of medication, the patient's condition has improved and he is expected to be discharged to his family, who reside locally. An initial meeting is scheduled with the student's parents and his 16-year-old sister. How can the clinician best address the needs of these family members and what ethical issues are likely to arise?

Following the discussion of the three levels of analysis, I will return to this case and offer some suggestions for working with families in a manner that is both clinically and ethically sound.

The Level of Ethical Rules

Several ethical rules merit particular consideration in professional practice with families of people who have mental illness. These include competence, relationships, informed consent, and confidentiality.

COMPETENCE

In their ethical codes, mental health professionals are mandated to maintain high standards of competence, recognize the boundaries of their competence, and provide only services for which they are qualified (American Psychological Association [APA], 1992). In addition to general clinical competence, when working with families that include a member with mental illness, practitioners need to be knowledgeable about serious mental illness and about relevant family issues.

Serious Mental Illness

Relatively few graduate programs prepare students adequately to work with clients who have serious mental illness (e.g., Johnson, 1990). Practitioners who work with this population need a basic understanding of the diagnostic categories that comprise serious mental illness; of etiological factors, including the strong evidence for a biological substrate (e.g., Torrey, Bowler, Taylor, & Gottesman, 1994); of current approaches to treatment and rehabilitation (e.g., Bedell, Hunter, & Corrigan, in press); of recent research concerned with prognosis (e.g., DeSisto, Harding, McCormack, Ashikaga, & Brooks, 1995); and of community resources. Clinicians also need understanding of the experience of mental illness from the perspective of clients themselves (see Frese, 1994; Hatfield & Lefley, 1994).

Based on 1996 prevalence data from the Center for Mental Health Services (Manderscheid & Sonnenschein, 1996), approximately 5.4 million or 2.7% of the adult population have a "severe and persistent" mental illness, including schizophrenia and serious affective disorders. These disorders may involve positive symptoms, such as hallucinations, delusions, disorganized thought and speech, and bizarre behavior; negative symptoms, which are characterized by a decline in normal thoughts, experiences, and feelings; disturbances of mood, including severely depressed mood, unusually elevated mood, or extreme mood swings; potentially harmful or self-destructive behavior; socially inappropriate or disruptive behavior; and poor daily living habits.

In spite of the devastating impact of these disorders on individuals, families, and society, only a minority of people with mental illness receive appropriate treatment (Wohlford, 1994). Researchers have found that only 21.9% of adults with mental illness receive treatment from health care or mental health care providers; only 12.7% receive services in mental health service settings (Regier et al., 1993). As many people with mental illness reside in our jails and prisons as in all of our hospitals, and at least one-third of the homeless are estimated to have a serious mental illness (Barker, Manderscheid, Hendershot, Jack, & Schoenborn, 1992; Torrey, 1995). The absence of effective treatment has devastating consequences for people with mental illness and for their families.

Many effective pharmacological and psychosocial interventions are now available for clients with mental illness (e.g., Bentley & Walsh, 1996; Scott & Dixon, 1995). In contrast to the message of hopelessness that often accompanied a diagnosis of serious mental illness in the past, long-term studies suggest a life process open to multiple influences and characterized by many outcomes, a majority of them positive (Wasylenki, 1992). Many people with mental illness are leading meaningful and productive lives in their communities, and they are increasingly open about their experiences. As a result, therapists are able to convey a sense of hopefulness to clients and their families.

Family Issues

In working with families of these clients, practitioners also need familiarity with new models and modes of professional practice, with family experiences and needs, and with effective intervention strategies. Although it is rarely included in graduate school curricula, extensive literature is available regarding these topics (Bloch, Szmukler, Herrman,

Benson, & Colussa, 1995; Lefley & Wasow, 1994; Marsh, Lefley, & Husted, 1995).

New Models and Modes

The new models of professional practice are competency-based, with emphasis on the strengths and resources of families (see Marsh, 1992). Similarly, the new modes of working with families are essentially collaborative partnerships that build on the expertise of clients, families, and professionals, with the objective of developing mutual goals for treatment and rehabilitation. Reflecting these new models and modes, practitioners should offer services to families in a manner that acknowledges their contributions, provides opportunities for them to enhance family functioning, and promotes a sense of intrafamilial mastery and control. The following family member benefited from this approach:

We have discussed my mother's illness with each other and with her therapist. Just because there is mental illness in a family doesn't mean the family has to stop growing as a unit or that the person cannot lead a constructive life. It was a strong family before my mother's illness. It's gotten much stronger since. (Marsh & Dickens, in press)

In addition to using a strengths-based and collaborative approach, clinicians need to understand the family experience of mental illness, including the essential needs of families and the special issues of parents, spouses, siblings, and offspring.

The Family Experience of Mental Illness.   The serious mental illness of a close relative is a catastrophic event for families (Marsh & Johnson, in press). As one family member attests, "This terrible illness colors everything—a family cannot escape." Another family member echoes this sense of family embroilment:

All family members are affected by a loved one's mental illness. The entire family system needs to be addressed. To assure us that we are not to blame and the situation is not hopeless. To point us to people and places that can help our loved one. The impact still lingers on. (Marsh & Dickens, in press)

Our current system of care is as much family- as community-based, and families generally serve as the first and last resort for their relatives, often with little professional guidance. Families fulfill crucial roles as primary caregivers for relatives who reside at home, as informal case managers who advocate for their relatives with service providers, and as crisis intervention specialists who handle relapses and emergencies. Whether their relatives live at home or in another setting, most families remain involved.

Researchers have consistently documented the devastating impact of mental illness on families, often defining the family experience of mental illness in terms of family burden, which has subjective and objective components (Lefley, 1996). Subjective burden refers to the personal suffering experienced by family members in response to their relative's illness; objective burden consists of the daily problems and challenges associated with the illness.

In response to their relative's mental illness, most family members experience a powerful grieving process that involves both real and symbolic losses; chronic sorrow that is woven into the familial fabric on a continuing basis; an "emotional roller coaster" in response to the alternating periods of relapse and remission that often characterize the course of mental illness; and empathic pain, as family members share in their relative's struggle against the forces of psychosis. The following mother portrays the depth of this subjective burden:

The problems with my daughter were like a black hole inside of me into which everything else had been drawn. My grief and pain were so intense sometimes that I barely got through the day. It felt like a mourning process, as if I were dealing with the loss of the daughter I had loved for 18 years, for whom there was so much potential. (Marsh, 1992, p. 10)

In addition to this powerful subjective burden, family members are confronted with the real-world challenges that comprise the objective burden. These include coping with their relative's symptomatic behavior, with caregiving roles for which they are unprepared and untrained, with family disruption and stress, with an often unresponsive and inhumane service delivery system, and with the social stigma that marginalizes and ostracizes people with mental illness and their families. The following man describes the objective burden that accompanied his father's mental illness during his own childhood and adolescence:

My father's paranoid schizophrenia meant we moved frequently, because he felt the conspiracy was closing in on him. He battered my mother, because he felt she was part of the conspiracy. I was too frightened to go to her aid. I couldn't have friendships with peers because my father felt they might "poison" my mind against him. (Marsh & Dickens, in press)

Although family burden is the most salient aspect of the family experience of mental illness, professionals should be aware of the potential for family resilience (Marsh et al., 1996). As with any catastrophic event, the illness may serve as a catalyst for family members to change in constructive ways as they learn to rebound from adversity and to cope with their altered circumstances. In recent research concerned with family resilience, we heard from many family members who affirmed the strengths noted by this sibling: "When a family experiences something like this, it makes for very compassionate people—people of substance. My brother has created a bond among us all that we will not allow to be broken" (Marsh & Dickens, in press).

In response to questions about any family strengths that had developed as a result of the mental illness, our survey participants noted their family bonds, commitments, strengths, growth, contributions, and gratifications. Our participants also affirmed their potential for personal resilience, noting that they had become better, stronger, and more compassionate people. The following family member conveys this sense of family and personal resilience:

I have become much more tolerant of imperfection in myself and others. I can face adversity with courage. . . . I have learned to appreciate the strengths of other people who appear to be different or are handicapped in some way. Our daughter's younger siblings accept her and make special efforts to help her feel a part of the family. My husband and I are closer and more honest with each other as a result of our shared grief and stress. . . . We are proud that our family has remained intact and strong. (Marsh et al., 1996, p. 10)

It is essential to place family resilience in the context of family burden, which is experienced by virtually all families. As one family member commented, "Any increased sensitivity to others or any other 'side effects' would be traded in an eyeblink for a healthy relative" (Marsh & Dickens, in press). Nevertheless, the potential for family resilience has important implications for practitioners, who can assist families in coping effectively with the mental illness and its consequences for their family.

In addition to family burden and resilience, clinicians need to understand the unique experiences and concerns of parents, spouses, siblings, and offspring, so that they can address the needs of individual family members. As Rolland (1994) has discussed, the impact of chronic illness on family members depends partly on its timing in their life span and on their roles and responsibilities within the family. As a result, individual family members have unique experiences, needs, and concerns in their role as parent, spouse, sibling, or offspring (Wasow, 1995). Thus, while addressing the needs of the family as a unit, practitioners can also offer services to individual family members. I will briefly mention each of these family roles.

As adult family members, parents and spouses share in the family burden, although they also have unique concerns. Parents generally experience a range of intense losses, both real and symbolic. They are most likely to assume responsibilities as primary caregivers or informal case managers, sometimes for a lifetime. Parents are also prone to feelings of guilt and responsibility, which may be intensified by professionals who espouse earlier conceptual models that incorporate unsupported assumptions of family pathogenesis or dysfunction. Spouses are subject to emotional, social, and financial losses similar to those that accompany spousal bereavement. They may face increased responsibility for parenting and other aspects of family life, as well as substantial conflict if they consider separation or divorce.

Because of their developmental status, young family members share a special vulnerability to the mental illness in their families (Marsh & Dickens, in press). It would be expected, for instance, that the disruption accompanying the mental illness of a parent or older sibling might undermine the acquisition of basic trust during infancy, the development of peer relationships and academic skills during childhood, and the establishment of a secure sense of identity during adolescence. A child who is confronted from birth with the mental illness of a close relative may be vulnerable to all of these risks.

Siblings may experience the dual losses of their brother or sister and of their parents, whose energy may be consumed by the mental illness; the sense that their own needs have been neglected; an effort to compensate their anguished parents for their own losses (the "replacement child syndrome"); and alienation from the world of their peers. Offspring may become enveloped in the psychotic system of their parent, with an adverse impact on their own perceptions; may move into a "parentified" role before they have finished being children; or may attempt to become perfect children to spare their beleaguered family additional problems. The losses of young family members may be profound, as the following sibling attests, "I lost out on my childhood"

(Marsh & Dickens, in press). Likewise, an adult offspring wrote about "my loss of a healthy mother, a normal childhood, and a stable home."

As a result of the mental illness in their midst, families have a number of essential needs, including their needs for information about mental illness and community resources, for skills to cope with the illness and its consequences for their family, and for support for themselves. A range of intervention strategies can address these needs as well as the unique concerns of individual family members.

Family Interventions

Like all families, families of people with mental illness are a diverse group and vary along a continuum of competence. Some of these families are effective in fulfilling all of their functions; others experience difficulty in solving even minor problems; and most families fall someplace in the middle of the continuum. Accordingly, professionals need to avoid making general assumptions about families of people with mental illness, to evaluate each family on its own terms, and to develop a service plan that provides an optimal match for a given family.

Reflecting a historical shift in perspective from the family as a cause of mental illness to the family as a source of support, a range of family interventions are now available. See Marsh and Johnson (in press) for a discussion of these interventions, which include family support and advocacy groups, family consultation, family education, family psychoeducation, and psychotherapy. At the time of their relative's diagnosis, clinicians can offer assistance to families through a referral to the local affiliate of the National Alliance for the Mentally Ill (NAMI), the largest mental health advocacy organization in the country, with over 1000 local affiliates in all 50 states. They can also recommend publications and other resources designed for families (e.g., Mueser & Gingerich, 1994; Torrey, 1995).

When working directly with families, practitioners can assume an initial role as a family consultant, offering assistance to families regarding a wide range of illness-related concerns and assisting them in making an informed choice regarding their use of other available services (Bernheim, 1989; Wynne, McDaniel, & Weber, 1987). Working with individual families or with multiple family groups, clinicians can also offer education about mental illness and its treatment, about caregiving and management issues, about the mental health system and community resources, and about family coping and adaption (see Anderson, Reiss, & Hogarty, 1986, for a sample educational program for families).

Working with a group of professionals as a team, practitioners might also offer family psychoeducation, which is a more intensive and long-term intervention that includes family education, skills training, and support (see Falloon, Boyd, & McGill, 1984). Finally, some family members may also be appropriate candidates for traditional clinical intervention, including individual, marital, and family therapy. Family members who pursue psychotherapy will also benefit from other services designed to meet their needs for information, skills, and support.

RELATIONSHIPS

Mental health professionals are required to clarify at the outset which individuals are clients and the relationship the clinician will have with each person (APA, 1992). Reflecting the intervention strategies already discussed, practitioners who work with families may serve as family consultants, as family educators or psychoeducators, or as psychotherapists. In addition to clarifying their own role, clinicians should clarify at the outset which family members are clients, the relationship the therapist will have with each, and policies regarding communication with family members who are not clients, such as the parents of an adult client with mental illness who resides at home. Especially if families are serving as primary caregivers, it is important to consider the impact of decisions on all members of the family and to involve families in decisions that affect them, whether or not they become clients themselves.

When working with families of people who have mental illness, practitioners should also clarify the differences among family consultation, education, psychoeducation, and psychotherapy, and assist families in making an informed choice about their use of professional services. As Bernheim (1989) has discussed, these families often do not see themselves as needing or wanting therapy and may object to being treated as "unidentified patients" in their contacts with service providers. At the same time, families may benefit from other professional services that address their educational and supportive needs.

INFORMED CONSENT

Mental health professionals are required to obtain appropriate informed consent to therapy or related procedures, using language that is reasonably understandable to participants (APA, 1992). When working with these families, consultants can assist them in making an informed decision about their use of services by discussing the available services, their potential risks and benefits, the risks of forgoing services, and possible alternatives. Research support for various services might also be shared with families.

There is empirical evidence, for example, that certain family variables are related to increased relapse rates of clients with serious mental illness (Dixon & Lehman, 1995; Lefley, 1992). These family variables (criticism, hostility, and over-involvement) are called *expressed emotion.* Researchers also have found that psychoeducational programs designed to decrease an initially high level of expressed emotion in family caregivers can significantly reduce the risk of client relapse. Thus, if there is a high level of conflict in a particular family, it might be appropriate to explain that people with serious mental illness are unusually vulnerable to high levels of stress and to encourage the family to participate in a psychoeducational program.

Knowledgeable practitioners can also share information about community resources and professional services. As a unit, families can then decide which services best meet their needs in the present and in an uncertain future. As individuals, family members may elect to receive a referral for additional services, such as a specialized support group for siblings or spouses, or for personal psychotherapy.

CONFIDENTIALITY

At the outset and thereafter as new circumstances warrant, mental health professionals are required to discuss confidentiality and its limitations, as well as the foreseeable uses of information generated in therapy and evaluation (APA, 1992). Confidentiality often poses challenges for clinicians who work with family members who are not clients (e.g., Petrila & Sadoff, 1992). Especially if family members are serving as primary caregivers for clients who reside at home, the right of clients to a confidential therapeutic relationship may conflict with the right of families to be involved in decisions that affect them.

Families often complain that professionals fail to communicate with them and to address their legitimate concerns. For example, family members often feel cut off from essential information that would increase their understanding, improve their coping effectiveness, and assist them with long-term planning. Practitioners sometimes justify this failure to communicate with families on the basis of confidentiality, an explanation that evokes frustration among families:

A major problem in the mental health system is the exclusion of relatives under the guise of client confidentiality. Involve them! Acknowledge them and their grief, their loss, anger, and frustration. They are hungry for information. Give them concrete ways to deal with their relatives. Do not blame. (Marsh & Dickens, in press)

As Zipple and his colleagues discuss (see Chapter 13), a number of strategies are available to resolve problems related to confidentiality. These include providing nonconfidential information to families about mental illness and making referrals to family support and advocacy groups, such as NAMI. When dealing with confidential information, practitioners can use release of information procedures (Marsh, Lefley, & Husted, 1995 provide a sample release form designed specifically for family members), include family members on the treatment team (with the permission of the client), or serve as mediators who negotiate the boundaries of confidentiality to meet the needs of particular clients and families. In institutional settings, separate staff may be assigned to serve as family advocates who work directly with families.

Confidentiality does not prohibit professionals from listening to family members, although it may be clinically unwise in certain cases. Even when clinicians feel it is best not to have contact with families (for example, to protect a fragile therapeutic relationship), family members should have an avenue to express their concerns and share their observations, perhaps with another staff member who can consult with the therapist. Family members might wish to share observations about the risk of imminent harm, indications of substance abuse, evidence of treatment or medication noncompliance, or other serious matters. I recently heard from a mother who had tried unsuccessfully to communicate her concern about her daughter's potential for suicide. Her daughter did in fact attempt suicide, which might have been avoided if there had been better channels of communication.

Another case illustrates the problems that can result when potential conflicts regarding confidentiality are ignored. A mother called a taxi to return her son to his community residence after a weekend visit at home. When she contacted the agency to make sure her son had arrived safely, she was told that the staff were not permitted to give out any information about the residents. A policy that encouraged residents to contact families upon arrival might have prevented this situation which was understandably frustrating for the mother. Moreover, decisions regarding the information to be shared with families should be made not by staff but by clients, who should be given an opportunity to make an informed choice about these matters as early as possible.

The Level of Ethical Principles

At the first level of ethical rules, dilemmas may arise that offer no obvious resolution. In a given case, for example, the practitioner might believe that the welfare of the client is best served by working closely with the family, with whom the client resides. Perhaps there has been much conflict in the family during this difficult period, and the client does not wish to have the family involved, threatening to terminate treatment if the therapist talks with his or her parents. At the same time, the parents, who are understandably concerned about their adult child, are asserting their right to be kept fully informed about the nature and course of treatment, for which they are paying. Another dilemma might arise if the clinician recommends family therapy, but the parents respond that they do not wish to participate in this form of intervention. Or perhaps some family members are willing to attend family sessions, but others refuse, such as one parent or a sibling. The clinician believes that all family members must participate for family therapy to be effective. What is the best—and most ethical—course of action under each of these circumstances?

These dilemmas offer no easy resolution at the first level of analysis. Accordingly, practitioners may need to shift the second and more general level of ethical principles, which include autonomy, beneficence, and nonmaleficence.

AUTONOMY

Reflecting the principle of autonomy, families have a right to choose their degree of participation in therapy, to decline to participate at all, to set or alter goals, and to withdraw without undue pressure (Lakin, 1988). However, the right of families to make an informed choice about the use of services may conflict with other ethical concerns, such as the welfare of a client with mental illness. Based on the assumption that family involvement is essential for effective treatment of a client, for example, an agency or individual practitioner might require other family members to participate in family therapy as a condition for obtaining treatment for their relative. Such a requirement is not uncommon in professional practice with children and adolescents, although this policy may increase the potential for negative treatment effects if the needs and desires of parents are ignored (see the discussion in Chapter 1).

A flexible approach to working with families is generally best. There are many ways for families to be involved in their relative's treatment and to meet their own needs. Assuming an initial role as a family consultant, the practitioner can discuss the available services, perhaps referring the parents to a family support and advocacy group in the community and addressing their illness-related questions and concerns on an as-needed basis. A formal educational or psychoeducational program might also be recommended if appropriate, as well as individual, marital, or family therapy. Services are more likely to be accepted and beneficial when families have made an informed choice based on their own needs and preferences.

BENEFICENCE

Consistent with the principle of beneficence, professionals are mandated to contribute actively to the good of others. Given the diversity among families of people with mental illness, the goal of professional practice is to achieve an optimal match between the needs, desires, and resources of particular families and the available services. An initial consultation can allow practitioners to educate families about available services and encourage families to share their needs and concerns.

Consultants should conduct a cost-benefit analysis of various alternatives and discuss this analysis with families. Reflecting the principle of least intervention (Thompson, 1990), they should recommend the form of intervention that offers maximum benefits with fewest risks and reasonable costs.

An important consideration is the research support for the effectiveness of various services, as well as familial perception of their value. For example, families who have a member with serious mental illness consistently rate educational and supportive resources as more helpful than individual, marital, group, or family therapy (Marsh, 1995). Thus, a family consultant might make an initial referral for a family support group or educational program, which can jointly meet many family needs. Families whose needs are not met by these resources might be referred for additional services, such as a psychoeducational program or psychotherapy for one or more members.

Nonmaleficence

Nonmaleficence is the directive to do no harm, which is defined broadly to include a range of adverse consequences, including negative treatment effects. The literature describing clinical practice with families of clients with mental illness suggests that the potential for negative treatment effects is relatively high among this population (Marsh, 1992). For example, there is the risk of adverse effects when clinicians inappropriately assume that families are pathogenic or dysfunctional (e.g., Carr, 1990; Lewis, 1989). Such unsupported assumptions, which often guided professional practice in the past, are likely to intensify the subjective burden of family members and to undermine their relationships with professionals. Although current practitioners are more likely to work collaboratively with families and to acknowledge their supportive role, family members continue to report that the system is unresponsive to their needs (e.g., Lefley, 1996). As one family member asserted, "Caring families get socked with most of the responsibility and blame but little legal or therapeutic support. We must change the system" (Marsh & Dickens, in press).

Additional risks are associated with general prescriptions of family therapy that do not take into account the needs, desires, and resources of specific families (Marsh, 1992). As noted, the most compelling needs of families are for information about mental illness and its treatment, for skills to cope with the illness and its consequences for their family, and for support for themselves. As a result, psychotherapeutic interventions that focus on intrapsychic or intrafamilial phenomena may be experienced by families as irrelevant or even intrusive. In addition, both family and marital therapy carry potential risks, including loss of privacy and increased family disruption in family therapy, and deflection from personal problems and concerns in marital therapy.

The Level of Ethical Theories

If professionals find they cannot resolve an ethical conflict at the level of ethical rules or principles, they can shift to the third level of ethical theories. This metalevel of analysis facilitates resolution of ethical conflicts through an examination of all possible consequences of decisions and defines the scope of ethical practice to include all relevant parties, including family members who are not clients. For instance, parents who are serving as primary caregivers for an adult child who resides with them are likely to be affected by discharge and treatment plans. Similarly, they may be expected to monitor medication compliance and to remain alert for signs of impending relapse. Although these parents may not be clients themselves, they cannot serve as effective caregivers in the absence of relevant information. Yet practitioners may assume that client confidentiality prevents them from working with parents.

The ethical theories of universalizability and utilitarianism can be used to resolve ethical dilemmas at the third level of analysis. Universalizability postulates that ethical decisions are consistent with those that individuals would make under the same circumstances for themselves or others whom they love. Professionals who work with families of people who have mental illness are well aware of the powerful burden borne by these families. It is not difficult to empathize with them or to imagine what it must be like to confront this tragic and life-transforming diagnosis in a beloved relative. Such an empathic perspective can offer a useful vantage point for considering ethical dilemmas and striving for the most appropriate resolution. For example, with their relative's consent, it may be appropriate for parents who are primary caregivers to serve on the treatment team, which can offer them an opportunity to share their insights and concerns and to be involved in decisions that affect their family.

Utilitarian theory requires that all possible benefits be weighed against all possible costs for all affected individuals, which certainly includes families of clients with mental illness, especially if they are serving as primary caregivers. Following an assessment of the potential impact of a decision on the family as a unit and on all individual members, the ethical course of action is that which results in the least amount of avoidable harm. When families are clients themselves, clinicians have the opportunity to encourage all members of the family to examine various courses of action and their implications for the family as a unit and for each member. As families improve their skills in problem solving and conflict resolution, their ability to achieve equitable solutions will improve. Even when family members are not clients, therapists can maintain a family systems perspective when working with the relative who has mental illness, encouraging the client to consider the perspectives of other family members. The clinician can also offer consultation to the family as needed or, if appropriate, refer the family to another practitioner who can establish a separate relationship with the family.

From Theory to Practice

Let us return to the case of the 18-year-old college student with schizophrenia who is planning to return home following his initial hospitalization, focusing on the ethical issues already discussed. The ethical theories of universalizability and utilitarianism encourage practitioners to maintain a family systems perspective and to consider the impact of professional decisions on the family as a unit and on all individual members. Indeed, such a perspective is already legally and ethically mandated under some circumstances (for example, when there is risk of imminent harm), and is the standard approach when working with families that include a member with a developmental disability (e.g., Turnbull & Turnbull, 1990) or chronic medical condition (e.g., McDaniel, Hepworth, & Doherty, 1992). Applying the theory of utilitarianism, the parents and younger sibling are clearly "affected individuals" who merit consideration in clinical and ethical decision making.

Examining some of the relevant ethical rules and principles, what issues are likely to arise in working with this family? Initially, in order to work effectively with this family, professionals need to maintain (or to develop) *competence* regarding serious mental illness and relevant family concerns. For example, they should be able to meet family needs for information, skills, and support, and to address the unique concerns of individual family members, including the 16-year-old sibling.

As early as possible, issues related to *confidentiality* need to be addressed in a manner that respects the need of the college student for a confidential relationship in therapy, as well as the needs of a family that is assuming a caregiving role under challenging circumstances. The practitioner might explain to the client the importance of having informed parents who can support his treatment and facilitate his recovery. At the same time, the son needs to be encouraged to discuss with his therapist the information that will be shared with his parents and the nature of their involvement in his treatment.

Reflecting the importance of clarifying *relationships* and promoting a process of *informed consent*, the professional will need to establish which family members are clients and the relationship to be established with each. The family consultant should inform the family of the range of services available to them, the potential benefits and risks of these services, and the available alternatives. Once the parents and sibling have made a decision about their use of services, the practitioner can make appropriate referrals or offer direct services to the family.

The approach thus far is consistent with the ethical principles of *autonomy*, which appears to ensure the right of the parents to make an informed choice about their involvement in services, although this right may conflict with other ethical concerns, such as the welfare of their son. For instance, their son's therapist may believe that parent involvement is essential for his recovery, but the parents do not wish to participate in family therapy. It is important to aim for a resolution of this dilemma that acknowledges both ethical concerns (informed choice and welfare of the client), and that respects the rights and preferences of all parties.

Under these circumstances, family consultants might discuss the various ways in which the parents can be involved in their son's treatment and assist them in evaluating their options. For example, the parents might be interested in a referral to a family support and advocacy group in the community and in periodic consultation with a professional who can offer assistance with illness-related questions and problems. Similarly, the needs and preferences of the 16-year-old sister should also be addressed. She might appreciate a referral to a specialized support group for siblings or for personal counseling as she comes to terms with her brother's mental illness and its meaning for her life.

Consistent with the principle of *beneficence*, the goal with this family—as with all families—is to achieve an optimal match between their needs, desires, and resources and the available services. Based on the expressed needs of the family and on a cost-benefit analysis of available services, practitioners should recommend the course of action that offers maximum benefits with fewest risks and reasonable costs. The initial intervention for most families should address their informational and supportive needs. For example, during the first session with this family, the practitioner might recommend useful publications and make a referral to a community organization such as NAMI, which offers education and support to families, as well as opportunities for advocacy.

The practitioner should also discuss other available services with the family, assist them in deciding which services best meet their needs, and help them to access those services. As noted elsewhere (Marsh & Johnson, in press), when working with such families practitioners can assist them in:

- Understanding and normalizing the family experience of mental illness;

- Focusing on the strengths and competencies of their family and their relative;
- Learning about mental illness, the mental health system, and community resources;
- Developing skills in stress management, problem solving, and communication;
- Resolving their feelings of grief and loss;
- Coping with the symptoms of mental illness and its repercussions for their family;
- Identifying and responding to the signs of impending relapse;
- Creating a supportive family environment;
- Developing realistic expectations for all members of the family;
- Playing a meaningful role in their relative's treatment, rehabilitation, and recovery; and
- Maintaining a balance that meets the needs of all members of the family.

The family service plan might consist of a single intervention or a combination of services. The plan might also change over time, as family members learn to cope with their relative's mental illness and as their own needs and concerns evolve. Thus, professionals should maintain a lifespan perspective when working with families who are likely to benefit from professional services on an as-needed basis, perhaps in response to a rehospitalization or relapse on the part of their relative or to stressful events in their own lives.

The suggested approach is likely to decrease the potential for *nonmaleficence,* including negative treatment effects. The family consultant has worked collaboratively with the family in designing a service plan that addresses their expressed needs and respects their preferences. Similarly, the consultant has focused on the supportive role of the family and on their strengths and potential contributions. This competency-based approach to professional practice reduces the risk that the family will be harmed by the application of earlier models that held families accountable for their relative's mental illness and that often served as the rationale for a recommendation of family therapy, sometimes without the consent of the family. In contrast, should this family choose to participate in family therapy, their choice will be an informed one designed to address their specific needs and concerns.

Finally, both clinically and ethically, the overarching concern in professional practice is to establish a constructive alliance with families who have a member with mental illness. Such an alliance is likely to be facilitated by a collaborative and competency-based approach to professional practice, by an understanding of family experiences and needs, and by an individualized family service plan designed to address their expressed needs.

References

American Psychological Association. (1992). Ethical principles of psychologists and code of conduct. *American Psychologist, 47,* 1597–1611.

Anderson, C. M., Reiss, D. J., & Hogarty, G. E. (1986). *Schizophrenia and the family.* New York: Guilford.

Barker, P. R., Manderscheid, R. W., Hendershot, G. E., Jack, S. S., & Schoenborn, C. A. (1992). Serious mental illness and disability in the adult household population: United States, 1989. In R. W. Manderscheid & M. A. Sonnenschein (Eds.), *Mental health, United States, 1992* (DHHS Publication No. SMA 92-1942). Washington, DC: U.S. Government Printing Office.

Bedell, J. R., Hunter, R. H., & Corrigan, P. W. (in press). Current approaches to assessment and treatment of persons with severe mental illness. *Professional Psychology: Research and Practice.*

Bentley, K. J., & Walsh, J. (1996). *The social worker & psychotropic medication: Toward effective collaboration with mental health clients, families, and providers.* Pacific Grove, CA: Brooks/Cole.

Bernheim, K. F. (1989). Psychologists and families of the severely mentally ill: The role of family consultation. *American Psychologist, 44,* 561–564.

Bloch, S., Szmukler, G. I., Herrman, H., Benson, A., & Colussa, S. (1995). Counseling caregivers of relatives with schizophrenia: Themes, interventions, and caveats. *Family Process, 34,* 413–425.

Carr, A. (1990). Failure in family therapy: A catalogue of engagement mistakes. *Journal of Family Therapy, 12,* 371–386.

DeSisto, M. J., Harding, C. M., McCormack, R. V., Ashikaga, T., & Brooks, G. W. (1995). The Maine and Vermont three-decade studies of serious mental illness. *British Journal of Psychiatry, 167,* 331–342.

Dixon, L. B., & Lehman A. F. (1995). Family interventions for schizophrenia. *Schizophrenia Bulletin, 21,* 631–643.

Falloon, I. R. H., Boyd, J. L., & McGill, C. W. (1984). *Family care of schizophrenia.* New York: Guilford.

Frese, F. J. (1994). Psychology's role in a consumer-driven system. In D. T. Marsh (Ed.), *New directions in the psychological treatment of serious mental illness* (pp. 79–98). Westport, CT: Praeger.

Hatfield, A. B., & Lefley, H. P. (1993). *Surviving mental illness.* New York: Guilford.

Johnson, D. L. (Ed.). (1990). *Service needs of the seriously mentally ill: Training implications for psychology.* Washington, DC: American Psychological Association.

Kitchener, K. S. (1984). Intuition, critical evaluation and ethical principles: The foundation for ethical decisions in counseling psychology. *Counseling Psychologist, 12,* 43–55.

Kitchener, K. S. (1986). Teaching applied ethics in counselor education: An integration of psychological processes and philosophical analysis. *Journal of Counseling and Development, 64,* 306–310.

Lakin, M. (1988). *Ethical issues in the psychotherapies.* New York: Oxford University Press.

Lefley, H. P. (1992). Expressed emotion: Conceptual, clinical, and social policy issues. *Hospital and Community Psychiatry, 43,* 591–598.

Lefley, H. P. (1996). *Family caregiving in mental illness* (Family Caregiver Applications Series, Vol. 7). Thousand Oaks, CA: Sage.

Lefley, H. P., & Wasow, M. (Eds.). (1994). *Helping families cope with mental illness.* Newark, NJ: Harwood Academic.

Lewis, W. (1989). How not to engage a family in family therapy. *Journal of Strategic and Systemic Therapies, 8,* 50–53.

Manderscheid, R. W., & Sonnenschein, M. A. (Eds.). (1996). *Mental health, United States, 1996.* Rockville, MD: Substance Abuse and Mental Health Services Administration, Center for Mental Health Services.

Marsh, D. T. (1992). *Families and mental illness: New directions in professional practice.* New York: Praeger.

Marsh, D. T. (1995). Families and serious mental illness: Ethical issues in professional practice. *Family Psychologist, 11*(1), 17–19.

Marsh, D. T., & Dickens, R. M. (in press). *Troubled journey: Coming to terms with the mental illness of a sibling or parent.* New York: Tarcher/Putnam.

Marsh, D. T., & Johnson, D. L. (in press). The family experience of mental illness: Implications for intervention. *Professional Psychology: Research and Practice.*

Marsh, D. T., Lefley, H. P., Evans-Rhodes, D., Ansell, V. I., Doerzbacher, B. M., LaBarbera, L., & Paluzzi, J. E. (1996). The family experience of mental illness: Evidence for resilience. *Psychiatric Rehabilitation Journal, 20*(2), 3–12.

Marsh, D. T., Lefley, H. P., & Husted, J. R. (1995). Families of people with mental illness. In M. Harway (Ed.), *Treating the changing family: Handling normative and unusual events* (pp. 171–203). New York: Wiley.

McDaniel, S. H., Hepworth, J., & Doherty, W. J. (1992). *Medical family therapy: A biopsychosocial approach to families with health problems.* New York: Basic Books.

Mueser, K. T., & Gingerich, S. (1994). *Coping with schizophrenia: A guide for families*. Oakland, CA: New Harbinger.

Petrila, J. P., & Sadoff, R. L. (1992). Confidentiality and the family as caregiver. *Hospital and Community Psychiatry, 43,* 136–139.

Regier, D. A., Narrow, W. E., Rae, D. S., Manderscheid, R. W., Locke, B. Z., & Goodwin, F. K. (1993). The de facto U.S. Mental and Addictive Disorders Service System: Epidemiologic Catchment Area prospective 1-year prevalence rates of disorders and services. *Archives of General Psychiatry, 50,* 85–94.

Rolland, J. S. (1994). *Families, illness, and disability: An integrative treatment model*. New York: Basic Books.

Scott, J. E., & Dixon, L. B. (1995). Psychological interventions for schizophrenia. *Schizophrenia Bulletin, 21,* 621–630.

Thompson, A. (1990). *Guide to ethical practice in psychotherapy*. New York: Wiley.

Torrey, E. F. (1995). *Surviving schizophrenia: A manual for families, consumers, and providers* (3rd ed.). New York: HarperCollins.

Torrey, E. F., Bowler, A., Taylor, E., & Gottesman, I. (1994). *Schizophrenia and Manic-Depressive Disorder*. New York: Basic Books.

Turnbull, A. P., & Turnbull, H. R. (1990). *Families, professionals, and exceptionality: A special partnership* (2nd ed.). Columbus, OH: Merrill.

Wasow, M. (1995). *The skipping stone: Ripple effects of mental illness on the family*. Palo Alto, CA: Science & Behavior Books.

Wasylenki, D. A. (1992). Psychotherapy of schizophrenia revisited. *Hospital and Community Psychiatry, 43,* 123–127.

Wohlford, P. (1994). National perspectives on clinical training for psychological services. In D. T. Marsh (Ed.), *New directions in the psychological treatment of serious mental illness* (pp. 3–20). Westport, CT: Praeger.

Wynne, L. C., McDaniel, S. H., & Weber, T. T. (1987). Professional politics and the concepts of family therapy, family consultation, and systems consultation. *Family Therapy, 26,* 153–166.

CHAPTER 13

Client Confidentiality and the Family's Need to Know

Strategies for Resolving the Conflict

ANTHONY M. ZIPPLE, SUSAN LANGLE, WAYNE TYRELL,
LEROY SPANIOL, and HARRIET FISHER

In an era of ongoing efforts to enhance the level and frequency of communication with one another, the distinction between what is uniquely personal and what others need to know about our lives becomes increasingly difficult to distinguish and preserve.

A basic foundation of any therapeutic relationship is confidentiality. Without the recognized respect for the privacy of patients and the holding of patient confidence, the helping relationship will be unable to fully reach its therapeutic potential.

Each year an estimated 250,000 psychiatrically disabled adults are discharged from inpatient settings and return to live with their families (Zipple & Spaniol, 1987). A survey of National Alliance for the Mentally Ill members found that 42 percent of the families reported having their ill family member living with them (Steinwachs, Kasper, & Skinner, 1992). When the patient and his or her family are mutually involved in the rehabilitation program, there are no clear and easy guidelines to balance the dilemma of patient privacy or confidentiality and the family members' genuine need to be informed and included in treatment strategies. Even the strongest and most resourceful of these families may experience extreme levels of stress, frustration, anger, grief, and pain as they attempt to provide support for their loved one who has a mental illness. Families struggle to provide adequate assistance to the mentally ill member who recently required the support and control of a professionally-staffed hospital unit; the strain of their efforts can become unbearable (Wasow, 1994a). As Maryellen Walsh (1985), the mother of a young man with schizophrenia wrote, a major mental illness can "ransack their lives with a ferocity unimagined outside of the family circle" (p. 21).

Mental illness is a complex and puzzling phenomenon. Families have a myriad of questions concerning their loved one's impairment and they want and need information on the diagnosis, etiology, treatment, and prognosis of the illness. Providing such information can be of enormous assistance to families as they work to understand and support their relative (Hatfield, 1987; Lefley, 1996; Mueser & Gingerich, 1994; Torrey, 1995). In addition, there is significant evidence that providing information in these areas to families decreases the frequency of relapse among the ill members (Anderson, Reiss, & Hogarty, 1986; Falloon, Boyd, & McGill, 1985; Leff, Kuipers, Berkowitz, Eberbein-Vries, & Sturgeon, 1982; McFarlane, 1990, 1994).

In spite of the importance of providing such information to families and the evidence that it benefits both the person who has a mental illness and his or her family, professionals frequently fail to give this information to families. For example, Spaniol, Jung, Zipple, and Fitzgerald (1987) found that 58 percent of the families they surveyed reported that professionals did not adequately assist them in understanding their family member's illness. Holden and Lewine (1982) found that one-third of the families in their study were given no diagnostic information for two years or more after their family member's initial breakdown, 47 percent were given no information about the reasons for prescribing medications, and 76 percent received no information about the possibility and nature of medication side effects. Bernheim and Switalski (1988) found that although mental health practitioners and family members had somewhat favorable attitudes about each other, there was limited direct contact between families and practitioners. This severely limits the ability of practitioners to provide meaningful information.

A significant factor in the reluctance of professionals to disclose such basic information seems to be concerns about protecting the confidentiality of their clients (Dearth, Labenski, Mott, & Pelligrini, 1986; McElroy & McElroy, 1994). Although it is important to respect the client's right to confidentiality, an impermeable wall of confidentiality between the client and practitioner and the client's family is not generally in the interest of any of the parties. In this chapter, we attempt to provide strategies for resolving the conflict between the client's right to confidentiality and the family's need to know.

Legal Issues in Confidentiality

Mental healthcare providers are often caught between their desire to be supportive of families and their ethical and legal obligations to protect the confidences of their clients. Complicating this potential conflict is a fear of legal liability for improperly disclosing information, as well as fear of liability for failing to warn or take other protective action in emergencies that might demand disclosure of confidences.

Confidentiality laws must be seen in the context of an American society that protects the individual rights and liberties of all citizens as evidenced by the federal Bill of Rights, as well as such other protections contained in the constitution of each state. The concept of personal privacy protected from invasion by the government is elaborated in the many court decisions interpreting the First Amendment, which protects freedom of speech, exercise of religious beliefs, and right of assembly; the Fourth Amendment, which provides for security of persons, houses, and papers from unreasonable searches or seizures; and the Fifth, Ninth, and Fourteenth Amendments. Indeed, the Supreme Court has read these provisions together as supporting a general right of privacy for married couples to make family planning decisions (*Griswold v. Connecticut*, 1965).

With this firm commitment to the rights of the individual in mind, it is understandable that the confidentiality provisions protecting the privacy of clients who receive mental health services focus on the right of the clients rather than the legitimate and understandable interest of family members of such clients.

Mental health professionals may rely on the principle of confidentiality as the basis of their refusal to share information with the families of their clients. This principle is inherent in the professional ethics of service providers, as first articulated in the Hippocratic Oath: "All that may come to my knowledge in the exercise of my profession or in daily commerce with men, which ought not to be spread abroad, I will keep secret and will never reveal." This ethical obligation is likewise embodied in the codes of ethics of the American Medical and American Psychiatric Associations and is incorporated into the licensing requirements and disciplinary codes of service providers such as medical doctors, psychologists, rehabilitation counselors, pastoral counselors, and social workers who are licensed and regulated by state bodies.

This ethical commitment to protecting the secrets of clients of mental health services is furthered by the privilege laws enacted by the majority of states, which prevent the forced disclosure of information confided by the client to a mental health practitioner during the course of treatment. These state laws define the class of professionals who will not be required to testify about such confidences. Such laws also may indicate whether information given only by the client or whether information gleaned from others in the context of treatment will be protected from forced disclosure.

Conditions of Disclosure of Privileged Information

Some professionals believe that there is a difference between patient privacy and secret keeping. Privacy concerns an individual's choosing not to share something about himself or herself with the rest of the family. Secret keeping, on the other hand, is choosing to share with one family member certain thoughts that he or she feels should not be shared with all members of the family (Freeman, 1981).

In all states, there are instances where the privilege protections are overridden by other societal interests. Most common is the requirement that suspected child abuse be reported by a mental health professional, even if the information about such suspected abuse is obtained during mental health treatment of the suspected abuser. In some states, concerns about abuse, neglect, or exploitation of elderly, disabled, or other vulnerable adults must be reported in the same manner as suspected child abuse notwithstanding confidentiality provisions. The justification for this reporting is the societal interest in assuring that its most vulnerable and dependent members are protected from harm and in providing supportive services to families to assist them in caring for their dependent members.

A second area where confidential communications may properly be revealed is in the context of civil commitment proceedings. Many states' laws regarding involuntary hospitalization permit mental health practitioners to disclose otherwise confidential information in commitment petitions and their attendant court hearings. The justification for such disclosure is the need to provide treatment for those who may be dangerous to themselves or others and who are unable or unwilling to seek voluntary hospitalization for their illness.

The third major exception to the confidentiality protections afforded to clients of mental health services is the legal obligation to warn potential victims or take other protective action when a client confides a serious threat against an identified or identifiable victim or victims. This provision is illustrated by the case of *Tarasoff v. Board of Regents of the University of California* (1976) where legal liability was imposed upon a therapist who failed to take protective steps out of fear of violating his obligations of confidentiality to his client, Ms. Tarasoff's former boyfriend, who had threatened to kill her. The therapist did not alert Ms. Tarasoff and was subsequently sued by Ms. Tarasoff's family after the client followed through on his threat. The family recovered substantial monetary damages in compensation for the failure to warn that resulted in her death.

Courts have interpreted the confidentiality statutes of several states within the contexts of lawsuits seeking monetary awards by clients against their physicians for improper disclosure under a breach of privacy or for breach of confidentiality argument. Invasion of privacy is a legal theory that may impose liability on individuals for wrongful disclosure of embarrassing private or confidential information regardless of whether the disclosing person has a special duty of trust, such as a physician-patient relationship, to the person whose secrets are disclosed.

In *Horne v. Patton* (1973), for example, disclosure by a physician to the patient's employer contrary to the specific wish of the patient was found to constitute an invasion of privacy for which the patient could be compensated. Other courts have found that disclosing private information may not constitute an invasion of privacy for which damages can be recovered, if the court finds a sufficient reason for disclosure. In *Bratt v. International Business Machines Corp.* (1984), a physician's disclosure of an employee's mental condition, without consent, to the patient's employer was found by the court to be justified by the valid interest and reasonable necessity of the employer to have access to such information. In this case, an employee was referred to a physician, also employed by the employer, who made a report regarding the employee's mental condition to the employee's supervisor.

Breach of confidentiality is a legal theory that may impose liability on those who have a special relationship of trust for disclosing information in violation of that trust. When such legal actions are brought before the courts, the justification for the disclosure and the relative need of the recipient for the information is compared with the expectation of confidentiality of the patient or client. Clinicians need to be aware that breach of confidentiality is considered a high-risk area in clinical practice, which could be brought within a "low profile" malpractice configuration by adopting certain risk management techniques. These techniques include awareness of and adherence to established professional standards, to applicable administrative policies and procedures, and to applicable federal, state, and local law (Watkins, 1989).

There are no instances in which access by parents has been challenged, but in two reported cases, access by a spouse to mental health information was addressed. For example, in Missouri in the case of *Mikel v. Abrams* (1982) a physician was not held liable for discussing a husband's condition with his wife because the disclosure was not unreasonable and the wife had a legitimate interest in the issues discussed. The court ruled that under state law, a spouse has a right to access medical information regarding his or her partner by virtue of the marital relationship. However, more recently in New York, in *MacDonald v. Clinger* (1982), disclosure by a psychiatrist to a spouse was deemed improper absent consent of the spouse in treatment or other justification such as danger to the spouse or others.

With these legal interpretations of confidentiality laws and practices providing less than clear guidance to mental health professionals, it is understandable that they react cautiously to requests for information from the family members of their clients. Disclosure with the consent of the client becomes the most desirable way to accommodate the rights and interests of all involved. The client may share information regarding his or her own treatment with interested family members, or the client may give authorization to the service provider to share information with the person(s) of his or her choice.

Providing Nonconfidential Information

When a relative becomes mentally ill, the family needs to become educated about the disorder, its implications, and its treatment. This can be an enormous and confusing task, especially for the family that is experiencing the crisis of having a member become mentally ill. Families will usually turn to mental health practitioners for the information they need.

Frequently, the information needs of families can be met by providing them with information that is helpful but not confidential. Consider a parent who calls a mental health clinic and says, "My son is attending your clinic and was just told that he has schizophrenia. What does that mean and what can be done about it?" Many clinics have policies that require staff to refuse to speak to the parent without the express permission of the client. This is done to prevent the clinic from acknowledging that the family member is a clinic client and from divulging other protected information.

Although it is clear that the clinic is required to guard against the unauthorized release of information, the questions of family members can often be answered by providing relevant but nonconfidential information to them. In response to the question posed by parents of a clinic client, a practitioner can tell the parent that by law he or she cannot acknowledge that their adult child is a clinic client. (This will not be troubling to the parents because they probably already know that their adult child attends the clinic.) However, the practitioner can go on to answer the question, "What is schizophrenia and what can be done about it?" without ever referring to a specific individual or any confidential information.

Approaches for addressing the question include the following:

1. Discuss the treatment, and prognosis on the phone or in person. As a public education service, the practitioner is free to provide didactic presentations on mental illness to community members. It would be a simple matter to give the family basic information on the causes, diagnosis, treatment, and prognosis of a particular mental illness as a public service and without reference to the particular client. The practitioner initially giving the information should be someone other than the direct care provider for the ill family member. This protects the practitioner's relationship with their client prior to discussing with the client what he or she is willing to have disclosed. Families can respect the limits placed on the practitioner by confidentiality more easily if someone is willing to be as helpful as possible within those limits.

2. Provide written information. Many families want and appreciate written information. Although the level and depth of the information is determined by the family's needs and ability to understand it, many families seem to want and be helped by specific and relatively technical written material. For example, simple fact sheets on medications, clinic services, and specific disorders can be developed by the clinic and distributed to family members. These can also be translated into other languages for family members who do not speak English. The liberal use of family-oriented educational books is also helpful. There are many of these now available, and families often find them helpful (Atkinson, 1986; Bernheim & Lehman, 1985; Bernheim, Lewine, & Beale, 1982; Hatfield & Lefley, 1987; Hyde, 1980; Korpell, 1984; Lefley, 1996; Mueser & Gingrich, 1994; Vine, 1982). In addition, reprints of

articles from mental health periodicals can be useful, such as *Psychiatric Services, Psychiatric Rehabilitation Journal, Schizophrenia Bulletin,* and *New Directions for Mental Health Services.* Copies of newsletters of the National Alliance for the Mentally Ill (NAMI) and its state and local chapters contain useful information that is written specifically for families. Finally, sharing written information from mental health texts on diagnosis, psychopharmacology, etiology, treatment, and prognosis is frequently appropriate. Giving families access to the clinic library can be a valuable and appreciated service to families.

3. Refer families to educational groups. Many clinics have educational seminars specifically for families (Hatfield, 1984; Plummer, Thornton, Seeman, & Littman, 1981; Walsh, 1985). These seminars cover much of the basic information needed by families.

In addition, there are currently over 1000 local affiliates of NAMI throughout the United States. Families can be referred to these groups for support and education. Finally, families can be invited to clinic in-service workshops, conferences, hospital grand-rounds, and other educational forums.

Providing Confidential Information

Although the provision of nonconfidential information is useful in a broad range of situations, it often does not meet the entire need for information. When an individual is disabled for any reason, that person's family frequently plays a critical role in helping him or her to cope with the limitations imposed by the disability. This assistance may be reliably provided over a period of many years (and often for a lifetime), far longer than most professional-client relationships endure. These families have a legitimate interest in knowing specific details concerning the disability.

This is certainly true when an individual is disabled by mental illness. The person's family wants and needs to know information related to their loved one's impairment if they are to be supportive of their relative and assist in the management of the illness. For example, the family cannot provide assistance related to medication management, monitoring for side effects, and observing the effects of medication unless they have been told what the medication is, what it does, and what the side effects are. The family cannot support the goals of treatment and rehabilitation plans unless they are informed about the goals and the proposed methods of achieving them.

Practitioners who are caught between the client's right to confidentiality and the family's need to know must develop practical strategies for helping families access information while still protecting the rights of the client. In an effort to respond to these dilemmas, the judicial system has held to four fundamental conditions, set forth by Tahn Henry Wigmore (as cited in Watkins, 1989) and referred to as Wigmore's Four Criteria, which are necessary for the establishment of a privilege:

1. Communications must originate in the confidence that they will not be disclosed.
2. The element of confidentiality must be essential to the maintenance of the relationship between the partners.
3. The relation is one which in the opinion of the community ought to be fastened.
4. The injury that would inure to the relationship as a result of disclosure must be greater than the benefit gained in regard to the correct disposal of litigation.

Strategies that are useful in resolving this tension include the following:

1. Use release of information procedures. When a person is discharged from a hospital or transferred to another program, relevant information about the client is expected to be shared with the receiving agency. Practitioners routinely release confidential information about their current or former clients to other practitioners or agencies serving these clients. An integral part of this process is some form of client release or permission for one practitioner to disclose the specific confidential information to another specified party. As long as the client grants permission (and such permission should be documented) these transfers of confidential information are legal and reflect the right of the client to control access to his or her clinical records.

Although such release procedures are routinely used to allow other practitioners to access information, they are infrequently used to grant family members access to their ill relative's treatment information even when the person is discharged to the family home and the family becomes the primary caregiver. Such procedures can be useful in encouraging the family to be a strong and useful support. As noted earlier, clients and families are often not notified that such release procedures can be employed. In our experience, when clients are approached in a supportive way by a practitioner who believes in the value of involving families, most clients are willing to grant some degree of access to family members.

During an intake process at a clinic or program, clients can be encouraged to grant permission to one or more of their relatives to access the clinical records. As long as the release process specifies the parties to whom information can be released, the information that can be released, and the effective time limit of the release, these releases are legal. Once a formal release is obtained, the practitioner is free to disclose information in person, by phone, or in writing to families within the limits of the release.

The use of a formal release is also useful in cases where the family is attempting to locate a relative with a mental illness who has moved or dropped out of sight. Legally, the agency cannot disclose whether it is treating the client. However, when the family calls a mental health agency in an effort to locate a family member who is possibly being served by the agency, the family can be told that the agency will make every effort to locate the client and secure a release *if the person is being served by the agency.* The family should be informed about the limits of client privilege, but must be assured that the agency will investigate and assist in any way possible. This will help to reduce the family's level of anxiety. The agency should then take strong steps to solicit the client's permission to contact the family or arrange for the client to contact the family directly.

2. Include family members on the treatment team. Clinical care in most mental health agencies and hospitals is directed by clinicians organized into treatment teams. These teams are responsible for planning, coordinating, and delivering appropriate interventions to consumers. Although most team members are employees of the agency or hospital providing the service, the team may also include representatives from vocational rehabilitation, medical centers, or other groups who have an interest and role in supporting the person with the disability. These outsiders on the team may be suggested by the primary provider. However, the client must grant them permission to be included on the team and to have access to confidential treatment information.

Although agencies and hospitals routinely include practitioners from other agencies on the treatment team, they frequently fail to consider encouraging family members to join. Family members often have a significant role to play in the support of the client and, as such, are appropriate treatment team members. Families can share their perceptions of their relative's current strengths and deficits and information on his or her premorbid functioning. Practitioners can encourage clients to permit family members to attend treatment team meetings and to have access to confidential information. In turn, the practitioner can also encourage the family member to attend meetings by scheduling them at convenient times and by helping the family member to understand and participate in the working of the team.

Agencies can and should develop policies and procedures that support the role of family members on the treatment team. In agencies where this occurs, the question of "Should the family be involved in the treatment?" evolves into the question of "How do we help family members to participate fully on the treatment team?" As team members, they play critical roles in the treatment of their relatives and, with their relative's permission, have access to information relevant to treatment. Once the client grants permission for the family member to be on the team and involved in his or her treatment, the family member also can have ongoing contact with other providers regarding treatment, and the issue of confidentiality tends to disappear. The client can retract permission to have the family member be a part of the treatment team. However, this occurs infrequently when the family member plays a substantive role on the team.

3. Use practitioners as mediators. As noted earlier, a client has a clear right to the protection of confidential information. In contrast, a family member does not have an automatic right to access such information. When a conflict between the client's right to confidentiality and the family's interest in accessing such information occurs, practitioners often focus only on the client's right and juxtapose this right with the family's lack of a right. In such a *positional bargaining* situation (Fisher & Ury, 1981), only one position can win and the other must lose. If discussions between the family and the disabled member are allowed to become win-lose contests, the client's right to confidentiality must be protected even if it is not in the client's or the family's interests to withhold information.

Positional bargaining, however, is not the only way to frame the situation. It is possible to bargain from a recognition of the shared interests of the parties and to develop options that satisfy the interests of both parties, shifting the win-lose solution to a win-win one.

In the case of confidentiality, the practitioner can assume the role of mediator and assist the consumer to explore his or her interests and develop proposals for sharing information that meet both the client's and family's interests. For example, the family of a someone receiving medication may have an interest in knowing what the medication is, what it is prescribed for, and if the patient is taking it as prescribed. The patient may have an interest in taking the medication regularly and in recognizing early signs of unpleasant side effects or prodromal symptoms. The practitioner can help the parties discuss their interests, define the areas of shared interests, and develop strategies to meet these mutual interests.

Such solutions may involve the sharing of some limited area of confidential information (such as medication information) while protecting other areas of confidential information (such as information related to sexual behavior). The release of information document can be specifically tailored to reflect such an agreement. This process may also involve time-limited trials of information sharing or trades, such as the sharing of specified information in exchange for less family interference in some other specified area. The successful development of such a win-win solution in one area will tend to breed a willingness to use this approach to solve other conflicts. A practitioner who is a skilled mediator can, over time, help the client and the family resolve most problems related to confidentiality and to develop arrangements that meet the needs of all.

4. Employ family advocates. It is possible and appropriate for a single practitioner to be an advocate for the interests of both the person with the disability and his or her family. Although this is feasible in most situations, there are instances where the disabled individual and the family are so far apart on issues that it becomes impossible for the practitioner to represent the rights and the interest of the client who is in therapy and to advocate for the family's interest in accessing confidential information. In these situations, the practitioner is ethically bound to serve the client even if it means failing to help the family meet its needs for information. When this occurs, the practitioner must find some other method of assisting the family.

One strategy for meeting the needs of families in this situation is the use of family advocates. A family advocate is any person with the authority and the ability to represent the interests of the family and to effectively advocate for their needs. These advocates should be chosen by the family and can be employees of the agency, volunteers, or members of some other organization, such as a local affiliate of the National Alliance for the Mentally Ill. They can help the family define its wants and needs for confidential information, develop strategies for accessing it, and represent the family in correspondence and in meetings related to the problem. The use of family advocates leaves the practitioner free to represent his or her client while ensuring that the family still has a voice and is supported. Even in cases where the family is not granted the access to confidential information that they desire, the act of providing a supportive advocate can in and of itself be helpful and comforting. Agencies should develop policies that encourage the use of such procedures and the establishment of legitimate positions for these advocates in the service planning process.

Training and Supervision

Families and practitioners share a common interest in supporting the success of their respective relatives and patients with mental illnesses. A major element of working collaboratively is the ability to share experiences, expertise, and information about mental illness and treatment. Although there are several strategies discussed in this chapter for sharing important information without breaching confidentiality, real situations in clinical settings may include elements that challenge the ability of practitioners to decide when and what information can be shared with families.

In these situations, there is no substitute for excellent training and supervision. During the past several years, models for practitioner training have begun to emerge in the area of working with families with mentally ill members (Bowker, 1988; Warren, 1994; Wasow, 1994b). These models and the work of the NAMI Curriculum and Training Committee have begun to influence preprofessional training and to open the door to greater understanding about the importance of communication between practitioners and families.

Practitioners need to continue to educate themselves and their peers about these issues. More important, clinical supervision and peer review related to confidentiality should be expanded from discussions of "Is it legal?" to "Is it in the interest of the patient and the family and, if so, how do we support and negotiate the sharing of information?" The answer to the latter question is not simple. Attempts to answer this question force us to make our way through legal and ethical uncertainties. However, thoughtful discussion, skilled consultation, and an openness to being guided by the needs of those we serve will usually help us find a solution that allows for sharing some level of helpful information.

Conclusion

A person who is severely disabled will need special supports for a protracted period, and families can be a crucial resource. Without ongoing contact with loved ones, a person with a mental illness may never achieve his or her potential. In a service system that relies on service providers who have short job expectancies, it is even more important to assist the client to preserve his or her natural caregivers and advocates. Accordingly, it is essential to inform and involve the family in the service planning and service delivery process. Caregivers have an absolute obligation to be informed and aware of their state's licensing and regulatory statutes that address the issues of confidentiality and privileged communication.

Professionals likewise should assist agencies in developing policies on confidentiality that they can use in their practice. The policies need to be based on the professional codes of ethics as well as advice from the agency's legal counsel (Watkins, 1989). If practitioners are committed to helping families become informed about and involved in their relative's treatment and rehabilitation, the practitioner must develop strategies for sharing information without violating confidentiality. However, the functional standard in regard to the legal consequences for the possible breach of confidentiality remains as follows: "Erring on the side of confidentiality is the more preferred risk" (Watkins & Watkins, 1983, pp. 55–69). The exercise of the strategies discussed in this chapter help accomplish this goal.

References

Anderson, C., Reiss, D., & Hogarty, G. (1986). *Schizophrenia and the family.* New York: Guilford.

Atkinson, J. (1986). *Schizophrenia at home: A guide to helping the family.* New York: New York University Press.

Bernheim, K., & Lehman, A. (1985). *Working with families of the mentally ill.* New York: Norton.

Bernheim, K., Lewine, R., & Beale, C. (1982). *The caring family: Living with chronic mental illness.* New York: Random House.

Bernheim, E., & Switalski, T. (1988). Mental health staff and patients' relatives: How they view each other. *Hospital and Community Psychiatry, 39,* 63–68.

Bowker, J. (1988). *Services for the chronically mentally ill: New approaches for mental health professionals.* Washington, DC: Council on Social Work Education.

Bratt v. International Business Machines Corp., 392 Mass 508 (1984), 467 N.E.2d 126.

Dearth, N., Labenski, B., Mott, M., & Pellegrini, L. (1986). *Families helping families*. New York: Norton.

Falloon, I., Boyd, J., & McGill, C. (1985). *Family care of schizophrenia*. New York: Guilford.

Fisher, R., & Ury, W. (1981). *Getting to yes: Negotiating agreement without giving in*. New York: Penguin Books.

Freeman, D. S. (1981). *Techniques of family therapy*. New York: Jason Aronson.

Griswold v. Connecticut, 381 vs. 479 (1965).

Hatfield, A. (1984). *Coping with mental illness in the family: The family guide*. Arlington, VA: National Alliance for the Mentally Ill.

Hatfield, A. (1987). Social support and family coping. In A. Hatfield & H. Lefley (Eds.), *Families of the mentally ill: Coping and adaptation* (pp. 191–207). New York: Guilford.

Hatfield, A., & Lefley, H. P. (1987). *Families of the mentally ill: Copying and adaptation*. New York: Guilford.

Holden, D., & Lewine, R. (1982). How families evaluate mental health professionals, resources and effects of illness. *Schizophrenia Bulletin, 8,* 626–633.

Horne v. Patton, Ala. 201, 287 (1973), 502 S.O.2d 824.

Hyde, A. (1980). *Living with schizophrenia*. Chicago: Contemporary Books.

Korpell, H. (1984). *How you can help: A guide for families of psychiatric hospital patients*. Washington, DC: American Psychiatric Press.

Leff, J., Kuipers, L., Berkowitz, R., Eberbein-Vries, R., & Sturgeon, D. (1982). Controlled trial of social intervention in the families of schizophrenic patients. *British Journal of Psychiatry, 141,* 121–134.

Lefley, H. P. (1996). *Family caregiving in mental illness*. Newbury Park, CA: Sage.

MacDonald v. Clinger, 84 App. Div. 2d 482 (1982), 446 N.Y.S.2d 801.

McElroy, E., & McElroy, P. (1994). Family concerns about confidentiality and the seriously mentally ill: Ethical considerations. In A. Hatfield & H. Lefley (Eds.), *Helping families cope with mental illness* (pp. 243–258). Newark, NJ: Harwood Academic.

McFarlane, W. (1990). Multiple family groups in the treatment of schizophrenia. In H. Nasrallah (Ed.), *Handbook of schizophrenia* (pp. 167–189). New York: Elsevier.

McFarlane, W. (1994). Families, patients, and clinicians as partners: Clinical strategies and research outcomes in single and multiple family psychoeducation. In H. Lefley & M. Wasow (Eds.), *Helping families cope with mental illness* (pp. 195–222). Newark, NJ: Harwood Academic.

Mikel v. Abrams, 541 F. Supp. 591 (WD MO 1982), *aff'd* without OpN 716 F.2d 907.

Mueser, K. T., & Gingerich, S. L. (1994). *Coping with schizophrenia: A guide for families*. Oakland, CA: New Harbinger.

Plummer, E., Thornton, J., Seeman, M., & Littman, S. (1981). Coping with schizophrenia: A group approach with relatives. *Journal of Psychiatric Treatment and Evaluation, 3,* 257–262.

Spaniol, L., Jung, H., Zipple, A., & Fitzgerald, S. (1987). Families as a central resource in the rehabilitation of the severely psychiatrically disabled: Report on a national survey. In A. Hatfield & H. Lefley (Eds.), *Families of the mentally ill: Coping and adaptation* (pp. 167–190). New York: Guilford.

Steinwachs, D., Kasper, J., & Skinner, E. (1992). *Family perspectives for meeting the needs for care of severely mentally ill relatives: A national survey.* Baltimore: Johns Hopkins University School of Hygiene and Public Health.

Tarasoff v. Board of Regents of the University of California, 529 P.2d 533, Cal. Reptr. 14 (1976).

Torrey, E. F. (1995). *Surviving schizophrenia: A manual for families, consumers, and providers* (3rd ed.). New York: HarperCollins.

Vine, P. (1982). *Families in pain.* New York: Pantheon Books.

Walsh, M. (1985). *Schizophrenia: Straight talk for family and friends.* New York: Morrow.

Warren, N. (1994). Training psychiatric residents and psychology interns to work with families of the seriously mentally ill. In H. Lefley & M. Wasow (Eds.), *Helping families cope with mental illness* (pp. 295–308). Newark, NJ: Harwood Academic.

Wasow, M. (1994a). Professional and parental perspectives. In H. Lefley & M. Wasow (Eds.), *Helping families cope with mental illness* (pp. 27–38). Newark: Harwood Academic.

Wasow, M. (1994b). Training future clinicians to work with families. In A. Hatfield & H. Lefley (Eds.), *Helping families cope with mental illness* (pp. 277–294). Newark, NJ: Harwood Academic.

Watkins, S. A. (1989). Confidentiality: An ethical and legal conundrum for family therapists. *American Journal of Family Therapy, 17,* 291–302.

Watkins, S. A., & Watkins, J. C. (1983). Malpractice in clinical social work: A perspective on civil liability in the 1980's. *Behavioral Sciences and the Law, 1,* 55–69.

Zipple, A., & Spaniol, L. (1987). Current educational and supportive interventions with families: A review and suggestions for their use. In A. Hatfield & H. Lefley (Eds.), *Families of the mentally ill: Coping and adaptation* (pp. 261–277). New York: Guilford.

PART FOUR

Professional Issues

CHAPTER 14

An Ethics Policy for Family Practice Management

MICHAEL C. GOTTLIEB

Over the last 40 years, family therapy has become extraordinarily popular as a treatment modality among practitioners. Despite this popularity, little has been written about the unique ethical dilemmas that this approach presents. Only isolated efforts have been made to resolve these problems, and there are few references practitioners can consult that will provide them with ethical rules or decision-making guidelines to assist them. This lack of information leaves practitioners with the task of carrying on as best as they can with little guidance from scholars or their profession.

In this chapter, I review these unique issues and highlight those that have been resolved. Second, I suggest some reasons why we have made so little progress in this area. Third, the need for more specialized training for both students and practitioners is emphasized. Finally, until greater consensus is reached on these matters, I propose that practitioners develop their own ethical decision-making policies and conclude with specific steps to follow in developing a personal ethical decision-making policy.

In presenting this position, I am making the following assumptions. First, I assume that the reader has the authority to implement my recommendations, that is, that he or she is an independent practitioner or institutional administrator. Policy making is not a task that can be imposed on those who do not have decision-making authority.

An earlier version of this chapter was presented at the 1995 annual meeting of the American Psychological Association, New York. Thanks to Howard Liddle for his thoughtful comments.

Second, I presume the reader has training or experience with the ethical issues involved in multiperson therapy and is familiar with the issues to be discussed.

Third, when discussing actual clinical problems, clear distinctions between ethical issues are seldom possible. The issues discussed here are divided arbitrarily for the purpose of discussion.

Unique Ethical Dilemmas

For many years, psychotherapy was conducted on an individual basis, ethical principles were written accordingly (Lakin, 1994; Woody, 1990), and professional responsibility was generally clear. A psychologist's primary obligation was to his or her patient, whose autonomy and welfare he or she was expected to promote (American Psychological Association [APA], 1990).

Practitioners from various disciplines began to treat couples and families in the early 1950s (Hoffman, 1981), and over the years this treatment modality received much empirical support. Perhaps due to its "exasperating nature" (Lakin, 1994), many years passed before scholarly articles appeared regarding the ethical issues involved in this approach (e.g., Boszormenyi-Nagy & Krasner, 1980; Grosser & Paul, 1964; Hines & Hare-Mustin, 1978; Karpel, 1980; Rinella & Goldstein, 1980). It was not until 1982 that two works defined and organized four major ethical issues in the area (Margolin, 1982; O'Shea & Jessee, 1982), and it was another ten years before psychology made its initial effort to address this type of work in its ethical principles (APA, 1992).

Margolin (1982) recognized three issues unique to treating couples and families. First, who is the patient? Is it an individual, a particular dyad, or the family system? How is the decision to be made, and what relationship is the therapist to have with family members who are not patients?

Second, if there is more than one patient, how is the therapist to maintain therapeutic neutrality so that all feel treated equally and triangulation is avoided? Furthermore, under what circumstances must neutrality be abandoned in favor of an individual family member?

Third, how is confidentiality to be managed? Should the therapist keep nothing secret from other family members, or is it acceptable to keep some information confidential? If so, on what basis should the decision be made?

Finally, iatrogenic risk—damage caused inadvertently in the course of treatment—is a problem usually associated with physical medicine. O'Shea and Jessee (1982) extended the concept to family therapy because, "a previously asymptomatic family member may become symptomatic during or subsequent to therapy" (p. 15). How much information should be provided as a matter of informed consent when treating families? For example, how will disclosing or concealing the "tricks" of strategic therapy (Lakin, 1994) affect family members?

Recently, I proposed the addition of two issues to the list: change of format, a term originated by Margolin (1982), and various issues surrounding the use of live supervision (Gottlieb, 1995a). A change of format occurs when the formal definition of the patient changes, for example, from individual to marital therapy. In these circumstances, what is the practitioner to do regarding confidentiality, professional responsibility, and the iatrogenic risks such decisions may incur?

In live supervision with teams, who is professionally responsible for the family and how is informed consent managed? Furthermore, how are the problems of group dynamics inherent in team functioning to be avoided?

Published papers address other ethical issues such as doing individual and family therapy concurrently (Gottlieb & Cooper, 1990); working with families with elderly members (Duffy, 1990); operating from a systemic perspective in hospitals (Gottlieb & Cooper, 1993); treating families who have a member with a chronic physical illness (Gottlieb, 1995b); working with gays and lesbians (Scrivner, 1995); and relational diagnoses (Gottlieb, 1996).

This literature raised complex and vexing issues that are inherent in family practice. (See Chapter 12 by Marsh in this volume for a more detailed discussion.) Unfortunately, little has been accomplished toward resolving these problems, and unambiguous decision-making guidelines are not available for practitioners. Nevertheless, some progress has been made.

Progress in Ethical Principles

Some organizations have published ethics codes (e.g., American Association of Marriage and Family Therapy, 1991). Unfortunately, they do not squarely confront the ethical dilemmas encountered in family practice. Psychology remained silent on the matter until the publication of its *Ethical Principles and Code of Conduct* (APA, 1992), which finally addressed some of these issues. The most significant addition for family psychologists was Section 4.03, which speaks to questions surrounding patient definition:

> (a) *When a psychologist agrees to provide services to several persons who have a relationship (such as a husband and wife or parents and children), the psychologist attempts to clarify at the outset (1) which of the individuals are patients or clients, and (2) the relationship the psychologist will have with each person. This clarification includes the role of the psychologist and the probable uses of the services provided or the information obtained.*
>
> (b) *As soon as it becomes apparent that the psychologist may be called on to perform potentially conflicting roles (such as marital counselor to husband and wife, and then witness for one party in a divorce proceeding), the psychologist attempts to clarify and adjust, or withdraw from, roles appropriately. (p. 1605)*

This section addresses some of the issues originally raised by Margolin (1982). It recognizes that psychologists may ethically provide services to several persons who have relationships with one another. It also emphasizes the need to clarify patient definition, as well as the psychologist's relationship with other family members. Finally, it acknowledges that these roles may conflict and that it is the psychologist's responsibility to try to resolve such conflicts. Unfortunately, it provides no guidance regarding the process of patient definition, how relationships with other family members are to be defined, or how conflict is to be resolved if it arises.

Section 5.01, concerning the limits of confidentiality, is also a helpful addition. It states:

> (a) *Psychologists discuss with persons and organizations with whom they establish a scientific or professional relationship (including, to the extent feasible, minors and their legal representatives) (1) the relevant limitations on confidentiality, including limitations where applicable in group, marital, and family therapy or in organizational consulting, and (2) the foreseeable uses of the information generated through their services.*
>
> (b) *Unless it is not feasible or is contraindicated, the discussion of confidentiality occurs at the outset of the relationship and thereafter as new circumstances may warrant. (p. 1606)*

This section correctly highlights the need to establish ground rules for management of confidential information, how it is to be used, and the necessity to clarify these rules as soon as possible. Unfortunately, it gives no guidance regarding which rules might be preferred or what "relevant limitations" might entail.

The final addition (Section 4.08) is concerned with the interruption of services:

> (a) *Psychologists make reasonable efforts to plan for facilitating care in the event that psychological services are interrupted by factors such as the psychologist's illness, death, unavailability, or relocation, or by the client's relocation or financial limitations. (p. 1606)*

This section was not written with the intention of dealing with the ethical concerns of family psychologists. Nevertheless, it is relevant because family practice commonly entails long interruptions of service when one works with families over the life span. Unfortunately, it does not explain "reasonable efforts" or the kind of planning required.

Since the publication of the revised code, two major works have appeared. The first, a book written by those involved in the code's revision, was designed to "communicate . . . our best understanding of what the 1992 ethics code was designed to communicate" (Canter, Bennett, Jones, & Nagy, 1994, p. xii). This volume devotes one and one-half pages to Couple and Family Relations (pp. 93–94). Section 4.03 is explained in somewhat greater detail, but little additional guidance is offered.

Second, a special section in *Professional Psychology: Research and Practice* was devoted to a critical analysis of the ethics code. Lakin (1994) was asked to comment on aspects of the code related to group and family therapy, and his trenchant criticism is worth reading. He raised many issues of concern to family psychology, most of which the code does not address, but offered no guidance as to their resolution.

The three sections of the ethics code and two brief commentaries comprise all the specific guidance presently offered to family practitioners. The additions address a very small portion of the issues noted above, and none offer specific guidance to practitioners. In my view, this situation is the result of certain basic limitations.

LIMITATIONS TO ETHICAL RULE MAKING

Many have been critical of APA for not addressing issues of family practice more thoroughly (e.g., Lakin, 1994), and this criticism is deserved in some respects. On the other hand, rule-making efforts may have gone almost as far as possible because of certain limitations inherent in family practice. These include the effect of family members upon one another, certain limitations regarding informed consent in family practice, and the interactive effects of clinical judgment and ethical decision making.

Interpersonal Relationships

The most fundamental limitation to ethical rule making was reviewed by Lakin (1994). He argued that the ethical challenges of multiperson therapy are considerably more complex than those encountered in individual treatment because therapists cannot anticipate the future course of therapy to the same extent that they can with individual patients. That is, therapists cannot know how interventions will affect individual family members or how the interventions will affect relationships among family members after therapy sessions.

For example, during an initial interview with a couple, a woman raised numerous relational issues. Her husband remained aloof and minimally engaged, despite the therapist's repeated efforts to join with him. The wife called the next day to inform the therapist that they would not be keeping their next appointment. She reported that after their session, her husband was overwhelmed by the number of issues she raised and that she shared these in front of a stranger. As a result of this experience, he decided that their differences were insurmountable, asked for a divorce, and moved out that very evening.

Training in systems-oriented therapy includes attention to the affect that interventions will have on all family members. Being aware of and trying to anticipate such outcomes is vital to good treatment planning and is consistent with O'Shea and Jessee's (1982) concern regarding iatrogenic risk. Can the profession write ethical rules regarding such matters? In my view, such an endeavor would be of dubious value and could risk placing therapists in a position of responsibility for matters beyond their control.

Informed Consent

Unfortunately, some misinformation surrounds certain aspects of informed consent. Many practitioners mistakenly view it as a necessary evil that detracts from the work of psychotherapy. Some try to meet its requirements by giving patients booklets to read and forms to sign. These concrete measures can create the illusion that informed consent is a discrete procedure. This notion may have been fostered inadvertently by the APA ethics code (APA, 1992), which noted the need to obtain informed consent for treatment, "as early as is feasible in the therapeutic relationship" (p. 1605) and "at the outset of the relationship" (p. 1606). Understanding informed consent in this fashion is an oversimplification. Consider the following example: A woman presents with symptoms of major depression. At the initial interview, she denies any history of childhood abuse. The symptoms begin to resolve with medication and psychotherapy. At the tenth session, she reports experiencing intrusive memories of childhood abuse and shortly thereafter complains of having dissociative episodes.

This common example raises fundamental questions about the nature of informed consent. How can informed consent obligations be fulfilled at the outset when the therapist had no idea of what was to be revealed? What is one to do when unanticipated events fundamentally change the diagnosis, treatment plan, and sometimes the professional relationship?

Contemporary ethics scholars now understand that informed consent can no longer be viewed as a single event. Instead, it is now seen as a recurrent process of interactive dialogue (Packman, Cabot, & Bongar, 1994) involving communication, clarification, and decision making (Pope & Vasquez, 1991) throughout the therapy process.

Consider the following example from family practice: A couple present with problems regarding power, control, and communications. The therapist recommends a focused, solution-oriented approach in which the couple will be seen conjointly. As part of her recommendations, the therapist informs them of her no-secrets policy regarding confidentiality. The couple agrees and work begins, but little progress is made. The therapist becomes concerned and decides to raise the issue to see if the treatment plan needs to be altered. Just as she introduces the issue, the husband blurts out that he is bisexual and HIV positive. He wanted to tell his wife for some time, and planned to use the therapy sessions as a vehicle to do so. He wanted to discuss the problem privately with the therapist, in the hope that she would help him confront his wife, but when he was informed of the no-secrets policy, his plan was disrupted, and he withheld the information.

In this example, the therapist followed both the letter and the spirit of informed consent guidelines. Nevertheless, her procedures were not sufficient to take account of the subsequent events that she could not have foreseen.

Problems with informed consent also arise as a result of some systems-oriented treatment approaches. Pure strategic therapists would argue that informed consent is tantamount to "discussing one's strategy with an opponent before the actual game" (Mills & Sprenkle, 1995, p. 372). To do so would reduce the power and maneuverability they need to be of help.

Similar problems arise with certain postmodern approaches such as collaborative language systems. Here the role of the therapist is to take a "not knowing" position, have no preconceived ideas about standards of health, and believe that problems are "dissolved through a natural consequence of dialogue" (Mills & Sprenkle, 1995, p. 370). How are we to write ethical guidelines regarding informed consent when certain approaches assume that too much patient or therapist knowledge may compromise treatment effectiveness?

Ethical Decision Making and Clinical Judgment

I and others (Gottlieb & Handlesman, in preparation) have concluded that ethical decision making and clinical judgment are not independent processes. Brown (1994) noted that ethics should be fundamentally integrated into practice, and Lakin (1994) argued that family practitioners must understand that ethical pitfalls are "inextricably embedded in the methods" (p. 348) used to bring about therapeutic change. Similarly, Sonne (1994) argued that both providing and withholding information from patients may produce risk.

Consider the following: A family presents with a teenage daughter who is acting out in ways that are potentially dangerous to her. After his assessment, the family psychologist recommends family therapy with a focus on strengthening the parental coalition to gain control over the daughter's behavior. The psychologist informs the parents that the situation is serious enough that he wishes to forego more extensive evaluation in order to gain control of the situation as soon as possible. The parents agree and treatment begins. Within a brief period, the parents regain control, the daughter's behavior improves, and the psychologist considers discussing termination at the next session. At the appointed hour, the mother arrives alone to inform the psychologist that her husband is so depressed that he has not gotten out of bed or gone to work in two days.

Reasonable practitioners might argue that the psychologist erred in not fully evaluating the family further before proceeding with treatment. Had he done so, he might have discovered the father's depression and recommended a different treatment plan. However, he would then have to justify the ethically questionable decision of postponing treatment for the daughter, who was in a potentially dangerous situation. But, even if we agree that his decision was clinically and ethically defensible, he is confronted with a deteriorated patient and now is vulnerable to the charge that he did not treat the family in a competent manner.

This example is only one of many in which ethical decision making and clinical judgment exist in dynamic interaction. Because such circumstances are common in family practice, it is necessary to understand that ethical choices may generate different clinical outcomes and that clinical decisions will present varying ethical dilemmas.

Is it reasonable to assume that ethical guidelines can be written to address the complex nature of family practice? Ethics codes can serve only as broad decision-making guidelines. We cannot expect them to do the hard work of ethical decision making for us. Instead, we must learn to rely upon ourselves to think through the practice dilemmas that face us. Toward this end, I make two recommendations: enhanced educational efforts and development of individual ethics policies.

Practitioner Education

In the past, there were no courses on ethics in graduate training programs, since it was not considered a substantive area of scholarship. Content was acquired in a piecemeal fashion as issues arose in the course of research and acquiring practice skills. Since then the area has grown into a distinct field of inquiry, and formal coursework is now required in a majority of APA-approved doctoral training programs (Vanek, 1990).

Unfortunately, few students will be exposed to the ethical issues surrounding family practice. Ethics teachers already complain of insufficient time to cover required material in the time allotted. Furthermore, it is unlikely that specialized courses in the area would be added to an already demanding training curriculum. As a result, few practitioners will have any formal educational experience in this vital practice area.

This is a highly undesirable situation, since the majority of psychologists do marriage and family work as a part of their practice. The result is that many practitioners are ill-prepared to cope with the ethical challenges they will encounter. Therefore, it behooves practitioners to educate themselves regarding these specific ethical issues before treating couples and families. This may be done through reading, attending continuing education seminars, and consulting with experienced colleagues. Such steps are necessary to avoid doing harm.

An Ethical Decision-Making Policy

Family practice seems to present a paradox. On one hand, psychologists should educate themselves regarding family practice ethics. At the same time, few of these matters have been resolved. How is one to educate oneself and practice ethically when so little information and guidance is available?

Although there is presently no answer to this problem, some resources may be of help. There are now good general ethical decision-making guidelines available (e.g., Haas & Malouf, 1989) as well as a helpful focus list for risk management (Bennett, Bryant, VandenBos, & Greenwood, 1990). More recently, policies have been suggested for specific situations, such as Tarasoff liability (Monahan, 1993). Until guidelines are created for family psychologists, individual practitioners will be forced to rely upon themselves. What follows is an interim measure that may be helpful.

I propose that each practitioner investigate the ethical dilemmas that commonly occur in his or her practice area and create an individualized ethics policy to address them. Certainly, such a policy will not resolve all ethical dilemmas, but it will be helpful in two ways. First, by thinking through potential dilemmas, some problems can be avoided altogether. Second, by addressing ethical issues that typically arise, the practitioner is in a better position to manage such problems when they occur. In an effort to assist colleagues in this task, I offer the following guidelines.

First, define the practice by considering theoretical orientation, populations served, practice setting, location, personal values, and any other relevant variables. For example, an altruistic family psychologist, working in a rural community mental health center serving a Native American population using short-term solution oriented approaches, will have few ethical problems in common with a family psychologist who does long-term organizational consulting to family business in a big city.

Second, determine which state laws, regulations, and institutional policies must be considered. Also, decide which professional ethics codes and specialty guidelines apply. For example, a family psychologist who works in the forensic evaluation unit of a state facility for adolescents would be subject to all relevant state law as well as the mental health code, state licensing board rules and regulations, institutional policies of the agency, the APA ethics code (APA, 1992), and guidelines for forensic psychologists (Committee on Ethical Guidelines for Forensic Psychologists, 1991). Finally, he must also be familiar with criminal law as it applies to adolescents.

Third, given the type of practice and relevant regulations, what kinds of ethical problems can be reasonably anticipated? For instance, the director of psychological services for a family guidance clinic knows that she will at least need to review institutional policy and state laws and regulations in order to write policies regarding confidentiality, release of patient information, and their exceptions.

Fourth, examine the specific practice in question. What ethical problems have arisen in the past? How frequently have they occurred? What problems have colleagues in the same practice area experienced? Does the frequency or seriousness of a particular problem require a policy statement? For example, a family psychologist works in a private practice in a wealthy suburb. He discovers that he experienced a high number of requests for records from divorcing partners in custody disputes whom he previously saw conjointly. He decides to establish the procedure of explaining his policy on the release of records with every couple who initiate marital or family treatment as a matter of informed consent.

Fifth, are there unique characteristics of the practice that make certain dilemmas more likely? For example, coping with definition of the patient may be a more serious problem for a family practitioner in a hospital-based setting. Or, one may have to pay special attention to confidentiality issues when working in the area of infidelity.

Sixth, brainstorm. Read the regulations and codes that govern both the profession and practice area. See if issues present themselves that would apply. For example, review the issues in the first section of this chapter and Chapter 12 by Marsh in this volume. This step is more abstract and theoretical, but it may help generate issues not previously considered. For example, in reviewing state regulations, a family psychologist discovers that rules regarding mandated reporting of child abuse may apply to her 18-year-old patient who told her that he was sexually involved with his 16-year-old girlfriend.

Seventh, write an initial draft of the policy and share it with coworkers, administrators, and colleagues who are in similar practice settings. Ask them to review it critically, and revise as needed.

Eighth, after the policy has been reviewed and revised, show it to a sample of current, well-integrated patients who are well-known to you. Ask them to review and criticize the policy from their perspective, and revise as needed. For example, a couple informed a psychologist that they never read the informed consent form they were asked to sign at the first session because they were too distressed. They recommended that the practitioner follow up at a later date when anxiety would not interfere so much with processing the information.

Ninth, pilot the policy with a sample of new patients. Solicit feedback, and revise as needed.

Tenth, implement the policy.

Eleventh, review the policy at least annually in light of new laws, regulations, ethical codes, and advances in knowledge.

Finally, if an obstacle arises at any step in the process, seek ethics consultation.

Conclusion

In this chapter, I acquainted the reader with the more salient ethical dilemmas faced by family practitioners and the limited help that ethics codes offer in addressing them. I argued that there are inherent limits that may prevent much further rule making and suggested that practitioners educate themselves regarding these matters. I concluded with guidelines practitioners may follow to develop ethical decision-making policies for their individual practice situations.

It is not possible to know all the ethical issues a practitioner will face in his or her practice lifetime. Nevertheless, it serves us well to remain mindful of the issues that may confront us. I have tried to help the reader anticipate what may lie ahead and how to more effectively cope with these developments.

References

American Association of Marriage and Family Therapy. (1991). *AAMFT Code of Ethics*. Washington, DC: Author.

American Psychological Association. (1990). Ethical principles of psychologists. *The American Psychologist, 45*, 390–395.

American Psychological Association. (1992). Ethical principles of psychologists and code of conduct. *American Psychologist, 47*, 1597–1611.

Bennett, B. E., Bryant, B. K., VandenBos, G. R., & Greenwood, A. (1990). *Professional liability and risk management*. Washington, DC: American Psychological Association.

Boszormenyi-Nagy, I., & Krasner, B. (1980). Trust-based therapy: A contextual approach. *American Journal of Psychiatry, 137,* 767–775.

Brown, L. S. (1994). Concrete boundaries and the problem of literal-mindedness: A response to Lazarus. *Ethics and Behavior, 4,* 275–281.

Canter, M. B., Bennett, B. E., Jones, S. E., & Nagy, T. F. (1994). *Ethics for psychologists: A commentary on the APA ethics code.* Washington, DC: American Psychological Association.

Committee on Ethical Guidelines for Forensic Psychologists. (1991). Specialty guidelines for forensic psychologists. *Law and Human Behavior, 15,* 655–665.

Duffy, M. (1990, August). Ethical issues in intergenerational family therapy. In M. C. Gottlieb (Chair), *Ethical issues in treating families from diverse populations.* Symposium conducted at the meeting of the American Psychological Association, Boston, MA.

Gottlieb, M. C. (1995a). Ethical dilemmas in change of format and live supervision. In R. H. Mikesell, D. Lusterman, & S. H. McDaniel (Eds.), *Integrating family therapy: Handbook of family psychology and systems therapy* (pp. 561–569). Washington, DC: American Psychological Association.

Gottlieb, M. C. (1995b). Ethical issues in the treatment of families with chronically ill members. In S. McDaniel (Ed.), *Counseling families with chronic illness* (pp. 69–84). Alexandria, VA: American Counseling Association.

Gottlieb, M. C. (1996). Some ethical implications of relational diagnoses. In F. W. Kaslow (Ed.), *Handbook of relational diagnosis and dysfunctional family patterns* (pp. 19–34). New York: Wiley.

Gottlieb, M. C., & Cooper, C. (1990). Treating individuals and families together: Some ethical considerations. *Family Psychologist, 6,* 10–11.

Gottlieb, M. C., & Cooper, C. (1993). Some ethical issues for systems oriented therapists in hospital settings. *Family Relations, 42,* 140–144.

Gottlieb, M. C., & Handlesman, M. (in preparation). *Clinical judgment and ethical decision-making: At the crossroads.*

Grosser, G., & Paul, N. (1964). Ethical issues in family group therapy. *American Journal of Orthopsychiatry, 34,* 875–884.

Haas, L. J., & Malouf, J. L. (1989). *Keeping up the good work: A practitioner's guide to mental health ethics.* Sarasota, FL: Professional Resource Exchange.

Hines, P., & Hare-Mustin, R. (1978). Ethical concerns in family therapy. *Professional Psychology: Research and Practice, 9,* 165–171.

Hoffman, L. (1981). *Foundations of family therapy.* New York: Basic Books.

Karpel, M. (1980). Family secrets: I. Conceptual and ethical issues in the relational context. II. Ethical and practical considerations in therapeutic management. *Family Process, 19,* 295–306.

Lakin, M. (1994). Morality in group and family therapies: Multiperson therapies and the 1992 ethics code. *Professional Psychology: Research and Practice, 25,* 344–348.

Margolin, G. (1982). Ethical and legal considerations in marital and family therapy. *American Psychologist, 37,* 788–801.

Mills, S. B., & Sprenkle, D. H. (1995). Family therapy in the postmodern era. *Family Relations, 44,* 268–376.

Monahan, J. (1993). Limiting therapist exposure to Tarasoff liability. *American Psychologist, 48,* 242–250.

O'Shea, M., & Jessee, E. (1982). Ethical, value and professional conflicts in systems therapy. In. J. C. Hansen (Ed.), *Values, ethics, legalities and the family therapist* (pp. 1–22). Rockville, MD: Aspen.

Packman, W. L., Cabot, M. G., & Bongar, B. (1994). Malpractice arising from negligent psychotherapy: Ethical, legal and clinical implications of *Ösheroff v. Chestnut Lodge. Ethics and Behavior, 4,* 175–197.

Pope, K. S., & Vasquez, M. J. T. (1991). *Ethics in psychotherapy and counseling.* San Francisco: Jossey-Bass.

Rinella, V., & Goldstein, M. (1980). Family therapy with substance abusers: Legal considerations regarding confidentiality. *Journal of Marital and Family Therapy, 6,* 319–326.

Scrivner, R. (1995, August). Family therapy ethical issues in working with lesbians and gays. In R. Scrivner (Chair), *Ethical issues in lesbian and gay family therapy.* Symposium conducted at the meeting of the American Psychological Association, New York.

Sonne, J. L. (1994). Multiple relationships: Does the new ethics code answer the right questions? *Professional Psychology: Research and Practice, 25,* 336–343.

Vanek, C. A. (1990). Survey of ethics education in clinical and counseling psychology. *Dissertation Abstracts International, 52,* 5797B. (University Microfilms No. 91-14, 449)

Woody, J. D. (1990). Resolving ethical concerns in clinical practice: Toward a pragmatic model. *Journal of Marital and Family Therapy, 16,* 133–150.

CHAPTER 15

Professional Liability and Risk Management in an Era of Managed Care

SAMUEL KNAPP

This chapter focuses on risk management techniques for psychologists who work with families. Risk management refers to actions that psychologists can take that would reduce their risk of liability in the form of an ethics charge before an association ethics committee or a state licensing board, a malpractice suit, or a disciplinary action before an institutional review board. The principles of risk management presume that all professional activities incur some form of risk. However, proper risk management activities can reduce the risks to an acceptable level. A basic assumption of this chapter is that sound clinical practices conducted within the context of the APA ethics code normally provide the best risk management protection. Failure to follow ethical principles may undermine the effectiveness of treatment, disrupt the family unit, or precipitate the alienation of family members.

The most important risk management strategies are for psychologists to: (1) focus on their relationship with the patients and their families, (2) anticipate problems, (3) document carefully, and (4) consult with knowledgeable peers. These four content areas overlap considerably.

The views expressed do not necessarily represent those of the Pennsylvania Psychological Association.

Focus on the Relationship

Psychologists provide the most effective treatment when they maintain a positive and collaborative relationship with the patient and the patient's family. This positive relationship also reduces the likelihood that a psychologist will be charged with negligence. Practitioners who traditionally have more intense and personal relationships with patients tend to have lower rates of malpractice. Psychologists who treat patients and have the opportunity to build a personal relationship are less likely to have complaints lodged against them. Psychologists who work in court-ordered or forensic settings (such as child custody evaluations) have higher risks of malpractice complaints because they lack the therapeutic relationship that acts as a buffer against a malpractice suit (Stromberg et al., 1988).

Relationships can be maintained and improved through the use of listening and reflecting skills. It is hard to overemphasize their therapeutic effectiveness and relationship-building qualities. Even among physicians of the same specialty, patients tend to have more complaints when there was "impersonal, rushed, and unsatisfactory interpersonal interacting between the patient and physician" (Weyrauch, 1995, p. 23).

Focusing on the relationship with the patient also means considering the psychologist's relationships with other family members and the patient's relationship with his or her family. There are pathological and toxic families with whom the patient may voluntarily decide to restrict contact. On the whole, however, most patients will desire to have regular contact with their families.

The general rule is that psychologists are in a fiduciary relationship with their patients and owe no duty to any other person, except in rare cases where a patient may present imminent threat of harm to an identifiable third person (see VandeCreek & Knapp, 1993), and in a few other unusual situations. However, family members who were not identified patients have been indirectly harmed by the actions of psychologists. For example, psychologists treating adult patients with serious mental illnesses may inadvertently allow harm to other family members by failing to involve them in treatment decisions (see Chapter 12 by Marsh in this volume). Also, allegations have been made of psychotherapists falsely implanting memories of childhood abuse in patients (see Chapter 11 by Strand and Nash in this volume).

ADULT CHILDREN WITH SERIOUS MENTAL ILLNESSES

Many adult children with serious mental illnesses depend on their parents for caregiving and support or to monitor their ability to care for themselves. The development of appropriate boundaries between family members is difficult because most adults want independence, but the nature of their illnesses sometimes makes it difficult for them to live independently without risking harm to themselves or others.

Although the person with the illness is the primary patient, consideration needs to be given to the perspectives and needs of their caregiver relatives. For example, parents may wish to receive information about the progress or problems of their adult children, or may have information they want to share with the psychotherapists. Despite a movement toward increased caregiver involvement with the treatment of the patient, Biegel, Song, and Milligan (1995) found that many caregivers continue to feel dissatisfied with the quantity and quality of their contacts with mental health professionals. Specifically, they would like to have been asked for their observations about their family member, to have been consulted about treatment, or to have been given adequate information about the family member's illness.

However, parents do not intrinsically have the right to that information and, in many cases, the failure of family members to obtain that information has led to unnecessary hardships and tragedies. Some of these difficulties occurred because psychologists and other healthcare professionals misunderstand or misapply the general rules about confidentiality. The purpose of confidentiality rules is not necessarily to keep all information private, but to give the patient maximum control over the release of that information. The issue is best addressed by having a release of information form signed as early as possible in treatment. It may be prudent to have the psychologist wait until the patient is stable and coherent, explain the benefits of the release, and get it signed. In some instances, the patient may refuse to authorize a disclosure or allow their family members to be involved in treatment.

ALLEGATIONS OF CHILDHOOD ABUSE

A growing area of litigation is that of adult children identifying childhood abuse and confronting, even suing their perpetrators, who are often parents or other family members. Most knowledgeable practitioners agree that it is not the role of the psychologist to encourage confrontations or suits against family members. Those issues must be left to patients to decide for themselves (Knapp & VandeCreek, in press).

Confrontational sessions of child abuse have the potential to disrupt family relationships, sometimes for life. Lawsuits can be very expensive and often leave the winner emotionally exhausted and, when attorneys fees are deducted, only a little bit wealthier.

A more basic issue arises concerning the credibility of the allegations. Hypnosis, sodium amytal interviewing, and age-regression therapy all lack scientific support as techniques to retrieve accurate memories and are often implicated when allegations of implanting false memories of abuse occur. Patients who acquire or recover memories of abuse through these techniques should be informed ahead of time of the potential for false or illusory beliefs.

ALTERNATIVE ACTIONS

No absolute rule can be made concerning the desired role of family members in therapy. Sometimes family members can represent interests that are antithetical to those of patients. However, on balance, it is far preferable to involve family members in positive discussions than to assume an adversarial perspective.

Psychologists are permitted to solicit other family members for participation in psychotherapy when it is clinically indicated. The provision against in-person solicitation of vulnerable persons "does not preclude attempting to implement appropriate collateral contacts with significant others for the purpose of benefiting an already engaged therapy patient" (American Psychological Association [APA], 1992, Principle 3.06).

MULTIPLE RELATIONSHIPS

As with individual patients, it is desirable to avoid multiple relationships. Kaslow (1992) identified situations where multiple relationships may be forced upon a clinician by circumstances, such as, a business acquaintance of a husband turns out to be the spouse of a client of the psychologist-wife. The APA *Code of Conduct* (1992) anticipates these potential scenarios and notes that the psychologist should try to avoid multiple relationships but if, "due to unforeseen factors, a potentially harmful multiple relationship has arisen, the psychologist attempts to resolve it with due regard for the best interests of the affected person and the maximal compliance with the ethics code" (APA, 1992, Principle 1.17).

Multiple relationships can be especially problematic in child custody cases. Psychologists working in child custody cases lack the strong psychotherapeutic relationship that often deters patients from making public allegations of negligence. Although patients may be forgiving of the indiscretions of a psychologist whom they like or trust, they are not likely to be so forgiving when they are on the losing end of a child custody case.

APA's *Guidelines for Child Custody Evaluations in Divorce Proceedings* (APA, 1994) state that "psychologists generally avoid conducting a child custody evaluation in a case in which the psychologist served in a therapeutic role for the child or his or her immediate family or has had other involvement that may compromise the psychologist's objectivity" (p. 678).

Anticipating Problems

Closely related to the issue of focusing on the relationship is that of anticipating problems. Families are better able to make informed decisions about psychotherapy and become more trusting of their psychologist when they are informed of potential problems and pitfalls.

AREAS OF COMPETENCE

Psychologists may sometimes find themselves in difficult situations when they attempt to treat patients or address problems outside of their areas of skill or competence. Some of the previous chapters in this book deal with the unique needs or perspectives in dealing with minority families (Goodwin), gay or lesbian couples (Scrivner), families where a member has a serious mental illness (Marsh), when being asked to provide couples therapy (Magee) or a child custody evaluation (Mannarino).

At times, practitioners in rural or otherwise underserved areas may receive requests to provide services that are outside of their area of expertise. In these situations, "treatment referred is treatment denied." These practitioners should seek consultation or continuing education to improve the quality of service as much as possible.

EXPLAINING THE TREATMENT RELATIONSHIP

One of the best risk management techniques is to provide structure to the treatment relationship as early as possible. This includes informing the family of the important elements of treatment and ensuring that family members (including minors) understand applicable limits to confidentiality. Competent treatment also requires psychologists to be aware of effective ways to deal with threats to harm oneself or others, to know how to avoid implanting false memories of (or failing to identify) past sexual abuse, and to avoid blurred boundaries.

Many potential problems can be avoided if psychologists take time at the beginning of therapy to explain the structure and nature of the relationship. The APA *Code of Conduct* states that "Psychologists discuss with clients or patients as early as is feasible in the therapeutic relationship appropriate issues, such as the nature and anticipated course of therapy, fees, and confidentiality" (APA, 1992, 4.01 [a]). It further elaborates that "Psychologists make reasonable efforts to answer patients' questions and to avoid apparent misunderstandings about therapy. Whenever possible, psychologists provide oral and/or written information, using language that is reasonably understandable to the patient or client" (1992, Principle 4.01 [d]). At times, it may be helpful to provide patients with a service brochure that describes essential information about the services being provided.

SUPERVISION

The need to provide structure to the relationship is no less important when the patient or family is being treated by a supervisee. In a supervisory relationship, the psychologist assumes total responsibility for the case. The supervisee has no legal status other than as an extension of the psychologist. Any failure on the part of the supervisee is presumed to be a failure on the part of the psychologist.

The term *supervision* needs to be distinguished from the term *consultation*. In a consultation relationship, the practitioners receiving the consultation may accept or reject the opinions of the consultant as they wish. Those practitioners are presumed to have the legal ability to conduct treatment by themselves and do not relinquish any of the independent authority by engaging a consultant.

Patients should be informed ahead of time if there is a supervisor involved in the case, and they should have access to that supervisor.

However, patients do not need to be informed ahead of time if there is consultation with another provider, as long as identifying information about the patient is not revealed.

MANAGED CARE LIMITATIONS

Given the limitations that managed care companies sometimes place on the treatment of patients, it is important for psychologists to discuss these limitations as soon as it is feasible. It would be desirable, for example, for a psychologist to alert a family with a serious problem that their benefits typically include 20 sessions (and may be reduced upon the discretion of a case manager). If the psychologist believes that the family will need more intense treatment, then it is necessary to inform the family of that (and the limitations of their policy, if known) as soon as possible.

ACCEPTABILITY OF TREATMENT TECHNIQUES

The selection of treatment also involves the description of risks that may be entailed in the treatment. For example, engaging a couple in marital therapy may include the risk that one of them may decide that he or she wants a divorce. A husband may want to keep the status quo, whereas the wife wants to have the resources or gain the courage to leave the relationship.

Psychologists should also consider the acceptability of treatment techniques. Although most patients have a general notion of what is involved in psychotherapy, some family therapy practices may engender particular opposition or concern among family members.

Paradoxical Techniques

Paradoxical techniques attempt to eliminate the patient's (or family's) symptoms by encouraging them. Although they are often used by systems-oriented family therapists, they may also be used by behavior therapists, logotherapists, and others. Although some paradoxical techniques involve openly explaining the rationale to the patient, others involve deliberate manipulation or deception. Psychologists need to balance the anticipated effectiveness of the technique against the harm that could occur if the technique were to undermine the credibility of the therapist, or backfire and actually increase the symptomatology.

Mandatory Attendance in Therapy

Another common family therapy practice is to require all family members to attend family therapy sessions and to refuse treatment if one or more of the family members refuses to attend. A question arises as to whether this policy ultimately discourages effective treatment for some families where one or more members may not want to participate in treatment. The reasons for nonparticipation in family therapy may vary widely. Perhaps the person is an older child who is developmentally emancipating from the family; or it may be a person who, rightly or wrongly, has misconceptions or fears about psychotherapy process.

It may be argued that mandatory attendance could be ethically acceptable in some situations, such as where the provider has solid grounds to believe that services would be useless or harmful without the involvement of the family. Nevertheless, mandatory attendance would be therapeutically contraindicated in other situations. For example, it may appear coercive to require the attendance of all family members when a therapist has developed a hopeful or dependent relationship on the part of patients, only to terminate treatment because their other family members refused to cooperate. Mandatory attendance may also be contraindicated when patients live in an area without easy access to other psychotherapists who can provide similar services, or when the continued hospitalization of a patient depends on the attendance of all family members in treatment.

Medical Involvement

A significant portion of hospitalized patients have coexisting physical disorders that may not have been recognized by their referring provider. For example, Pies (1994) reported that over one-third of the depressed patients evaluated in a general hospital for depression had a medical condition related to their depression.

However, insisting on a physical examination ahead of time for every patient (or every family member of a patient) would be unnecessarily burdensome. The general rule is that nonmedical psychotherapists should adopt a low threshold for referring patients to physicians for an evaluation of possible medical problems. It would be useful to request a physical examination when patients complain of physical symptoms that are not easily explained by recent environmental events (e.g., a patient who did not sleep well last night complains of being tired), when they have an atypical symptom profile (such as the vegetative symptoms of depression without the concurrent depressed mood), or when they fail to improve for no obvious reason. Generally, psychologists use good discretion in making referrals to physicians. Dörken (1990) found that the major malpractice carrier for psychologists had never been paid any claims against psychologists for failure to refer for a physical problem.

CONFIDENTIALITY

Confidentiality is another issue that needs to be anticipated and addressed early in the treatment relationship. The common problems with confidentiality come from subtle threats. They can occur when multiple family members are being treated or have a role in the treatment of the patient. Some of the issues that need to be addressed include: policies regarding handling of family secrets, disclosure of information generated by adolescents, confidentiality limits imposed by managed care contracts, and confidentiality when there is suspected child abuse or threats to identifiable third persons.

Confidentiality and Managed Care

Confidentiality may be compromised by managed care companies who may require release of records as a condition of payment for services. Psychologists need to inform the patients of these limits as soon as possible, and should be discreet about what to include in the records. Generally speaking, the records should focus on justifying the diagnosis and describing how the treatment is related to the diagnosis. Precise language is preferable. If the managed care company does require the records as a condition of payment, the psychologist should inform the patient and, if necessary, review the general nature of the information in the records.

Family Secrets

The failure to address this issue early could lead to considerable problems. Sometimes one family member may reveal a confidence in secret only to find it discussed openly later on. Or, some family members may want to disclose a secret because they want to develop an alliance between themselves and the therapist at the expense of the other family members. Keeping secrets can become therapeutically burdensome because it is often difficult to know which bit of information is secret, to whom secrecy is promised, and so on.

The optimal response is to define the policy regarding family secrets at the beginning of therapy. Some psychologists state that they will not guarantee to keep any secrets at all, including extramarital affairs. Others may not disclose the information, but would insist upon discussing the resistance to sharing the information. Regardless of the particular position taken, the policy toward family secrets should be discussed as early in treatment as feasible. Unless it is a major focus of treatment or necessary to justify a diagnosis, family secrets or other embarrassing information should not be included in the records.

Confidentiality and Adolescents

Some states permit adolescents to seek psychotherapy without parental consent. In most other states, however, children must have parental consent before they can seek psychotherapy on their own. The traditional assumption is that the ability to seek therapy implies the ability to control information generated in psychotherapy. This rule does not apply in life-endangering circumstances where healthcare providers may provide treatment in emergency situations without the consent of the parents.

How should psychologists deal with confidentiality issues of adolescents who are seeking psychotherapy? The most common question concerns the request of adolescents to have the contents of their psychotherapy remain private and confidential from their parents. While the request may be clinically appropriate, there may be no legal protection for keeping the information confidential. Although it may not be stated explicitly in any statute or regulation, an argument is often made that the ability to authorize or consent to treatment implies the ability to access or control the information generated from such treatment. Consequently, if parental consent is needed to institute treatment, the parents would also have a right to obtain information generated from such treatment, whether it be psychotherapy or psychological testing. Sometimes it may be clinically indicated to get an adolescent to sign a release of information form ahead of time, although it is not required and would be legally meaningless.

The optimal manner for psychologists to handle this issue is to discuss it openly at the start of psychotherapy. At times, psychologists may be able to persuade the parents to withhold their requests for complete information to allow the adolescent a greater sense of privacy, and thus encourage a stronger therapeutic alliance. When discussing this issue with parents, psychologists need to be candid and note that the information generated (and withheld from the parents) may include highly sensitive information, such as the use of drugs or sexual activity. Nonetheless, in situations where parental consent to treatment is required, the parents may continue to insist upon obtaining the information generated within the therapeutic setting.

Families and Violence

Confidentiality may be limited when patients threaten serious physical harm to themselves or others through child abuse, spouse abuse, elder abuse, or by threats to other identifiable persons.

Again, it is desirable to address limitations to confidentiality ahead of time, although patients need not receive a laundry list of every conceivable exception to confidentiality, however remote. The information provided to patients should reflect the nature of their concerns. Consequently, it seems appropriate, for example, to mention the child-abuse exception when dealing with parents. It is also prudent to include basic information about confidentiality and its exceptions in any service brochure that may be given to patients.

The most famous case dealing with threats to harm others was *Tarasoff v. the Regents of the University of California* (1976). The *Tarasoff* decision, which has been adopted by many other states, requires psychotherapists to try to prevent imminent danger of harm to identifiable third parties. Although the well-publicized cases (such as John Hinckley) deal with threats to public figures, the most common scenario is that the threat is against a family member, other relative, former lover, or relative.

The criteria established by the *Tarasoff* decision are reasonable. According to *Tarasoff* (1976), "a therapist should not be encouraged routinely to reveal such threats . . . unless such disclosures are necessary to avert danger to others" (p. 347). Psychotherapists are required to use state-of-the-art methods to assess dangerousness. Courts recognize that psychotherapists cannot predict dangerousness with complete accuracy. Instead, psychotherapists must use acceptable professional judgment in making these decisions (Appelbaum, 1985).

In situations where psychologists are treating a battered wife, for example, they need to determine whether the expression of the intent to harm on the part of the wife indicates an actual intent to harm her husband or is merely an expression of anger. Although no exact score card exists by which to formulate an opinion, the determination of dangerousness includes factors such as past history of violence, access to lethal weapons, degree of intent, availability of opportunity, and so on.

Even if psychologists determine that the threat is real, the *Tarasoff* decision does not necessarily require disclosure of the threat. Instead, the *Tarasoff* decision requires that the psychologist take "reasonable precautions" to diffuse the violence. These reasonable precautions could include increasing the frequency of psychotherapy, referring the patient for medication, seeking a voluntary hospitalization, etc. Although warning the intended victim is one option, it could be counterproductive and actually precipitate the violence the psychologist is trying to prevent. Often, therapeutic actions can reduce the violence and a warning or other extreme intervention is not required.

Finally, it should be noted that several states have passed "duty to warn" laws that eliminate liability on the part of providers who do warn intended victims. Many of these laws are poorly written and do not provide similar immunities for other protective actions besides warning intended victims.

To reduce their legal liability in the event that an unforeseen tragedy should occur, psychologists should document their interventions carefully. Consultations with other professionals are especially encouraged. Seeking a consultation may provide important information about the optimal manner of diagnosing or treating the patient and gives evidence that the psychotherapist is acting responsibly in treating the patient. Often, psychologists may want to receive the consultation from a psychiatrist who, with different training, may provide a pharmacological perspective on treating the patient.

If possible, psychologists should consider giving a warning with the patient present or at least with the consent of the patient (Beck, 1985). When giving a warning, it is necessary to give the minimal amount of essential clinical information, but make the warning meaningful.

It is prudent for a psychologist to develop a contingency plan or to take additional actions if the patient does not adhere to the treatment plan. A revised strategy might be necessary for a patient who, for example, stops taking medication or fails to attend outpatient appointments as determined in the treatment plan.

Record Keeping

Although records are used primarily to self-monitor treatment, they are also the psychologist's best defense in case of litigation. An axiom of risk management is that if it is not documented, it did not occur. The American Psychological Association (1993) developed general guidelines for record keeping, although these general guidelines still allow much provider discretion.

What to Include

Records should be comprehensive and objective. They should, in correspondence with APA guidelines, include the name of the patients, fee arrangement, dates and substance of service, test results, results of formal consultations, correspondence, release of information forms, copies of reports, intake sheets (if any), notations of phone calls and all other therapeutic contacts. Psychologists should attempt to secure the previous treatment records of patients. Failure to do so could be seen as negligence.

Every record should include the patient's diagnosis (or presenting problem), the treatment plan, and the information used to make the diagnosis and reach the treatment plan. Future mental health professionals reading the records should be able to understand generally what the psychologist was doing in treatment and why.

Substance of the Record

Psychologists should be certain to document high-risk situations carefully, such as when there is suspected child abuse, threats of violence towards others, transference problems, and so on. If possible, psychologists should have a standardized procedure or use standardized tests to clarify the clinical situation (e.g., the Beck Depression Inventory with a suicidal patient). Psychologists should include a discharge summary or note for each patient reviewing the course of treatment and relating the diagnosis to the manner in which you implemented the treatment plan.

If the family is relying on an insurance company to provide reimbursement for services, the psychologist may be requested to provide a *DSM-IV* diagnosis for one of the family members. Some clinicians and family members may prefer a relational diagnosis instead of intrapsychic diagnoses, which are more common in the *DSM-IV* (Kaslow, 1993). Unfortunately, many insurance companies do not reimburse unless the patient is given a *DSM-IV* diagnosis. Whatever decision the psychologist makes should be shared with patients so they understand their options for insurance reimbursement.

WRITING RECORDS

Although the psychotherapeutic process is subjective in and of itself, remarks in the chart should be as objective as possible. Psychologists should use behavioral descriptions whenever possible and only record statements relevant to treatment.

Although the records belong to the psychologist, the patient has a property interest in them. If litigation were to occur, the patient or the patient's attorney would probably have access to the records. Contrary to a common belief, most state courts do not offer special protection for a second set of private records or personal notes. Notes should be written as though the patient might see them sometime in the future. Pejorative comments, if seen by the patient, may provoke anger and create a perception of the psychologist as insensitive and uncaring.

Psychologists should try to maintain some internal consistency within their records. It is acceptable, for example, to diagnose a patient as having a panic disorder on one day and then to refer to the patient as having a social phobia three weeks later. However, the treatment record should document the reasons for the change in the diagnosis. Failure to document changes in the diagnosis or presenting problem could be interpreted as sloppiness.

Although psychologists may comment on previous notes and include clarifications, under no circumstances should a psychologist alter or destroy a previous note. Altered or destroyed notes give an impression of distorting information and admitting to culpability.

COMINGLED FILES

Some psychologists prefer to keep a chart only on one identified patient in the family, whereas others prefer to keep separate charts for each family member, and still others prefer to keep a single chart for multiple family members. Each has advantages and disadvantages. If the chart is kept only on one identified patient, there is a risk that the patient information will be hopelessly comingled with information about other members of the family. Comingled files raise confidentiality issues if a release is requested, because it is difficult to tease out what belongs and what does not belong in the chart of one person. On the other hand, keeping several individual charts can be burdensome if more than one family member is being treated. It can become difficult to separate individual from family issues at times.

There is no absolute answer as to when or whether to comingle charts. The decision should be based on a variety of factors, including the possibility that third-party reviewers may determine the necessity and level of intensity of treatment. Also, psychologists need to be aware that if a couple decides to divorce, one spouse may wish to use the information contained in the records in legal proceedings related to the divorce, property settlement, or child custody cases. In the case of marital therapy (as opposed to treatment for one patient), records should not be released without the consent of both spouses.

RECORDS AND NONCUSTODIAL PARENTS

Most states recognize the parental right to have access to the records of their minor children. Although this right generally poses few problems, difficulties may arise if a noncustodial parent seeks access to the information generated in treatment authorized by the custodial parent. Just because the child lives with one parent does not mean that the other parent has given up his or her parental rights and has no involvement in the health care that their child received. Under these circumstances, the psychologist should obtain information regarding the determination of legal and physical custody, which defines parental rights (see Chapter 7 by Mannarino). It is seldom necessary to give access to the complete record; rather, it is sufficient to keep the parent informed of the general nature of treatment.

PATIENT ACCESS TO RECORDS

Court cases and state laws are increasingly permitting patients to have a right to copies of their mental health records. Many times, patient requests for records reflect clinical issues, such as "What does my psychologist think of me?" or "What is wrong with me?" It is usually sufficient to deal with these issues directly in therapy without having to show patients their records.

In some circumstances, however, patients will insist on seeing their records. In these situations, psychologists will need to know the applicable state law or institutional policy. Many states permit providers to withhold information that would be harmful for their patients to see. If the law permits or requires the patients to see their records, then misunderstandings could be reduced if the records were written in concrete behavioral terms, with specific goals and minimal jargon or gratuitous comments. Also, if a decision is made to show the records to the patient, it is prudent for the psychologist to be present to review the records with the patient, which can reduce the likelihood that the patient will misunderstand or feel confused about the content in the records. Sometimes, psychologists can use the records review positively to focus on the treatment procedures and goals.

Consultation

Consultation is one of the best ways psychologists have to reduce their legal liability. Documented consultation with another competent professional is an excellent way to maintain high standards of care.

CLINICAL CONSULTATION

It is prudent for psychologists to consult in difficult cases at the very start of treatment. Very often, the opinion of another colleague may be very helpful in obtaining insights or perspectives on intervention strategies. Also, if patients are not responding to treatment and the reasons are not clear to the treating psychologist, it may be appropriate to get consultation from another professional. If the patient is not improving and has a disorder for which medication has proven effective, then a consultation (and perhaps an eventual referral) to a psychiatrist is indicated. It is important to document all consultations that a psychologist receives and to document all cases in which he or she provides consultation.

ONGOING CONSULTATION

In addition to consultation on a specific case, it is desirable for psychologists to receive ongoing consultation from peers and colleagues. Some psychologists are involved in peer consultation groups where they share cases and treatment perspectives with other providers. These groups often form a basis of self-education and self-monitoring of professional treatment.

LEGAL CONSULTATION

At times, psychologists may encounter situations in which legal or ethical issues are ambiguous or contradictory. The APA *Code of Conduct* cannot anticipate every conceivable set of circumstances that could arise, and some discretion and interpretation may be required.

Fortunately, several state psychological associations and the APA Insurance Trust provide legal consultation services for its members and subscribers. These organizations have often acquired a background of opinions from state licensing boards and other regulatory bodies relevant to the practice of psychology. In other cases, it may be prudent to solicit a formal opinion from a state ethics committee or a licensing board. Most boards that respond to inquiries include a disclaimer that their response is only based on the information given to them, and a different set of circumstances may result in a different conclusion.

Conclusion

Accusations of negligence occur when there is an unfortunate synergy of ill feelings toward the therapist and a perception of inadequate care. Psychologists can greatly reduce the likelihood of being accused of negligence by focusing on their relationships with family members, anticipating issues and problems, documenting treatment carefully, and seeking consultation. More important, these risk management procedures lead to a higher level of care for patients and their families.

References

American Psychological Association. (1992). *Ethical principles of psychologists and code of conduct.* Washington, DC: Author.

American Psychological Association. (1993). *Record keeping guidelines.* Washington, DC: Author.

American Psychological Association. (1994). Guidelines for child custody evaluations in divorce proceedings. *American Psychologist, 49,* 677–680.

Appelbaum, P. (1985). Tarasoff and the clinician: Problems in fulfilling the duty to protect. *American Journal of Psychiatry, 142,* 425–429.

Beck, J. (Ed.). (1985). *The potentially violent patient and the Tarasoff decision in psychiatric practice.* Washington, DC: American Psychiatric Press.

Biegel, D., Song, L., & Milligan, S. (1995). A comparative analysis of family caregivers' perceived relationships with mental health professionals. *Psychiatric Services, 46,* 447–482.

Dörken, H. (1990). Malpractice claims against psychologists: Policy issues, cost comparisons with psychiatrists, and prescription privilege implications. *Professional Psychology: Research and Practice, 21,* 150–152.

Kaslow, F. (1992). Legal issues of psychotherapy practice. *Independent Practitioner, 12*(3), 131–135.

Kaslow, F. (1993). Relational diagnosis: Past, present, and future. *American Journal of Family Therapy, 21,* 195–204.

Knapp, S., & VandeCreek, L. (in press). *Legal and ethical issues in the treatment of adult survivors of childhood abuse.* Washington, DC: American Psychological Association.

Mannarino, A. P. (1997, this volume).

Marsh, D. T. (1997, this volume).

Pies, R. (1994). Medical "mimics" of depression. *Psychiatric Annals, 24,* 519–520.

Strand, P. S., & Nash, M. R. (1997, this volume).

Stromberg, C., Haggarty, D., Leibenluft, R., McMillian, M., Mishkin, B., Rubin, B., & Trilling, H. (1988). *The psychologist's legal handbook.* Washington, DC: Council for the National Register of Health Service Providers in Psychology.

Tarasoff v. Board of Regents of the University of California, 529 P.2d 533, Cal. Reptr. 14 (1976).

VandeCreek, L., & Knapp, S. (1993). *Tarasoff and beyond: Legal and clinical issues in treating life endangering patients* (Rev. ed.). Sarasota, FL: Professional Resource Press.

Weyrauch, K. (1995, July 5). [Letter to the editor.] *Journal of the American Medical Association, 274,* 23.

CHAPTER 16

Professional Training in Ethics

LINDA K. KNAUSS

W hat makes teaching ethics particularly challenging is that it is not just teaching a body of knowledge, it is teaching a way of problem solving, decision making, and thinking. If they are not made to come alive through the use of case materials, vignettes, and real life situations, ethics courses can be extremely stagnant, academic, and theoretical. Most courses in professional ethics are complemented by including professional issues, such as dealing with insurance regulations, establishing a private or group practice, and dealing with hospital or organizational politics. Writings and training materials dealing with ethics instructions are virtually nonexistent. Thus, students often have little or no experience in applying ethical principles to actual cases and situations that they personally experience or witness.

In this chapter I examine professional training in ethics in psychology, which is representative of other mental health professions. In the past 20 years, there has been an increased emphasis on ethics training in graduate programs in psychology, and more programs are offering specific courses in ethics. This is considered to be a very positive trend, especially from a risk management perspective. Since 1979, every graduate program training professional psychologists seeking to be accredited by the American Psychological Association (APA) has been required to offer instruction in ethics and to familiarize students with whatever version of the APA ethics code is current (Bersoff, 1995). However, this standard was initiated 31 years after the APA began to accredit clinical psychology programs. This modification of the standards to include ethics training reflects the profession's growing recognition of the importance of ethical behavior and of the need for more explicit instruction in ethics during graduate school. This recognition also grew out of the violations of ethical standards by some therapists.

Should Ethics Be a Separate Course?

There was an old and widespread belief that ethics could best be taught in the context of supervised clinical work, rather than as a separate, formal course. This has been called ethical training by osmosis (Handelsman, 1986). It was assumed that ethical issues would come up in the course of clinical work and then be discussed in context, thus making ethics training more relevant. However, this approach assumes that adequate supervision is available, and that supervision is being provided by an ethically competent supervisor. Often one or both of these aspects are compromised by the needs and time constraints of a hospital, an agency, or a busy practice. Another shortcoming of this model is that it does not guarantee that a broad range of ethical issues will arise. It also seems preferable to learn about the multitude of ethical dilemmas that could occur and be prepared to face these situations, rather than learning about ethical issues during or after a crisis situation. Handelsman (1986) also stated that it is necessary to treat ethical thinking as a skill that must be developed and that is not intimately bound to the process of therapy or testing. However, there were no data available to compare whether ethics was best taught in a separate ethics course or integrated into existing courses in the curriculum. The momentum to initiate separate courses in ethics in graduate programs was based on the assumption, rather than on any empirical data, that such courses would have a positive impact.

In 1992, Gawthrop and Uhlemann provided such empirical data. They presented a vignette containing an ethical dilemma to undergraduate students who were preparing for careers in mental health professions. The treatment group received a 3-hour workshop on ethical decision making using a problem-solving approach. In comparison with two control groups, the treatment group performed significantly better on a rating scale designed to measure the quality of the decision-making process. Gawthrop and Uhlemann concluded that formal exposure to ethics education had a significant positive effect. It is also of note that a significant effect took place with only 3 hours of instruction.

The problem-solving approach used in this study was supplemented with elements of other ethics teaching models. The workshop goals were to sensitize participants to ethical issues and to maximize the quality of ethical decision making. Strategies included reading and discussion of ethical codes and case vignettes, self-generation of ethical dilemmas from experience, and generating and justifying ethical decisions about specific vignettes (Kitchener, 1986). Discussions of ethical dilemmas during the workshop often included an exploration of how values form the basis of codes (Abeles, 1980). The case vignettes also made participant evaluation and accountability an integral part of ethics education.

This study makes it clear that informal teaching methods are not the most effective way to teach ethics. It also shows that just providing information about ethics is not sufficient, because ethics education needs to include the process of teaching ethical decision making. The results of this study suggest that trainees who do not receive formal exposure to ethics education cannot be assumed to possess the same ethical decision-making skills as trainees who have gone through formal ethics education. In addition, the study suggests that separate sections of courses or full courses devoted to professional ethics be included in all training programs and that educators consider using a problem-solving approach to ethical decision making. Although this study provides conclusive evidence that formal coursework in ethics is more effective than informal teaching methods, several researchers caution that it cannot be assumed that ethics education will generalize to ethical behavior in clinical practice (Bernard & Jara, 1986; Pope, Tabachnick, & Keith-Spiegel, 1987, 1988).

When Should a Course in Ethics Be Offered?

Once a decision has been made to offer a formal course in ethics during a training program, the timing must be considered. Such a course can be offered early in the program so that students become familiar with ethics issues and principles and practice ethically from the beginning of their careers. On the other hand, it is very difficult to appreciate the subtlety of ethical dilemmas if one has no clinical experience. Thus, the course can be offered near the end of the program, or at least following practicum or internship experience.

Regardless of when the ethics course is offered, one course may not be sufficient. A model that addresses all of these issues, but is not widely used, would be to offer a didactic course early in a training program, which provides familiarity with principles and issues, and then to offer a seminar near the end of the training program, using a discussion format to examine dilemmas that have been encountered and subtleties not easily understood without clinical experience. Learning to practice ethically cannot be effective in an atmosphere that does not value or respect being ethical. Making a commitment to ethics education needs to be part of the foundation and philosophy of every graduate training program in psychology.

Where to Begin

Ethics courses often begin by teaching the APA ethics code; however, it quickly becomes apparent that this is not enough. A more experiential model is needed to cover the huge leap from ethical theory to daily clinical practice. This experiential model helps students develop a more realistic and practical understanding of both ethics and professional issues through the use of vignettes and the students' own case material.

"Decision making in the trenches" requires critical thinking, but this is difficult to teach. An ethics course requires students to examine their own values, beliefs, and definitions of right and wrong. Ethics, morals, laws, and even etiquette are all standards for determining whether an action is right, good, or proper; and each specifies penalties for deviation. Although these standards reflect the consensus of the society or culture that promotes it, moral frameworks are developed largely through rational processes, legal standards are primarily developed through political processes, and norms of etiquette are developed by historical precedent (Haas & Malouf, 1989). Ethical standards focus on behavior and motivations that aim at the highest ideals of human behavior. Criminal law, in contrast, focuses primarily on behavior that may harm other members of society, and etiquette focuses on behavior that establishes one's standing within a subgroup. Actions that violate moral or ethical standards can result in censure, guilt, or social criticism. Illegal behavior results in punishment, and impolite behavior results in social ostracism, or at least in mild social criticism (Haas & Malouf, 1989).

There are three main features that distinguish ethics (Haas & Malouf, 1989). First, ethics is based on principles. Second, the principles have universality. Finally, proper behavior can be deduced from the principles by reasoning. Thus, ethics should involve adherence to a consistent set of principles, assumed to be relevant for all people in similar situations and that result in the obligation to take particular action. However, professional ethics in psychology is not pure ethics but a combination of ethics, law, and etiquette. There is also no theory of professional ethics that meets the above standards (Haas & Malouf, 1989).

Understanding these concepts allows one to put psychology's ethics into perspective. The *Ethical Principles of Psychologists* is a code of conduct formulated by a select group of psychologists, based on their experience in the field, passed by the APA Council of Representatives, and acknowledged and accepted (by joining APA) by psychologists who are members of the APA. Psychologists who are members of the APA must conduct themselves according to the ethical principles, and many psychologists who are not APA members follow the ethical principles either by choice or because the ethical principles or a similar code has been incorporated into their licensing law (Bennett, Bryant, VandenBos, & Greenwood, 1990).

Ethics Codes Are Ambiguous

There is a widespread belief that ethics are absolute rules of conduct. However, because psychology is a continually evolving science and profession, new or better standards, principles, or guidelines may be developed to meet changing needs (Bennett et al., 1990) as time passes and circumstances change.

The APA ethical standards have been revised eight times since they were first published in 1953. Through these revisions, the standards have become much more practical and less philosophical. Initially, the standards intermixed aspirational aspects (the highest levels to which a professional should aspire) with minimal standards, below which one's professional behavior should not fall. In 1992, the APA *Ethical Principles of Psychologists and Code of Conduct* separated six General Principles, which were primarily aspirational, from the Ethical Standards, which define minimal standards of behavior for psychologists. Although this version is dramatically different in its format from any of the previous versions and far more specific, a problem with interpretation remains.

There are few, if any, sets of guidelines that are not at least somewhat ambiguous. This is because no set of rules can cover every situation; an exception can always be found. Thus, the standards need to be flexible enough to apply in a wide variety of situations, but they also must be specific enough to give adequate guidance. Other than forbidding sexual intimacies with current therapy patients or those whose treatment ceased within two years, and precluding the abandonment of patients, there are no absolute rules in the current APA code (APA, 1992). This leaves a tremendous amount to the judgment of the practitioner who must constantly balance the best interests of organizations, institutions, research participants, clients, and the public.

Problem-Solving Approaches

It is because of this ambiguity that it is necessary to teach ethics from a problem-solving approach. Since the APA ethical standards cannot prescribe the proper course of action for every situation, it is important for ethics courses to teach students to be aware of possible ethical conflicts and to reason out the most ethical solution to their dilemmas.

Several writers have proposed models to teach this skill (Haas & Malouf, 1989; Keith-Spiegel & Koocher, 1985; Kitchener, 1986; Sinclair, Poizner, Gilmour-Barrett, & Randall, 1987; Tymchuk, 1986). According to Eberlein (1987), many teaching models focus on the correct answer approach. The questions that comprise the Examination of Professional Practice in Psychology (the licensing exam) use this approach. Although forced-choice responses make this exam easier to score, it does not necessarily provide the opportunity to think about ethical questions in ways that could lead to more productive resolutions. It also gives the impression that every ethical dilemma has a right answer, a situation that is clearly not the case when listening to an ethics committee discuss a case or when examining the different decisions made by various ethics committees in similar situations. Eberlein (1987) concludes that when psychologists cannot refer to a specific standard, they fall back on their own value systems and their interpretation of the spirit of the code. It is extremely difficult to apply a limited set of rules to problems of human relationships, which almost always involve some conflict among values, morals, rights, and ethics.

KITCHENER'S APPROACH

Karen Kitchener (1986) showed how the work of Rest (1982), a moral philosopher, could form the basis of ethical decision making in psychology. Rest defined four components of moral behavior:

1. *Interpreting the Situation as a Moral One.* This involves the ability to perceive whether one's actions are affecting the welfare of

others and to imagine the consequences of one's actions on the lives of the people involved. Thus, a psychologist who schedules a client during the dinner hour and asks that client to join him or her at a restaurant must consider the ethical implications of the situation, not only the pragmatic issue of getting something to eat.

2. *Formulating a Moral Course of Action.* This is the process of deciding what is right or fair once the ethical issue is recognized. This decision is based on the current code of ethics, current literature, the philosophical principles underlying the code, and the psychologist's level of moral reasoning. Sometimes the ethics code does not provide adequate guidance. In this case, the outcome is a result of the use of mature moral reasoning.

3. *Deciding What to Do.* Research has shown that what people think they should do morally is not always what they decide to do. How people decide to act is not only influenced by moral values, but also by money, ambition, and self-interest.

4. *Implementing a Plan of Action.* It is not enough to be aware of and concerned about ethical issues, nor is it enough to think wisely about ethical issues. Professional practice requires that individuals take responsibility for acting and for the consequences of their actions. It involves what is often called ego strength. This theory provides a framework for ethical decision making.

Kitchener (1984) also suggested that the limitations of professional codes can be addressed by considering more fundamental ethical principles. Based on the work of Beauchamp and Childress (1983, 1989), she selected the following five ethical principles as most relevant to psychology: autonomy, nonmaleficence (do no harm), beneficence (benefit others), justice, and fidelity.

Autonomy means that individuals are free to act in the ways that they choose as long as their actions do not interfere with similar actions of others. Thus, if a person wishes his or her choices to be respected by others, then that person must similarly respect the right and choices others make, even if they appear mistaken.

The principle of nonmaleficence has its roots in the history of medical practice. It includes not inflicting intentional harm as well as not engaging in actions that risk harming others. Thus, it is a principle that forbids certain kinds of actions in contrast to beneficence, which is a positive obligation. This principle is not absolutely binding because it may be appropriate to harm another person if one's own life is in danger. However, it is generally considered one of the strongest ethical obligations.

The concept of beneficence or doing good for others is critical to ethical issues in psychology. It is reflected in psychologists' dedication to promoting human welfare. It is important to balance this principle with the one of autonomy and not insist on helping someone who does not want help or doing something against a person's will because you believe it is for his or her own good.

Justice refers to the fair treatment of an individual. It seems psychologists should have a commitment to being fair that goes beyond that of the ordinary person. Psychologists agree to promote the worth and dignity of each individual and are required to be concerned with equal treatment for all individuals.

The issue of fidelity is especially critical in psychology because issues like truthfulness and loyalty are basic to trust. While trust is vital to all human relationships, it is especially vital to the client-therapist relationship, which is dependent on honest communication. Psychologists have a unique ethical obligation to fulfill their commitments because a lack of trust could have serious consequences for all professional relationships and the profession itself.

These five ethical principles allow psychologists to analyze ethical issues when the ethics code does not give clear advice. However, to demonstrate that these five principles are embodied in the APA ethical standards, Donald Bersoff and Peter Koeppl (1993) have indicated where each of these concepts is reflected in the code.

KEITH-SPIEGEL AND KOOCHER

Keith-Spiegel and Koocher (1985) described a decision-making process to permit a systematic examination of a situation and the factors that may influence a final decision. It was adapted from a basic procedural guideline developed by Tymchuk (1981).

1. Describe the parameters of the situation. This includes obtaining information from the parties involved and/or from relevant sources.
2. Define the potential issues involved. From the information assembled, the critical issues should be described.
3. Consult the guidelines, if any, already available that might apply to the resolution of each issue. These guidelines may include the

APA ethical principles or other codes or policy statements. This process may lead to contradictions, or there may be no relevant source. However, it is critical to take this step because to disregard existing policy could have serious consequences.

4. Evaluate the rights, responsibilities, and welfare of all affected parties (including institutions and the general public). It is not unusual to discover that a flawed decision resulted from the lack of awareness of a party's right to confidentiality, informed consent, or evaluative feedback.

5. Generate the alternative decisions possible for each issue. This phase should be conducted without a focus on whether each option is ethical or feasible. Thus, a decision initially considered unacceptable may later be the best one after all.

6. Enumerate the consequences of making each decision. Whenever relevant, these consequences should include economic, psychological, and social costs; short-term, ongoing, and long-term effects; the time and effort necessary to effect each decision, including any resource limitations; any other risks, including the violation of individual rights; and any benefits.

7. Present any evidence that the various consequences or benefits resulting from each decision will actually occur. To the extent possible, estimate the probability of such occurrences, although often no evidence exists. Lack of evidence is itself a risk.

8. Make the decision. If possible, share this information with all people affected by the decision. Their input should be solicited and considered. The plan should be monitored through its completion and followup may be desirable.

Intertwined in most sources of variability in ethical decision making are differences in value systems among psychologists. Keith-Spiegel and Koocher (1985) recommend using this ethical decision-making model to the extent possible, given time and other constraints. They also suggest that each decision be carefully documented for the psychologist's protection, as well as for possible future use.

HAAS AND MALOUF

Haas and Malouf (1989) have developed an explicit framework for ethical decision making. The clinician must identify three elements before being able to make an ethical decision: (a) the nature of the problem,

(b) the identities and preferences of those persons who have a legitimate stake in the outcome of the problem, and (c) the relevant professional and legal standards (if any) that bear on the case at hand.

Once enough information is gathered to adequately identify the ethical nature of the problem, a five-stage decision making process is implemented.

1. Does a relevant professional, legal, or social standard exist? This question obligates psychologists to engage in a literature review or consultation with colleagues if they are not already aware of an existing standard.

2. Is there a reason to deviate from the standard? This could occur either because the standard is so vague it is not useful, or the specifics of a given case may lead to more harm than benefit by adhering to the standard. If there is no single ethical standard or principle that pertains, the practitioner must identify the relevant ethical issues. For example, what are the dimensions that make the issue problematic? If it is because of competing ethical principles, they must be defined and classified before they can be reconciled.

3. Can a primary ethical dimension be specified? For example, when a clear and present danger exists, the obligation to protect potential victims overrides that of upholding a client's confidentiality. However, in the case of informed consent versus competence, neither principle overrides the other. In cases where no single ethical dimension outweighs all others, a variety of actions may be ethically appropriate. If that is the case, the next step is to generate a list of possible actions, followed by a cost-benefit analysis. The alternative that results in the optimum resolution for the greatest number of interested parties should be chosen.

4. Does the new course of action appear to satisfy the needs and preferences of affected parties? The practitioner is obligated to render the services that he or she agreed to provide. These services are provided to satisfy some need of the consumer.

5. Is the course of action ethical and can it be implemented? In selecting a course of action, the question that must be asked is: Would you recommend that everyone do this? This differentiates the best choice from the most convenient choice. Although a therapist may be able to rationalize his actions in a particular situation, it is often helpful to think about how you would advise another person to act in a similar situation, and whether

this behavior would be justified if examined by a group of your peers.

Once a course of action is selected, it is also important that it can be put into effect. Thus, it needs to be practical. Suggesting that someone attempt to repeal a law or change contemporary social opinion is not a realistic course of action. In addition, it is important to consider all of the possible consequences even of acting ethically. For example, there could be serious consequences to a supervisee who confronts a supervisor who is acting unethically. In many cases, there are alternatives with less dramatic consequences.

Selecting the best course of action is not enough unless it is implemented. This often requires assertiveness, tenacity, and a strong network of support. Finally, it is recommended that practitioners review the appropriateness of any decisions that are made and consult with colleagues if necessary.

Haas and Malouf conclude that there will always be cases with unique features that puzzle practitioners. This framework is to guide practitioners in developing perspective on such puzzling cases.

OTHER PROBLEM-SOLVING APPROACHES

Tymchuk (1986) described a useful approach that includes seven steps. The decision of which alternative to implement was based on the short-term, ongoing, and long-term consequences and on the psychological, social, and economic costs, with a risk-benefit analysis of each alternative.

The problem-solving model recommended by the Canadian Psychological Association (CPA) Committee on Ethics (1986) is reflective of the Tymchuk approach and used the following six questions in the development of the new code (Sinclair et al., 1987).

1. Indicate the individuals and/or groups that need to be considered in arriving at a solution to the dilemma posed by the situation.

2. Take each of the individuals or groups that you feel should be considered, and explain in detail what consideration each is owed and why, particularly in terms of the rights and responsibilities involved.

3. What would be your choice of action, and why would you choose it?

4. What alternative choices of action would you consider, and why did you not choose them?

5. What is the minimal circumstance in the situation that you can conceive of that could lead you to a different choice of action? What would that action be, and why would you choose it?

6. Do you have any further thoughts or comments about this or similar situations? If so, explain.

The CPA Committee on Ethics (CPA, 1986), included an evaluation of the action taken as the seventh and final step. In teaching ethics, these questions are useful guidelines for evaluating any ethical dilemma and can lead to valuable class discussion.

Regardless of which problem-solving approach is selected, they all include the development of alternatives, analyses, choice of action, and evaluation (Eberlein, 1987). If there were a consensus on how to handle most ethical dilemmas, problem-solving guidelines would not be necessary. However, researchers have found that this is not the case. Tymchuk et al. (1982) found that aside from issues of sexual behavior, client identity, and client dangerousness to others, all of which are addressed in recent code revisions, there was not wide agreement about what constitutes ethical behavior. Also, in a study by Haas, Malouf, and Mayerson (1986), they presented a choice of at least two potentially viable alternatives and found 75 percent agreement on only three of ten vignettes presented. When psychologists cannot refer to a specific standard, they tend to fall back on their own value systems. According to Bersoff (1995), ethical behavior results from integrating didactic knowledge, including a thorough familiarity with the APA ethics code; an understanding of problem-solving and decision-making approaches; a clear conception of philosophical principles; and a basically sound character that leads a person to respond with maturity, judgment, discretion, wisdom, and prudence.

Why Do People Act Unethically?

In teaching students how to behave ethically, it seems important to understand what leads people to act unethically. Although psychology, like other fields, is not totally free from sociopaths, for the most part people do not plan to act unethically. Unethical behavior seems to sneak up on some people. Everyone knows it is not a good idea to fall asleep while driving, yet this still occurs fairly often. Similarly, most, if not, all practitioners know that it is unethical to have a sexual relationship with a client, yet this also still occurs. In some situations, rationalization and emotions seem to interfere with objectivity. Several studies suggest additional reasons for psychologists choosing unethical behavior while fully aware of the relevant ethical principles and problem-solving techniques.

Bernard and Jara (1986) asked clinical graduate students what they should and what they would do when confronted with two separate situations, each involving a clear ethical violation. One scenario depicted a clinical graduate student as being sexually involved with a client from a psychotherapy practicum. In the second scenario, a clinical graduate student was characterized as a problem drinker/alcoholic who was manifesting poor judgment and erratic behavior in various clinical practica. The data to be analyzed was the difference between what the reader said should be done and what he or she would actually do if confronted with these situations.

For both scenarios, at least half of the students stated that they would not live up to their own interpretation of what the ethical principles required of them as professionals. Although they knew what they should do as an ethical psychologist, they would not do it.

There were no significant differences based on any demographic variables, and most of the respondents had taken a course in ethics. Thus, it seems that a willingness to take action when confronted with an ethical violation that involves a colleague or friend is not something that can be taught. The problem here does not seem to be how to communicate the ethical principles to students, rather, how to motivate them to implement the principles that they understand.

Bernard, Murphy, and Little (1987) replicated this study with a sample of members of Division 12 (Clinical) of APA. Although approximately half of the students in the above study said that they would do less than they knew they should do whether the violation involved alcoholism or sex, this was not the case with clinical psychologists. In the case of alcoholism, 25 percent of the clinicians said they would do less than their understanding of the ethical principles demanded of them, whereas with the sexual scenario, one-third of the clinicians would not live up to their understanding of what should be done. Thus, although professionals say they would behave more responsibly than graduate students, significant numbers of clinical psychologists would not do what they know they should do when confronted with an ethical violation by a colleague.

Because there were no significant differences on any demographic variable, the decision to report the unethical behavior of a colleague seems to be a matter of personal values. The problem remains how to motivate more clinicians to implement the ethical principles, which they understand. It may be that a different thrust is needed in the teaching of ethics in graduate programs: one that emphasizes values, not only principles and problem-solving techniques.

Ethical slips also occur when professionals fail to take care of themselves and become impaired, either through substance abuse, burnout, or personal difficulties. It is important to recognize the signs that this is occurring and take the appropriate steps.

The following are some suggestions from Haas and Malouf (1989) and Bennett et al. (1990):

1. Be alert to increased stress at home and in the workplace.
2. Monitor your health and seek medical and dental attention as needed.
3. Take vacations and relax in other ways.
4. Recognize the signs and symptoms of substance abuse, including alcohol, prescription drugs, and over-the-counter drugs. Monitor your own use of alcohol and other substances.
5. Have consultants available to turn to for advice and feedback on your behavior.
6. Have a social support network that can provide resources in times of stress.
7. Consider personal therapy. (It is surprising how much resistance there is among mental health practitioners to receiving personal therapy.)
8. Have referral sources available to whom you can send cases beyond your competence or cases that might involve a special risk such as providing marital therapy while you are going through your own divorce.
9. Listen to family, friends, and colleagues if they indicate that you appear to be showing signs of distress.

Too often, psychologists assume they are capable of handling any situation, or they ignore problems out of fear of harming their image. It can't be stressed enough that clinicians should consciously monitor their functioning and seek feedback from others to recognize and correct potential impairment.

Ethical Principles and Personal Values

An individual may act differently than the APA ethical principles, or even the law, dictates when these rules and guidelines are contrary to his or her conscience. For example, although reporting a past crime is not an ethically acceptable reason to break confidentiality, many psychologists say that they could not live with themselves if they did not report to the police or other authorities certain information they have learned in the confidence of a therapy session. Although they recognize this is a violation of confidentiality, they are aware of the consequences of their behavior and are willing to accept the consequences if necessary.

Laws and personal values conflict when psychologists do not report cases of child abuse because they believe (often accurately) that it will be a deterrent to treatment. Psychologists also sometimes choose not to warn a potential victim of harm because they fear the potential victim may harm their client first (as in the case of an abused wife who threatened to kill her husband, but was in danger of more serious abuse if the husband knew of her intentions). Although many clinicians are willing to accept the consequences of their actions, a significant number simply believe their actions will not result in censorship or prosecution.

Pope and Bajt (1988) surveyed 100 senior psychologists, presumably acknowledged by their peers as knowledgeable and scrupulous regarding professional accountability. A majority of those surveyed acknowledged that they willingly violated laws or certain ethical principles and would do so again on the basis of client welfare or other deeper values. Whereas Ansell and Ross (1990) felt that the psychologists surveyed chose their client's welfare over obedience in this case to reporting laws, others point out the dangerousness of holding oneself as above the law (Kalichman, 1990; Pope & Bajt, 1988; Van Eenwyk, 1990). When choosing to disobey the law, it is difficult to ensure that your actions are based on sound professional judgment rather than on self-interest, prejudice, and rationalization (Pope & Bajt, 1988). Kalichman (1990) points out that it seems paradoxical that in the name of being ethical, psychologists so frequently choose to break the law.

The conflict between deeply held values and formal legal or ethical obligations needs to be addressed in education, training, and supervision, including a cost-benefit analysis of the consequences of both disregarding the law or ethics, as well as disregarding one's own values.

Ethical, Legal, and Clinical Issues

A course in ethics should help differentiate among ethical, legal, and clinical issues. Members of ethics committees are often asked questions that are primarily legal or clinical. It is extremely valuable to know when to consult an attorney, as well as when to seek supervision. Consultation and supervision are the most common recommendations made by ethics committees.

Although the APA ethical principles address confidentiality, issues such as how to respond to a subpoena, specifics of the mandated reporting law, and whether you can treat a minor without parental consent are all legal issues, subject to the laws of the state in which you are practicing.

In contrast, determining the suicide potential of a particular patient, selecting the proper assessment techniques, and making an appropriate diagnosis are all clinical issues, although failure to practice at the usual, customary, and reasonable level of the profession may be considered a violation of the ethical principle of competence.

ETHICS AND LAW

There are a few occasions where the law and ethical principles may be in conflict. One example of this is when a psychologist is subpoenaed to divulge information in court and the client refuses to give his or her consent for the psychologist to reveal the confidential information shared in treatment. If the patient does give consent, there is no ethical-legal conflict, although some people may feel a conflict with their personal values if they believe that revealing certain information is not in their client's (or former client's) best interest.

There are several steps that can be taken to resolve the above dilemma. Your client may consent to your discussing the problem with his or her attorney, with the opposing attorney, or with the judge in the case to attempt to come to an agreeable resolution in terms of the relevance and necessity of the records (Tepper, Rinella, & Siegel, 1991). However, if a client continues to refuse to consent to the release of information required by a subpoena or a court order, a psychologist is in the very difficult, and fortunately very rare, position of deciding whether to break confidentiality or to be held in contempt of court. It is a decision that should be made in consultation with your own attorney.

ETHICS COMMITTEES, LICENSING BOARDS, AND MALPRACTICE

There are several mechanisms to regulate psychologists. These include national, state, and local ethics committees; licensing boards; and malpractice suits. There is often confusion between the roles of an ethics committee and a licensing board. In terms of regulation, ethics committees determine whether the ethics code has been violated, licensing boards determine whether the licensing law that may contain an ethics code has been violated, and the jury in a malpractice case must determine whether the plaintiff has been harmed.

A licensing board is a legal entity, appointed by the governor. In cases that require adjudication, the board is the tryer of fact, making decisions on information that is presented to the members. Thus, they serve in the role of a judge, not an attorney or detective. This is very different from an ethics committee, which collects information, processes it, and reports a decision on whether the ethics code was violated.

Complaints to licensing boards are more common than malpractice suits. In order to substantiate a malpractice case, there must be liability, harm, and damages. If there is not a significant amount (of money) that can be claimed for damages, a situation probably will not become a malpractice case. However, it could go to the licensing board and be considered a violation of the licensing law, even if no harm occurred.

To succeed in a malpractice claim, a plaintiff must prove four distinct elements of malpractice. First, there must be a professional relationship between the psychologist and the client. Only then does the practitioner have a legal duty of care. Then, the practitioner must have breached a demonstrable standard of care; namely, he or she practiced below the standard of care. Next, the client must have suffered harm or injury, which must be demonstrated and established. The last element is the most difficult to prove. The practitioner's breach of the duty to practice within the standard of care must be the cause of the client's injury. In addition, the injury must be a reasonable and foreseeable consequence of the breach. It is the plaintiff who bears the burden of proving the existence of each element for successful malpractice litigation (Bennett et al., 1990).

The APA ethics code is used as a standard of care in malpractice cases. However, as such it can function as both a sword and a shield. When the code is used as a sword, practitioners fear being sued for malpractice if they do not conform to the code, which can cause anxiety, as the code is often ambiguous. However, the code can also be a shield, making actions defensible if they were taken to follow the code.

There is also a different standard of proof required to determine guilt in malpractice versus ethics cases. Because of this, it may not be appropriate to conclude that because someone was sanctioned for an ethics violation, they are necessarily guilty of malpractice. Civil malpractice cases are decided based on a preponderance of the evidence. Disciplinary proceedings are decided based on a preponderance of the evidence or on clear and convincing evidence. In contrast, criminal cases are decided on the basis of a still higher standard of proof: beyond a reasonable doubt.

Thus, a malpractice verdict against a psychologist for sexual relations with a patient, based on a preponderance of the evidence (for example, 51% certainty) might occur despite substantial doubt that the event occurred. However, this does not prove that the defendant would be convicted in a criminal proceeding in states with laws that make it a crime for mental health professionals to have sex with their clients. In these cases, proof beyond a reasonable doubt (for example, 95% certainty) would be required. Conversely, acquittal in a criminal case does not prove that a malpractice verdict or licensing board action would not be proper, because those do not require proof beyond a reasonable doubt (Stromberg et al., 1988).

Finally, the issue of bad conduct outside of the professional realm (such as spouse abuse, rape, or tax evasion) has been the issue of some controversy as to whether it should be considered by professional ethics committees. Such conduct shows poor self-control and impairs the public view of psychology, and as such, ethics committees are more likely to regard such behavior as potentially bearing on professional conduct (Stromberg et al., 1988).

In deciding on proper conduct, professionals need to consider many perspectives and sets of rules. These include ethical principles and standards, licensing laws, malpractice principles, criminal laws, clinical judgment, and personal values.

The value of acting ethically is not just to avoid punishment. It is a way of thinking to guide behavior in handling difficult situations. The questions to be considered go beyond just, "Is this an ethics violation?" Some people feel that as long as they follow the law they will be acting appropriately; however, it is not always that simple. Psychologists have the responsibility of weighing all sides of a question and resolving the dilemma in a way that, in his or her best judgment, upholds the ethical principles and practice guidelines of the profession as well as the law (Bennett et al., 1990).

An Ethics Educators' Conference

The members of the Ethics Committee of the Pennsylvania Psychological Association (PPA) felt that professional training in ethics was an important issue that did not receive enough attention. Thus, they organized a six-hour workshop for ethics educators. The purpose of the conference was to exchange ideas and to provide information on the evolving standards of the practice of psychology.

Attendance was by invitation only and included university, medical school, and professional school faculty who were teaching ethics courses in clinical, counseling, or school psychology programs. In addition, internship supervisors who taught seminars in ethics were invited. Also included were representatives from the APA Insurance Trust, the State Board of Psychology, PPA's Legal Consultation Plan, and PPA's Impaired Professional Program, as well as regional ethics committee members. Approximately 30 people attended the conference.

There were several workshops throughout the day, but rather than formal presentations, the emphasis was on the exchange of perspectives and information between the conference participants and the panel members. The topics for the panels were derived from responses to an informal survey of ethics education in Pennsylvania. That survey identified the following four general topic areas: the process of ethics education, the relationship of ethics to law and other regulatory bodies, real life issues, and specific content areas.

Many of the questions that were raised in the survey and in the workshop were discussed in this chapter. For example, teaching-process issues included when in the curriculum ethics should be taught, how ethics fits into a total curriculum, how to teach critical thinking and ethical decision making, and the challenge of teaching ethics to students who have not yet faced real life ethical questions.

The discussion of the relationship of ethics to law focused on what to do when state laws and ethics don't match; similarities, differences, and overlap in ethics and law; clarifying the differences among morality, ethics, and law; and identifying issues that have a common legal-ethical interface. Another issue that generated much discussion was how to do what is ethically responsible when the code conflicts with what is best for clients.

Real life issues were situations that caused ethical dilemmas and generated discussion on ambiguous situations, the process of ethical decision making, questions that come before the State Board of Psychology, and the personal struggles of psychologists. What made this particular workshop especially valuable was sharing case studies and collecting anecdotes for class discussion.

The panel on specific content areas discussed ethical dilemmas of school psychologists, ethics in supervision, interprofessional dilemmas, confidentiality, duty to warn, and abuse reporting. They also seriously considered the ethical dilemmas created by managed care, such as the issue of abandonment when a provider is dropped from a panel, or when further treatment is not authorized by the insurance company.

The need for training in the ethical and professional issues raised in managed care has recently emerged and is growing rapidly. Continuing education workshops have addressed this issue, which needs to be integrated into graduate training as well.

Many valuable suggestions were generated by the conference. Course syllabi were exchanged, as well as information on books and articles. It was suggested that practicing psychologists visit ethics classes and discuss their own ethical dilemmas and decision-making processes. This was considered especially relevant for classes where students had not yet faced their own ethical questions. Also, members of the Impaired Professionals Committee of PPA volunteered to speak to ethics classes and regional psychological associations on the value of good self-care skills and preventing burnout. Of particular interest was the idea of developing a collection of case studies, vignettes, and anecdotes to be used for class discussion.

The conference was considered a success by all who attended it, and a second conference is being planned. Future topics include different perspectives on the need for ethics education, ethics education throughout the career span, and ethics education through case examples.

Continuing Education

Although a major portion of ethics education should occur in graduate school and during internship, it should not stop there. Ethics education is a process that takes place over a career span. Once graduate education is completed, there are many continuing education workshops on ethics, professional issues, and risk management. Some states require a certain number of continuing education hours in ethics during each renewal period to maintain a license as a psychologist. Such a proposal is under consideration in Pennsylvania. Also, some insurance companies will give a discount on malpractice insurance to psychologists who have a specific number of hours of training in ethics.

Conclusion

Professional training in ethics is more than learning a code of behavior or teaching students to aspire to uphold the highest standards of the profession. Professional training in ethics is teaching critical thinking, problem solving, and decision making to prepare students for the clinical, legal, and ethical dilemmas they are sure to encounter as practicing researchers, academicians, or clinicians. In addition, professional training in ethics does not end in graduate school, but must continue throughout one's career as the field of psychology grows and changes.

References

Abeles, N. (1980). Teaching ethical principles by means of value confrontation. *Psychotherapy: Research and Practice, 17*, 384–391.

American Psychological Association. (1992). Ethical principles of psychologists and code of conduct. *American Psychologist, 47*, 1597–1611.

Ansell, C., & Ross, H. L. (1990). Reply to Pope and Bajt. *American Psychologist, 45*, 399.

Beauchamp, T. L., & Childress, J. F. (1983). *Principles of biomedical ethics* (2nd ed.). Oxford, England: Oxford University Press.

Beauchamp, T. L., & Childress, J. F. (1989). *Principles of biomedical ethics* (3rd ed.). Oxford, England: Oxford University Press.

Bennett, B. E., Bryant, B. K., VandenBos, G. R., & Greenwood, A. (1990). *Professional liability and risk management*. Washington, DC: American Psychological Association.

Bernard, J. L., & Jara, C. S. (1986). The failure of clinical psychology graduate students to apply understood ethical principles. *Professional Psychology: Research and Practice, 17*, 313–315.

Bernard, J. L., Murphy, M., & Little, M. (1987). The failure of clinical psychologists to apply understood ethical principles. *Professional Psychology: Research and Practice, 18*, 489–491.

Bersoff, D. N. (1995). *Ethical conflicts in psychology.* Washington, DC: American Psychological Association.

Bersoff, D. N., & Koeppl, P. M. (1993). The relation between ethical codes and moral principles. *Ethics and Behavior, 3,* 345–357.

Canadian Psychological Association Committee on Ethics. (1986). Code of ethics. *Highlights, 8*(1), 6E-12E.

Eberlein, L. (1987). Introducing ethics to beginning psychologists: A problem-solving approach. *Professional Psychology: Research and Practice, 18,* 353–359.

Gawthrop, J. C., & Uhlemann, M. R. (1992). Effects of the problem-solving approach in ethics training. *Professional Psychology: Research and Practice, 23,* 38–42.

Haas, L. J., & Malouf, J. L. (1989). *Keeping up the good work: A practitioner's guide to mental health ethics.* Sarasota, Florida. Professional Resource Exchange.

Haas, L. J., Malouf, J. L., & Mayerson, N. H. (1986). Ethical dilemmas in psychological practice: Results of a national survey. *Professional Psychology: Research and Practice, 17,* 316–321.

Handelsman, M. M. (1986). Problems with ethics training by "osmosis." *Professional Psychology: Research and Practice, 17,* 371–372.

Kalichman, S. C. (1990). Reporting laws, confidentiality, and clinical judgment: Reply to Ansell and Ross. *American Psychologist, 45,* 1273.

Keith-Spiegel, P., & Koocher, G. P. (1985). *Ethics in psychology: Professional standards and cases.* New York: Random House.

Kitchener, K. S. (1984). Intuition, critical evaluation and ethical principles: The foundation for ethical decisions in counseling psychology. *Counseling Psychologist, 12*(3), 43–55.

Kitchener, K. S. (1986). Teaching applied ethics in counselor education: An integration of psychological processes and philosophical analyses. *Journal of Counseling and Development, 64,* 306–310.

Pope, K. S., & Bajt, T. R. (1988). When laws and values conflict: A dilemma for psychologists. *American Psychologist, 43,* 828–829.

Pope, K. S., Tabachnick, B. G., & Keith-Spiegel, P. (1987). Ethics of practice: The beliefs and behaviors of psychologists and therapists. *American Psychologist, 42,* 993–1006.

Pope, K. S., Tabachnick, B. G., & Keith-Spiegel, P. (1988). Good and poor practices in psychotherapy: National survey of beliefs of psychologists. *Professional Psychology: Research and Practice, 19,* 547–552.

Rest, J. R. (1982). A psychologist looks at the teaching of ethics. *Hastings Center Report,* pp. 29–36.

Sinclair, C., Poizner, S., Gilmour-Barrett, K., & Randall, D. (1987). The development of a code of ethics for Canadian psychologists. *Canadian Psychology, 28,* 1–8.

Stromberg, C. D., Haggarty, D. J., Leibenluft, R. F., McMillian, M. H., Mishkin, B., Rubin, B. L., & Trilling, H. R. (1988). *The psychologist's legal handbook.*

Washington, DC: Council for the National Register of Health Service Providers in Psychology.

Tepper, A. M., Rinella, V. J., & Siegel, A. M. (1991). Subpoenas and court orders in the everyday practice of psychology. *Pennsylvania Psychologist Quarterly, 51*, 14.

Tymchuk, A. J. (1981). Ethical decision making and psychological treatment. *Journal of Psychiatric Treatment and Evaluation, 3*, 507–513.

Tymchuk, A. J. (1986). Guidelines for ethical decision making. *Canadian Psychology, 27*, 36–43.

Tymchuk, A. J., Drapkin, R., Major-Kingsley, S., Ackerman, A. B., Coffman, E. W., & Baum, M. S. (1982). Ethical decision making and psychologists' attitudes toward training in ethics. *Professional Psychology: Research and Practice, 13*, 412–421.

Van Eenwyk, J. R. (1990). When laws and values conflict: Comment on Pope and Bajt. *American Psychologist, 45*, 399–400.

Author Index

Subject Index